Down train passing Charlton Marshall between Blandford and Spetisbury about 1900 with Johnson 4—4—0 No 15 in original condition

THE SOMERSET & DORSET RAILWAY

by

ROBIN ATTHILL

with contributions on locomotives etc
by

O. S. NOCK

DAVID & CHARLES : NEWTON ABBOT

7153 4312 2

First published 1967
Second impression 1968

BY THE SAME AUTHOR

Old Mendip

TO THOMAS

Printed in Great Britain
by W J Holman Limited Dawlish
for David & Charles (Publishers) Limited
South Devon House Newton Abbot Devon

Contents

Illustrations

PLATES

IN TEXT

CHAPTER 1

The Character of the Line

As dusk fell on the evening of Sunday 6 March 1966, two Southern Pacifics stormed their way up to Masbury summit with their nine-coach special. I watched the red tail-lamp of the train disappear into the darkness. Only a minute before I had seen a glowing pillar of fire racing through Binegar; little flames flickered on embankments that were still sodden after six inches of rain in the last month. The night before, the signalbox at Evercreech Junction North had mysteriously burnt out only a few hours after the passing of the last service train.

This was the end—not merely the end of the Somerset & Dorset, but the end of the era of steam in the West Country. In the gathering darkness I had looked down from the windswept Mendip ridge to Glastonbury, the birthplace of the line and the site of its first headquarters, and beyond Glastonbury to the faint gleam of the Bristol Channel. My father had been born in the same year as the Somerset Central, the senior partner of the Somerset & Dorset; as a child he had travelled up from Glastonbury on excursions to the seaside at Burnham; now I had watched the line die, 111 years later.

The last weekend was a traumatic experience for all those who had worked on the line or lived near it and loved it. It is estimated that 2,000 people travelled over the line in chartered specials, which were pursued by streams of cars from vantage point to vantage point; every bridge and every cutting was manned with onlookers who had made the most complicated cross-country journeys, and infiltrated into the most impassable lanes, to reach an occupation bridge or crossing.

At Prestleigh the fields were black with figures rushing across country with cameras and tripods and tape-recorders to get their shots of the two immaculate green Southern Pacifics fighting their way up the 1 in 50 bank. This was quite distinct from the crowded three-coach service trains: no strengthening was possible in view of the run-down condition of the locomotives, and anyhow every vehicle of any kind had to be worked off the line by Saturday night.

I had made my own last journey earlier in the week, on an afternoon of brilliant sunshine and sharp showers. At almost every station there were old friends finishing their last week's work; dead engines filled the sidings at Bath; in the shedmaster's office the portrait of Alfred Whitaker still glowered from the wall; soon after 4 o'clock a porter moved along the platform with a long pole, turning up the gas-lights.

Things must have looked very much the same in 1874 except for the Ivatt 2—6—2T rostered to take the train up over Mendip and down to Templecombe. I spent the Saturday evening in the signal-box where I had struggled to pull the levers as a boy 40 years before. From this vantage point I watched the last regular passenger train on the line, double-headed and carrying the ceremonial coffin which had been put on board at Evercreech Junction. A light engine followed—No. 80037—and the box was switched out for the last time.

On the Sunday, two specials were run: I watched one pass Radstock, working on the wrong line because the Western Region engineer was already in occupation of the line, laying in the connection to the North Somerset line for working from Writhlington to Bristol next morning, at exactly the same point where the Somerset & Dorset had planned a connection under its 1871 Act.

The other I saw at Glastonbury, passing what was the old headquarters of the Somerset Central and for a while of the Somerset & Dorset, and setting out across the turf moor over the original twelve miles of line. And so to Masbury in the gathering darkness, where not more than a dozen people saw the last two trains over the summit. First came the northbound special carrying the traditional S & D head-code: this might have been any up excursion returning from Bournemouth, but the final southbound special with its blazing electric lights and its Southern Region head-code discs was something unique and unforgettable by reason of the spectacular driving which brought it up to the summit at express speed that it is unlikely had ever been seen before. Between them these two double-headed trains seemed to symbolise the joint and anomalous character of the line: two Southern Pacifics working back to Bournemouth, a British Railways 2—6—4T and an LMS 8F 2—8—0 designed by W. A. Stanier, who was born in 1876 in the far-off independent days of the Somerset & Dorset. For the purpose of historical record the locomotives concerned were 34013 *Okehampton* and 34057 *Biggin Hill*; 80043 and 48706.

What was the attraction of this line? Why was there such fury and excitement about its closure? What drew so many people from all over Britain during the last years, and particularly the last months, of its life?

To some extent the attraction was the beauty and variety of the scenery: the Somerset & Dorset was a supremely photogenic line to which the pages of post-war railway periodicals pay eloquent tribute. Even so, it could hardly compete with the dramatic splendour of the Settle & Carlisle line, or of the Brecon & Merthyr. Other smaller railway systems such as the Midland & Great Northern Joint, or the Midland & South Western Junction, never seemed to capture the imagination of the railway-lover or enthusiast in the same way—or did they die too soon to receive the full impact of the affection and interest in Britain's railways, kindled by the years of curtailment and closure, that was only accelerated by Dr Beeching? Perhaps the Brecon & Merthyr was nearest of kin to the Somerset & Dorset. D. S. Barrie's description of the Brecon & Merthyr as 'a poor relation with a distinctly murky past, which for half a century had struggled over mountains and against every kind of adversity to arrive at a modest usefulness' might well apply to the Somerset & Dorset. The Brecon & Merthyr was absorbed by the GWR in 1922, but the Somerset & Dorset, even though it lost its independence in 1875, retained its identity until 1948. Neither line ever lost its individuality; both were small enough to have retained something of the atmosphere of a family.

On the Somerset & Dorset everybody seemed to know everybody: I have talked to Driver Cook of Radstock who joined the railway in 1893, and to Frank Redman who served under the great Alfred Whitaker, Locomotive Superintendent at Highbridge from 1889 to 1911. Mention Edgar Smith or Tom Mogg, and faces light up; Alfred Dando, the signal boy at Foxcote on the night of the Radstock accident in 1876, is remembered as 'a quiet-spoken man who read his Bible every day'—this was from the late Ewart Gulliford who worked with Dando on the Somerset & Dorset between 1913 and 1916. They followed each other's careers with interest: 'I knew him when he was at Henstridge', or 'He's at Sturminster now—or up the branch'. There was the Newman family whose combined years of service to 'the Dorset' totalled well over 200: Walter Newman, who was signalman at Blandford—and Mayor and J.P. into the bargain—served for 55 years, and his son William, who finished up as stationmaster at Templecombe, for 51.

Another symbol of tradition on the line is the battered copy of the 1864 Rule Book which belongs to Driver Kemp of Radstock, who inherited it from Driver Flynn of Branksome, who inherited it from John Nutt, who signed for it in September 1872 on his appointment as fireman on the S & D. Even much of the day-to-day working was arranged verbally as between friends, and the telephone wires were a family grapevine: ring Bath Control to ask the whereabouts

I, the undersigned, having been appointed as Fireman *in the service of the* SOMERSET AND DORSET RAILWAY COMPANY, *do hereby bind myself to observe and obey the foregoing Regulations; and I hereby declare that I have carefully read them over (or) that they have been carefully read over to me, and that I clearly understand them, and have received a copy of the same.*

As witness my hand (or mark) this day of Sept 1872

Witness to Signature of the said } [illegible]

John Nutt

Fireman John Nutt's declaration from his copy of the S & D Rule Book of 1864

of No. 60 up, and some wayside signalman would chip in with 'Just off the Junction'. Of such stuff were railways made.

But the Somerset & Dorset was at the same time large enough to be considered a main line, if only by reason of the quantity of through freight and through passenger traffic that it handled, especially during the summer months. This was the deliberate policy of the companies who took over the line in 1875, and the 'joint' nature of the line, combining working methods derived from the Midland and the LSW with the older purely Somerset & Dorset tradition, was obvious in endless details. Lineside notices, for instance, might bewilderingly and inconsequently proclaim the Railway Executive, S. & D.J.R., Southern Railway, The Somerset & Dorset Joint Committee, L. & S.W.R., or even finally L. & S.**W**.**R**. or L. & **S**.W.**R**. with the relevant letters picked out in new paint to stress that the line was yet again under new management.

Near Cole, in Western Region territory, I once saw a train of Eastern Region stock from Cleethorpes to Bournemouth hauled by a Southern Pacific and an ex-Midland class 2P 4—4—0. This train would shortly be picking up the tokens for the single-line sections south of Templecombe by means of Alfred Whitaker's tablet-exchanging apparatus and would be carrying the unique S & D passenger head-code (one lamp at the foot of the chimney and one above the left-hand buffer). Freight train engines carried one lamp at the foot of the chimney and one above the right-hand buffer; light engines carried one lamp at the foot of the chimney. The exclusive S & D engine head-codes appear to have been used throughout the days of Joint ownership and even survived grouping and nationalisation.

Such operational details added to the fascination of the line for the railway-lover: the difficulties involved in passing heavy holiday traffic over long sections of single line, the fearsome banks up from Radstock and Evercreech to the 811 ft summit on the Mendip ridge, the extraordinary combinations of locomotives produced by the locomotive department for summer Saturdays, and the operation of the stud of Radstock bankers. Radstock drivers—and others—all had their 'jimmies', curved iron hooks which were wedged in the blast-pipes and weighted down to improve the draught and the steaming of their engines. It was all absolutely illegal, and there is the story of the blacksmith, under examination by an inspector as to whom he had made 'jimmies' for, scratching his head and saying 'It'd be easier to say who I didn't make'n for'.

There were other colourful local details of operation: 'Where's Frank to, then?' 'Up the bank doing the Binegar Calf', or 'She's late tonight because "the Perisher's" calling at the Junction for assistance'. The fact of the matter is that, long before the end, the Somerset & Dorset had become something of a period piece which was another reason for its attraction: one of the most easy ways of escaping into the Victorian period was to spend a winter's afternoon at Bath Green Park station or travelling along the branch whose whole atmosphere was unforgettably captured in John Betjeman's film *Let's imagine a Branch Line Railway* (BBC television 29 March 1963).

At Evercreech Junction there would be a coal fire burning in the waiting room, and later in the year bowls of primroses on the table. Presently a faint susurration of steam would suggest that the branch-line train was ready to start; at Edington Junction its approach might even be heralded by the ringing of a station bell belonging to the Somerset Central Railway. For the Somerset & Dorset had nothing whatever to do with the diesel era. It was somehow fitting that on the very day that the closure was announced, scenes from the film version of R. L. Stevenson's comedy *The Wrong Box* were being shot on location at Bath Green Park. A set of three flat-roofed coaches from the Burry Port and Gwendraeth Valley line and an ex-LMS 'Jinty' 0—6—0T were painted (one side only) what purported to be LSW green, and an LSW horse-drawn cart and a set of contemporary posters were all that was needed to transform the station into a nineteenth-century London terminus.

Over all there was a pathetic grandeur about the line. It had been planned with such courage and with such high ambitions which had never quite been fulfilled. Although the Midland and the South Western did all that they could to encourage through traffic, operational difficulties always made it an expensive line to work, and there can be no doubt that not nearly enough capital was put into it under the Joint Committee and, since 1930 at least, far too little was done to bring it up to date and to modernise the service and the image of the line. Hence its appeal to the connoisseur rather than to the genuine traveller, who was only likely to be irritated by the ludicrous manoeuvrings at Templecombe where a new joint station should have been built fifty years ago.

The closing decade of the line's history was marked by apparent mismanagement and neglect which has soured the memory of the railwaymen and the public alike. How far this was deliberate policy, fostered by an attitude of mind inherited from the GWR, we are now too close to the event to decide. The fact remains that in 1875 the GWR felt that the Somerset & Dorset, which had already deserted from the broad-gauge camp in 1862, had betrayed it, and that the new narrow-gauge link from the North to the South and West was

JOINT OPERATION AT MASBURY SUMMIT

(1) *Ex-Midland* 4—4—0 *No.* 509 *piloting a Southern Pacific on 'The Pines' in* 1954

EARLY BUILDINGS

(2) *Offices at Glastonbury 1861-77, built as an hotel, and later the district engineer's house*

(3) *Templecombe Lower: the original Dorset Central station building incorporated in the locomotive dept. Spur to the Upper station in background*

a deliberate stab in the back. Old memories die hard, and over the years there was never any love lost between the companies: no Somerset & Dorset man would ever speak of 'The Western' without a certain degree of acerbity. The Somerset & Dorset had become a legend in its own lifetime. By 1874 it was already known as the Slow & Dirty; slow and dirty it remained in popular prejudice, and though its loyal servants assured one that it was Swift & Delightful, they were to scrawl Sabotaged & Defeated in the dust that accumulated on the benches of their derelict stations.

CHAPTER 2

The Beginnings

THE SOMERSET CENTRAL

The Somerset & Dorset Railway came into existence on 1 September 1862 as a result of the amalgamation of two independent companies: the Somerset Central and the Dorset Central. The senior partner was the Somerset Central which had been incorporated under an Act of 17 June 1852.

When the centenary of the Somerset Central was celebrated on 28 August 1954, it was only appropriate that more than a hundred of the passengers who travelled by train from Glastonbury to Burnham-on-Sea should have worn a lapel badge bearing a portrait of James Clark. They were thus distinguished as members of a clan consisting of the 250 living descendants of James Clark (1812-1906), who is generally considered to be the Founding Father of the Somerset & Dorset.

In 1833 James Clark had been taken into partnership by his brother Cyrus who had set up business at Street in 1825 as fellmonger, skin-dresser and sheepskin rug manufacturer. James himself had initiated the making of wool-lined slippers, which was to lead to shoemaking becoming the firm's main concern. The firm had gone through hard times in the 1840s, but James Clark was nothing if not an optimist, and with the revival of confidence in the business he was eager to promote rail communication for the Glastonbury area.

A public meeting was held in the Town Hall at Glastonbury on 16 September 1850 with William Pinney of Somerton Erleigh in the chair. William Pinney had been a member of the provisional committee of the Somersetshire Midland Railway whose prospectus, issued during the Railway Mania of 1844-46, had proposed a line thirty miles long connecting Bruton, Wells, Glastonbury and Highbridge. The meeting was held to establish 'the desirableness of a railway communication from Highbridge to Glastonbury'. A committee was formed to forward the matter, preliminary surveys were made, and at another meeting, in the following June, the provisional committee proposed its scheme to an enthusiastic gathering.

The real genesis of the Somerset Central must be considered as the meeting of the promoters held at Hodge's Railway Hotel, Bridgwater, on 1 December 1851, 'for the purpose of constructing a line of railway from Highbridge to Glastonbury'. The meeting was presided over by George Warry of Shapwick House.

> 'I was voted to the chair pro temp.,' he recorded in his diary, 'and for a long time our advance to business was slow. There were long discussions but at last we . . . ended the day by launching our undertaking into the world and God grant that our efforts may be crowned with success; bona fides and good intentions are the basis of our conduct herein.'

The directors included James and Cyrus Clark and J. W. C. Clothier, all of Street, Ralph Neville of Butleigh Court, William Pinney, MP, of Somerton Erleigh, and the Hon Philip Pleydell Bouverie of Brymore House, Cannington, who was to be the chairman of the company for the first three years of its existence. There were also present two of the directors of the Bristol & Exeter Railway, which from the outset was eager to assist the new company, with the intention of extending the broad-gauge kingdom by means of a twelve-mile line striking eastwards into what was so far virgin territory as far as the railway was concerned.

Between the Mendip Hills and the low Polden range to the south stretches a large area of low-lying moorland, drained by the rivers Axe and Brue, which empty into the Bristol Channel at Uphill and Highbridge respectively. Describing this area, then known as Brent Marsh, in 1795, Billingsley said that in the previous twenty years more than 17,000 acres had been drained and enclosed; there remained however in the Brue valley alone about 9,000 acres of undrained turf bog. Billingsley's Agricultural Survey contains specific plans 'for more effectually draining the turf bogs and flooded land', and this was undertaken in the years immediately following an Act of 1801. A tide-sluice was built at Highbridge, and a North Drain and a South Drain were cut to carry away the water, with considerable success as far as agriculture was concerned.

Nothing could alter the contours, and large stretches of moor are still liable to flooding after heavy winter rain: Burtle 'Hill' rises to exactly 23 ft, and Glastonbury station, fourteen miles inland, is barely 20 ft above sea-level. Communications remained poor: the 1817 OS map shows a number of drove-roads serving the new enclosures, but no turnpike road had yet ventured into the area. In the mediaeval period the monks of Glastonbury had moved about the Somerset levels visiting their estates by water, and it was only appropriate that the next step in the development of the Brue basin should have been the construction of a canal.

The Glastonbury Canal, authorised by an Act of 1827, was triumphantly opened on 15 August 1833. A tide-lock was built at Highbridge and the navigation followed the Brue until past Bason Bridge, whence a new cut, with a single lock near Shapwick, continued to Glastonbury basin, fourteen miles from Highbridge. In 1848 the canal was bought by the Bristol & Exeter Railway for £7,000 with the proviso that it was to be maintained in good order and worked in connection with the railway.*

When the idea of a Central Somerset railway was first mooted in 1850, there were only three lines of railway in Somerset, all broad-gauge. The Great Western main line had been opened throughout from Bristol to London in 1841; the Bristol & Exeter (worked by the GWR until 1849) had reached Bridgwater in 1841, Taunton in 1842 and Exeter in 1844; the nominally-independent Wilts, Somerset & Weymouth, branching south from the GWR at Thingley Junction, two miles west of Chippenham, had struggled as far as Westbury by 1848 and then been absorbed in 1850 by the GWR which opened the line as far as Frome in that year.

Highbridge was preferred to Bridgwater as the terminal point of the Somerset Central as affording an entirely level route to Glastonbury along the valley of the Brue, whereas from Bridgwater, which was a very much more important town, with a population of 11,000†, and also affording an outlet to the sea, it would have been necessary to negotiate the Polden Hills. Beyond Glastonbury, extension eastwards towards the Wilts, Somerset & Weymouth was envisaged from the start, though whether this was to be effected by a line through Shepton Mallet to Frome, or further south near Castle Cary, was to be a matter of fierce dispute.

The Somerset Central's Act of Incorporation received Royal Assent on 17 June 1852, authorising a single line twelve miles twenty-six chains in length from Highbridge Wharf on the River Brue, thirty-three chains west of Highbridge station, to Glastonbury.

* Hadfield, Charles, *The Canals of Southern England*, 1955, pp. 221-23, 321, 358-9. (This work is being replaced by *The Canals of South West England* in 1967.)

† Highbridge was not at this time even a separate parish; its population was included in that of Burnham—1,701 in the Census returns for 1851.

The authorised capital was £70,000 in £20 shares, and towards this sum the Bristol & Exeter subscribed £10,000 of which £8,000, consisting of 400 paid-up shares, was held to be the purchase price of the Glastonbury Navigation & Canal which was transferred to the ownership of the Somerset Central on 16 September 1852. George C. Ashmead had already been appointed as surveyor and Charles Hutton Gregory as engineer; the contractors were Messrs J. & C. Rigby of Westminster.

The first sod was formally cut by the chairman at Highbridge on 18 April 1853 in the presence of the chairman and directors of the Bristol & Exeter, and 'a dejeuner in celebration of the event was afterwards partaken of in the Market Room at Highbridge by the Directors and a large number of their friends', and recorded in the minutes. Construction proceeded rapidly, though the engineer was experiencing considerable difficulty in building his road across the turf bog, as he reported to the general meeting in February 1854 with reference to the four miles eastwards from the canal lock at Shapwick: 'The treacherous nature of the peat has required great care in the work, but by the introduction of a large quantity of fagots, I believe that permanent security has been attained'. Two months later the directors walked over the line from near Bason Bridge to Glastonbury, and expressed themselves generally satisfied with the progress made. In anticipation of the opening of the railway, harbour tolls at Highbridge were reduced to encourage trade, with a special drawback on all coals carried over the line, and the Glastonbury Canal was closed to traffic on 1 July 1854.

The formal opening of the railway took place on 17 August 1854. It was a gloomy, wet morning, and driving into Highbridge together George Warry and James Clark had to shelter under a tree. Mercifully the rain had cleared off by 11 o'clock, and at Highbridge all was gaiety and decoration for the ceremony of the day, 'the opening of our railway', as Warry wrote in his diary.

> The directors of the B & E and our own arrived and a little after 2 we started with 6 first class carriages for Glastonbury and did the run in a little more than 35 minutes stopping a few minutes at the Shapwick station and taking in some of the natives for a trip.

A vast procession carrying banners emblazoned with such legends as 'Railway and Civilization' and 'Where ther's a will ther's a way' (*sic*) wound through the ruins of Glastonbury Abbey to a spacious tent where the inevitable cold collation was served to about 500 persons (see page 22). The repast and the speeches which followed occupied three hours, while 800 working-class dinners were served

The opening of the Somerset Central Railway, from *The Illustrated London News*, 26 August 1854

in another tent. The inhabitants of Glastonbury meanwhile took the opportunity of presenting a memorial (with which the Bishop of Bath & Wells entirely concurred), praying that the company would not allow the quiet of the town to be disturbed by excursion trains—referring apparently to Sunday trains. A Board of Trade inspection followed on 22 August, and the line was opened for regular traffic on Monday 28 August. George Warry rode down to Shapwick station before breakfast.

> An engine & carriages had gone up to make the start from Glastonbury. I waited and saw the first train go down. To a merciful and all-kind Father in Heaven I am in debt and for this favour His blessing has brought our work to its happy issue.

It was indeed a solemn and splendid moment for the promoters. There were two intermediate stations, at Shapwick and Ashcott, and a daily service of six trains in each direction was provided, with two on Sundays, thirty-five minutes being allowed for the twelve miles. The service duly appeared on the Bristol & Exeter timetable for December 1854 as connecting with its main-line trains at Highbridge, for although the Somerset Central Railway was always to remain an independent company, it was very much the foster-child of the Bristol & Exeter, which had undertaken to work the line for a term of seven years from its opening at a rent of £3,800 a year, at the same time guaranteeing 4 per cent on the capital for this term. The local company retained its right to the revenues from the harbour at Highbridge.

THE BURNHAM AND WELLS EXTENSIONS

No sooner was the line opened than the question of its extension at each end was brought forward. There was some truth in Louis H. Ruegg's sneer at the Somerset Central 'going from nowhere to nowhere over a turf moor, and with but one town on the whole line, and that having less than 4,000 people'. In fact the population of Glastonbury did not reach 4,000 until 1901, by which time it had been equalled in size by Street. When the railway was opened Street was no more than a large village with a population of about 1,700, though the directors expected heavy traffic from there, doubtless from C. & J. Clark's rapidly-expanding business. Burnham and Highbridge together were no larger, and neither Burnham nor Street was actually on the railway; Ashcott and Shapwick stations were two miles from the villages they served; and the intervening moors were sparsely populated with a few scattered hamlets and isolated cottages. It was therefore only logical that the directors' minutes for 7 October 1854 should refer to the possibility of extensions to Burnham and Wells.

On 24 October there is another significant minute to the effect that the secretary be permitted to apply for the position of secretary to the South Eastern Railway. If this application had been successful, the company would have lost one of its most loyal and energetic servants who in the next twenty years was to do more than any other single person towards the creation of the Somerset & Dorset system. This was Robert Arthur Read who came from the office of the secretary of the Bristol & Exeter, where he had had considerable experience, to succeed the first secretary of the Somerset Central Railway, J. F. Giles, in 1853 at a salary of £200 a year. It was largely due to Read's energy and vision that the extensions, first to Burnham and Wells, then to Cole to meet the Dorset Central, and finally northwards to Bath and southwards by means of running powers to Bournemouth West, were achieved. When Read finally retired in 1891 from the position of general manager and secretary of the Joint Committee which had taken over in 1876, the Somerset & Dorset was no longer a local line 'going from nowhere to nowhere': instead, its main line formed an important cross-country link between the North and the Midlands and the South and West, while the original section of the Somerset Central served as part of a through route from the Bristol Channel to the English Channel—an ambition which had been formulated from very early days.

The Burnham and Wells extensions were authorised by an Act of 30 July 1855 and opened in 1858 and 1859 respectively, by which time the further extension from Glastonbury to Cole to meet the Dorset Central, authorised by an Act of 21 July 1856, was also under way. The Burnham terminus was one mile fifty chains from Highbridge, and the branch diverged from the line to Highbridge Wharf immediately after crossing the Bristol-Bridgwater turnpike road on the level. Beyond the station at Burnham the line was extended along a 900 ft stone causeway or landing slip which had been substituted for the pier originally proposed.

Gregory reported to the directors on 22 August 1857 that the Burnham branch had been passed by the Government Inspector that day, but that difficulties were being experienced in forming a cut to admit coasting steamers to lie by the causeway, and experiments were being made with a sluicing pond to clear out deposits of mud in the cut. The foundation stone was laid on 5 September 1857 by one of the directors, George Reed, described as 'the foremost citizen of Burnham', and the landing slip was opened for public traffic at the same time as the Burnham branch on 3 May 1858, being worked by the Bristol & Exeter at a rent of £1,080 a year. On the opening day, the *Iron Duke* from Cardiff came alongside the pier and landed her passengers at about 10 o'clock. An hour later an excursion train from Bristol arrived at the station with 700 passengers who formed a procession to the pier headed by the railway brass band (*Sherborne Journal*, 6 May 1858). In the same month the Cardiff Steam Navigation Company's steamship *Taliesin* began to ply between Cardiff and Burnham, and at the next general meeting the shareholders of the Somerset Central were informed that

> the great convenience thereby afforded for speedy communication between the West of England and South Wales, and for the transmission of the agricultural produce of Somersetshire to that great market, has secured for it a large traffic.

Like its forerunner the Glastonbury canal, the Somerset Central had high hopes of the South Wales link. But to handle both passenger and cargo traffic on an open stone slipway with a gradient of 1 in 23, exposed to the weather and liable to the tidal limitations of the Parrett estuary and to constant silting on a completely open beach, was clearly not a practicable proposition. There is no evidence that passenger trains ever actually used the pier. There is no reference to special working arrangements in Bristol & Exeter Rule Books, nor in the very early Somerset & Dorset Rule Book for 1864 which contains elaborate regulations for other danger spots such as Highbridge Crossing or Pylle Bank.

At the opening ceremony, as we have seen, the train terminated at the station, and two very old inhabitants have independently recalled how in the 1880s passengers from South Wales walked up the pier and along the rails to the station to board their train at the excursion platform. For loading and unloading cargo, trucks were propelled to the pier by an engine and then lowered and hauled up again by a wire rope through a ring set in the stonework at the top of the pier. In 1884, rollers were ordered to be laid down between the rails for the protection of the wire rope on the pier.

Early photographs of ships at the pier show the sluicing pond with a controlling hatch, roughly on the site of the present Marine Lake, and mooring piles on the jetty itself, as well as a line of piles parallel with the jetty, to enable ships to be hauled off at various states of tide (see plates 4 and 5). Burnham's limitations as a seaport were clearly underlined by the failure of ambitious schemes to improve conditions for shipping there.

A nominally-independent subsidiary company was formed, the Burnham Tidal Harbour & Railway Company. The new company shared offices and officials with the Somerset Central, and was authorised under Acts of 6 August 1860 and 29 June 1865 to alter the course of the Brue and to construct a tidal harbour with quays and docks for cargo vessels—in short, to develop Burnham as a port and railhead. Nothing of all this seems to have been achieved, except that the Somerset Central was empowered by the Act of 1860 to run steamers, and under these conditions the Somerset & Dorset maintained a passenger service between Burnham and Cardiff on and off until 1888.*

In 1860, for instance, S.S. *Ruby* was purchased, a fast boat with 'very superior accommodation for the comfort and convenience of passengers'. George Warry made the crossing to Cardiff on 28 July 1860: 'A rough passage and I was wretchedly ill, fortunately the passage was short'. (Unfortunately *Ruby* eventually ran aground at Burnham and broke her back—or so the story goes. Watertight partitions were fitted, the two ends were towed to Bristol and put together, and *Ruby* crossed the Atlantic to become a blockade runner in the American Civil War—just the sort of romantic denouement one might have expected of a Somerset & Dorset steamer.)

Such profits as the Somerset & Dorset was to make as a seafaring company were to accrue from the harbour at Highbridge where cargo services to South Wales and to other Bristol Channel ports were maintained until 1933. From the outset, trade at Highbridge had steadily increased, and reference was made at a special general meeting held on 30 October 1855 to

> the great natural advantages possessed by Highbridge as a port for communication with Cardiff and the ports of South Wales, and the comparatively small outlay which would have to be incurred to render it available for an almost unlimited amount of traffic.

Agricultural and dairy produce were carried to the vast consumer market of the towns and mining districts of South Wales against cargoes of coal and other industrial products such as railway iron: locomotive coal, for instance, was supplied by contract from South

* For a full list of the Somerset & Dorset fleet and of the ferry services operated between Burnham and Cardiff see Appendix 5.

Wales through Highbridge, as were rails, and many Somerset & Dorset signal posts, boundary posts and fences were in later years economically constructed from old rails rolled at Dowlais.

The ultimate objective of the directors of the Somerset Central in developing the port of Highbridge was revealed at the same special general meeting:

> The connection of the Bristol and English Channels has for many years been considered to be of great importance particularly with a view to the more rapid conveyance of the produce of South Wales to the ports of the South Coast of England.

Towards the fulfilment of this aim the meeting considered two alternative proposals for extension eastwards: (i) through Wells (as already authorised by the Act of 1855) and Shepton Mallet to the Wilts, Somerset & Weymouth line (now Great Western) at Frome; (ii) to Week Champflower (*sic*) to make a junction with the Wilts, Somerset & Weymouth at Cole near Bruton.

Both these plans ostensibly envisaged reaching the south coast at Southampton by way of Westbury and Salisbury, but the second alternative was specifically and significantly recorded as 'having for its object an ultimate connection with the proposed line from Poole'. This can only refer to the scheme for the Dorset Central, whose prospectus proclaimed in large capitals JUNCTION OF ENGLISH AND BRISTOL CHANNELS, proposed a thirty-two-mile line from Wimborne to join the Wilts, Somerset & Weymouth at Week Champflower (*sic*), and adduced that the Somerset Central was already seeking powers for an extension from Glastonbury to the Wilts, Somerset & Weymouth.

Sharing a secretary and an engineer, solicitors and London offices, and publishing half-yearly reports that were identical in format, the Somerset Central and the Dorset Central were clearly hand-in-glove from the outset. The Dorset Central was planned as a narrow-gauge line, a factor of the greatest importance to the ultimate fate of the two companies; at this early stage it was the cause of the delay in completing the extension to Wells and of the nature of the extension when completed—a dead-end branch instead of a starting-point for further extensions.

At this date the cathedral city of Wells had a population of about 7,500. Enthusiastic support for an extension of the railway from Glastonbury had been shown at a public meeting in 1852, and disappointment followed when the Somerset Central's Act of 30 July 1855 provided only for a branch instead of the hoped-for eastward extension to Frome. At the vital special meeting of 30

October 1855, the case was argued against the route from Wells to Frome on the grounds of the high cost and fierce gradients involved—the East Somerset line from Witham to Wells was finally built with a ruling gradient of 1 in 46 and several miles at 1 in 50 or worse. The proposed line to Bruton could be constructed at little more than half the cost with a ruling gradient of 1 in 100. Despite strong opposition from the Wells faction, the Bruton proposal carried the day and the extension was ultimately authorised by an Act of 21 July 1856, misdated 29 July in the printed Act.

The inhabitants of Wells, feeling themselves abandoned by the Somerset Central, began to look towards the East Somerset, which was encouraged to add a Wells extension (authorised 27 July 1857) to its broad-gauge line already authorised from Witham to Shepton Mallet by its Act of Incorporation of 5 June 1856. This threat brought further pressure to bear on the directors of the Somerset Central, who were already being urged by shareholders representing the city to complete the branch before their powers lapsed. £17,000 additional capital was accordingly issued in the form of 5 per cent preference shares. Rigby, who had already been responsible for the Burnham extension, had also contracted to complete the Wells extension for £48,000, and this was to include a junction with the East Somerset. But this provision was cancelled before the East Somerset eventually reached Wells in 1862, and for sixteen years the two termini confronted each other across Priory Road.

By August 1858 the engineer reported 300 men and 80 horses at work on the Wells line; on 7 January 1859 the directors met at Glastonbury and 'went over the Wells line with an engine and carriage'; the formal opening took place on 3 March 1859, followed by a Board of Trade inspection, and the opening to the public on 15 March. Two petitions had been submitted by the inhabitants of Coxley requesting an intermediate station there, but the directors agreed on a single intermediate station at Polsham, though this was not opened until 1861. The Bristol & Exeter undertook to work the Wells extension as well as the Burnham extension at a rent of £3,950 a year until 28 August 1861, when its original lease of the Somerset Central expired.

In 1859, less than five years after its opening, the Somerset Central stood possessed of nineteen miles of single-line broad-gauge track, with a further thirteen and a half miles authorised on the Bruton extension. The next three years were to see changes which completely revolutionised the very nature of the company, and by 1863 it had been transformed from a purely local line into a trunk line seventy miles long, providing a through service between the Bristol Channel and the English Channel. These three vital years saw the termination of the company's lease to the Bristol & Exeter, the abandonment of the broad gauge, and finally the achievement of the goal towards which it had been striving—amalgamation with the Dorset Central, to whose history it is now time to turn.

THE DORSET CENTRAL

The independent life of the Dorset Central was even briefer than that of the Somerset Central, which it resembled in several ways: both concerns started as purely local lines, not more than a dozen miles long, linking country towns; both lines were worked from the outset by larger companies; neither was likely to become wealthy, but both evinced an immediate ambition to extend, and ultimately to amalgamate with one another, even if this intention was not always publicly and specifically proclaimed.

On the other hand, geographical and geological factors ensured that the original lines were very different in character and appearance: Dorset Central stations, for instance, were instantly distinguishable from the buildings of the Somerset Central. Again, there seems to have been no question of the Dorset Central ever standing on its own feet and working its own line; the Somerset Central seems always to have been regarded as the senior partner which would take charge when amalgamation was achieved. In fact, when this happened, the Dorset Central had not even completed its projected extensions—it existed in two isolated fragments, separated by a gap of sixteen miles which was not bridged for another year. The most important difference of all was the difference of gauge, the Dorset Central being as firmly linked to the narrow-gauge LSW as the Somerset Central was to the broad-gauge B & E—officially, at any rate. Whether it would ever have been practicable for the Dorset Central to link itself to the narrow-gauge LSW at one end and to the broad-gauge Wilts, Somerset & Weymouth at the other is perhaps a purely academic question.

Quite apart from the connection with the LSW, the Dorset Central's narrow gauge was part of its heritage from the abortive South Midlands Union Railway.* This was a project of 1852, leaving

* Contemporary newspaper reports include conflicting references to this project as the South *Midlands* Union and the South *Midland* Union Railway. The deposited plans state South *Midlands*; the Dorset Central prospectus refers to the South *Midland*.

the Midland Railway's Birmingham-Bristol line at Mangotsfield and following a route through Keynsham to Radstock, to give access to the Somerset coalfield, crossing the Mendip ridge by way of Holcombe and Stoke St Michael somewhat further east than the route ultimately followed by the Somerset & Dorset's Bath Extension, and then southwards through Blandford to Poole, giving access to 'the attractive watering place of Bournemouth'. A meeting of the promoters was held at Bristol on 29 December 1852, but in the face of considerable opposition and of the physical difficulties presented by the northern half of the route the scheme was abandoned, though some of the work done for the line—presumably the preliminary survey—was claimed as available in the Dorset Central's prospectus.

The Dorset Central traced its origin from meetings held at Blandford and Poole in 1854, and despite the protests of Dorset landowners against the desecration of 'the sacred valley of the Stour', an Act of Incorporation authorising the construction of ten and a quarter miles of narrow-gauge single line, from the LSW at Wimborne up the Stour valley to Blandford, was obtained on 29 July 1856, eight days after the Somerset Central had obtained the Act for its Bruton extension. Between the two systems there would be a gap of only twenty-four miles. The Dorset Central was authorised to raise £100,000 capital in shares and £33,000 on loan. The directors included Lord Rivers of Rushmore Lodge, Salisbury, Sir Ivor Bertie Guest of Canford Manor through whose lands the LSW's Wimborne line already passed, and George Reed of Burnham, under the chairman, H. D. Seymour, MP, of East Knoyle, who had already become a director of the Somerset Central. The secretary was Robert A. Read, the engineer was Charles Gregory, and the contractor was Waring Bros of London, a firm which was to have a long association with the Somerset & Dorset.

Sir Ivor Guest (1835-1914) was the son of Sir John Guest (1785-1852), the Dowlais ironmaster, who had bought Canford in 1846. This connection with the South Wales iron industry may explain the eagerness of the Dorset Central to link up with the Somerset Central and thus reach the Bristol Channel. Dowlais rails were exported all over the world and were to be one of the staple traffics on the Somerset & Dorset cross-Channel shipping services. In 1860 the Burnham Tidal Harbour & Railway Company was authorised to enter into agreements with the Dorset Central although the latter had not yet penetrated beyond Blandford.

The first sod of the Dorset Central was cut at Blandford St Mary on 13 November 1856 by Lady Smith of the Down House. The wheelbarrow and spade which she used on the great day were presented by Charles Waring and are still to be seen among the historical relics in the Transport Museum at Clapham. The expenses of the ceremony amounted to £224 13s 2d, including £71 for wine, a tidy sum in view of the company's uncertain financial prospects. In actual fact, the first eight months' traffic over the line left the directors with £898, which hardly looked like providing an adequate dividend on the authorised capital of £100,000. Nevertheless, the board was optimistic: the prospectus had claimed that the first section of the line would 'in itself be a profitable undertaking' from the large local traffic, while the first ordinary general meeting, held on 27 July 1858 at Wimborne, recorded undiminished confidence in the intrinsic value of the line and in its importance to the district through which it passed.

The Dorset Central had already set its sights on higher things. Its new Act of 10 August 1857 authorised the raising of a further £300,000 capital in ordinary shares and £100,000 in loans, and the building of an extension to meet the Somerset Central at Bruton, thus bridging the twenty-four-mile gap north of Blandford, and completing the Channel-to-Channel link. No such link could materialise so long as there was a difference of gauge, but at its own general meeting of 28 February 1857 the Somerset Central had already announced its intention of laying the narrow gauge in anticipation of the link-up to form a trunk line seventy miles long running from sea to sea, and this was authorised by an Act of 1 August 1859 which also allowed the Somerset Central to raise a further £75,000 capital, with loans to £24,000 and the conversion of debentures into 5 per cent stock.

The next problem was whether to convert to narrow gauge or to admit the mixed gauge by laying the third rail. On grounds of expense and convenience of working, it was decided to convert: the Bristol & Exeter's lease was due to expire on 28 August 1861, and the Somerset Central had no intention of renewing it or of acquiring broad-gauge stock for working its system: it therefore went ahead to obtain an Act which would allow it to abandon the broad gauge on the Bruton extension, while the proprietors' minutes somewhat naively recorded that 'no feeling of hostility to the neighbouring broad-gauge lines is entertained'.

It was not to be so easy to shake off the broad-gauge connection: parliamentary opposition by the broad-gauge parties resulted in modifications to the Somerset Central's 1861 Act—mixed gauge must be laid on the Bruton extension, and the connection with the broad-gauge Wilts, Somerset & Weymouth line near Bruton must be built as originally authorised. Yet more capital was authorised (£85,000 in shares and £29,300 in loans) and an extension of time allowed for completing the line to Bruton.

In spite of these setbacks to the Somerset Central's plans, it was recorded that the Bristol & Exeter directors had 'evinced a most kind and neighbourly spirit throughout the negotiations'. In view of the Somerset Central's complete change of front over the Bruton extension and its barefaced attempt to sever its broad-gauge connections, it is remarkable that no breach took place with the Bristol & Exeter: the latter had every reason to feel aggrieved by what had happened, yet within a few months it was to show remarkable generosity towards the Somerset Central in the great crisis in which it was involved in 1861-2, immediately preceding its amalgamation with the Dorset Central.

TOWARDS AMALGAMATION

The situation in the summer of 1861 was full of uncertainties. On 1 November 1860 the Dorset Central had opened its first section of line for traffic between Wimborne and Blandford, with intermediate stations at Sturminster Marshall and Spetisbury. This was worked by the LSW under an agreement to last five years, with the LSW taking 60 per cent of the gross receipts—a day's work for engines and carriages to be 140 miles or seven journeys each way. An extension of time had been obtained for the completion of the Blandford-Bruton section, with priority to be given to the Templecombe-Bruton section, which involved a junction at Templecombe with the Salisbury & Yeovil Railway. Pending amalgamation, a seven-year agreement had been approved for the Somerset Central to work the Bruton-Templecombe section in conjunction with its own proposed narrow-gauge extension from Glastonbury to Bruton, but there was small hope of this taking place before 28 August.

As soon as the Wells branch was opened in 1859, the engineer reported that Rigby had 470 men and 50 horses at work on the Glastonbury-Bruton extension. By the following February the number was increased to 600 men and 70 horses besides quarrymen, stonecutters, etc. Work was held up by unfavourable weather throughout the spring of 1860: a serious slip on Pylle bank was aggravated by persistent rains, and there was already talk of an application to Parliament for an extension of time. The bad weather continued into the autumn with an unusual amount of rain: a

BURNHAM PIER

(4) *Cardiff ferry: 'The Lady Mary' at the pier in 1883, showing mooring piles and sluicing pond (cf p. 25)*

(5) *Pleasure boat: Messrs P. & A. Campbell's 'Waverley' at the pier in 1908, showing* S & D *tracks still in position*

EARLY LOCOMOTIVES AT WORK

(6) S & D *No. 5, a Fox, Walker 0—6—0 saddle tank photographed at Radstock in 1875, was involved in the 1876 accident at Foxcote*

(7) SDJ *No. 12, a Johnson 0—4—4T of 1877, photographed at Evercreech Junction in its original cabless condition*

severe winter followed, and Pylle bank was still giving trouble.

It was now February 1861, and there was still the extra work and expense involved in laying the third rail on all the company's lines and in constructing the spur at Wyke Champflower, the engineer having already been instructed to communicate with the GWR about

DIVIDING TRAINS.

When it is necessary on any occasion to divide a Train in **Pylle Incline,** and to take it up the Incline in two parts, it must, when possible, be done in the following manner:—The part of the Train to be left must be pushed into the siding at West Pennard, clear of the Main Line, and the first part taken up and placed in the siding at Evercreech, when the Engine or Engines will cross over, to return on the proper Line, for the second part of the Train,—when this is taken to Evercreech, it must be left on the Main Line, clear of the Siding, and the first part of the Train taken out and coupled to it; by this means the Coaches or Waggons will be again in their proper positions in the Train. *Great care must be taken that the last portion of the Train is not allowed to run down the Bank after the Engine is uncoupled from it.*

Instructions for working Pylle bank—from the S & D Rule Book, 1864

the layout of the junction and the exchange of traffic. There was a station to be built at Highbridge, for Somerset Central trains had hitherto used a platform at the Bristol & Exeter station; there were offices to be provided at Glastonbury, fresh staff to be trained, and workshops to be built at Highbridge for the repair of engines and rolling-stock; and above all there were the narrow-gauge engines and rolling-stock to be purchased and paid for.

Tenders had been invited from Robert Stephenson, Kitson, Rothwell of Bolton, Slaughter Gruning of Bristol, Beyer Peacock, and George England of London, and were received from all but the two first-named. England's tender, which was the lowest, was accepted: eight engines at £1,850 each and six tenders at £300 each were to be supplied, one of the engines to be fitted as a tank engine at the additional cost of £150. Delivery was scheduled for July. Four first class carriages at £295 each, five composites at £268 each and four third class at £180 each were ordered from John Perry of Bristol; eight second class carriages at £228 each, and four luggage brakes at £220 each from Joseph Wright of Birmingham.

Tenders were also invited for goods stock from Brown Marshall of Birmingham, Hennet Spink & Else of Bridgwater, John Perry, Joseph Wright, and Rowland Brotherhood of Chippenham. The tenders of the last two were accepted, and four horseboxes at £120 each and six carriage trucks at £76 each were ordered from Wright. Thirty high-sided goods wagons at £58 each, forty low-sided goods wagons at £48 each, and six pairs of timber trucks at £84 each were ordered from Brotherhood.

These orders amounted in all to £27,794, and in February 1862 Counsel was to give his opinion that 'the Company have incurred debts for rolling-stock which they have no funds to discharge'. As a matter of fact neither the rolling-stock nor the line was ready by the long-awaited date when the Bristol & Exeter's lease was due to expire and the Somerset Central was to assume responsibility for working the new narrow-gauge service over its own metals and the metals of its neighbour: as late as 31 August 1861 the link-up with the Dorset Central was still scheduled for October. The Bruton-Templecombe section was ready for use by November, but it was not until 18 January 1862 that the formal opening to Templecombe took place, followed by a dinner at Burnham: public traffic over the narrow gauge began on 3 February 1862.

The five months' gap had been generously filled by the Bristol & Exeter, which in 'a most kind and neighbourly spirit' let the Somerset Central hire locomotives and carriages with which to maintain a service between Burnham and Wells during the final stages of the mixing of the gauge. Perhaps it was the least that the Bristol & Exeter could do, seeing that it had disrupted the Somerset

Central's plans and delayed the opening of its extension by insisting on the mixing of the gauge throughout: after all, it had invested a good deal of capital in the Somerset Central and one of its directors sat on the board. But the Somerset Central might well feel gratitude to the larger concern which had worked its line for seven years and regularly paid the agreed 4 per cent dividend on its share capital, which was considerably more than the shareholders were likely to receive in the immediate future.

From 3 February 1862 the Somerset Central was left to run its own house as best it could. At the fortnightly meeting of directors on 14 February it was agreed that one Robert Scott should be employed for one week at a wage of £5 'to teach the engine drivers the most economical way of using fuel'. The Somerset Central still had a lot to learn about running a railway.

Meanwhile, it had been agreed that the Bristol & Exeter should run a daily passenger train from Bristol to Wells *via* Highbridge and a daily goods train to Cole, taking 25 per cent and 40 per cent of the receipts respectively. Discussion was to continue for some years about the completion of the junction with the GWR at Cole, but even if it was completed—and there is no certainty on this point—it is certain that no broad-gauge traffic ever passed through on to the Wilts, Somerset & Weymouth line. The Bristol & Exeter trains continued to work until 1868, and the third rail was removed from the Somerset & Dorset system about 1870. The broad-gauge victory in the skirmish of 1861 had achieved little or nothing, for the amalgamation of the Somerset Central and the Dorset Central had been a foregone conclusion to the prolonged period of bargaining and negotiation.

As far back as the autumn of 1859 the board of the Somerset Central had discussed the question of subscription to the Dorset Central, the nomination of two directors to its board, and the conferring of mutual running powers over the whole of the two systems as soon as the extensions were completed, including the junction with the Salisbury & Yeovil at Templecombe, as authorised by the Dorset Central's 1860 Act.

In February 1861 the Somerset Central directors were stressing the mutual advantages of the two companies being worked as one, and proposing to undertake the working of the Dorset Central—which was approved at a special general meeting on 29 June. By August they were strongly of the opinion that it would be 'greatly to the interest of both companies that an amalgamation should take place at a future time, so as to secure entire unity of action and economy in management'. Another special general meeting on 9 May 1862 approved the Bill for Amalgamation, which received Royal Assent on 7 August, to take effect from 1 September. After an independent life of just over ten years, the Somerset Central Railway had ceased to exist.

The Dorset Central directors, after drafting an agreement for the working of their line by the Somerset Central for seven years, pending amalgamation, had also approved the proposal for amalgamation in August 1861. They met the Somerset Central directors in July 1862 at the Westminster Palace Hotel under the chairmanship of George Warry, and their final board meeting before the company's dissolution under the Act of Amalgamation was also held in London on 31 July 1862. At this meeting the directors passed a resolution recording their appreciation of the services of Robert A. Read during his seven years as secretary, testifying to the ability with which he had conducted the business of the company, *through a period of great financial difficulty*.

> The Directors feel that it would have been their duty to propose that this Resolution be accompanied by a gratuity had the financial position of the Company permitted it, but under the circumstances they can only record their unqualified approbation of the manner in which Mr. Read has discharged his duties.

On this significant note, stressing a state of financial stringency and the indispensability of Robert Read, the brief six years of the Dorset Central's independent life came to an end.

As a matter of fact it was Robert Read's life that had almost come to a sudden end on 25 January 1862 by the falling of a bridge at Pitcombe near Cole on the Dorset Central, 'which but for the merciful kindness of Providence', George Warry commented, 'would have involved all our railway labours in ruin and confusion, for the bridge gave way within a few minutes after Mr. Read had passed with an engine and one carriage over it. How can we be duly thankful to God for preserving us from that great calamity had it gone down under the train.'

CHAPTER 3

The Somerset & Dorset Railway

ASSETS AND LIABILITIES

The Somerset & Dorset Railway inherited to a marked degree both the assets and the liabilities of the parent companies from which it was born on 1 September 1862. It had fifty miles of well-laid track on which a regular service had been maintained for some years: admittedly the service had been maintained by other companies, and the line still existed in two distinct and separate sections, but work was progressing to complete the missing sixteen miles of track within the extension of time allowed by the Dorset Central's Act of 1860. Meanwhile the new company was firmly linked to the LSW and 'all parts of the narrow-gauge system' by means of the junction at Templecombe, and at the other end of the line ships were making the passage from Burnham to Cardiff in one and a quarter hours.

As soon as the Templecombe-Blandford section was completed, the Somerset & Dorset, with the co-operation of the LSW at the southern end, would be able to boast a Channel-to-Channel service: whether any worthwhile traffic would materialise was another question. To operate the service there was the new rolling-stock —even before amalgamation took place, the Locomotive Superintendent, Robert Andrews, had asked for additional engine power, and more carriages had already been ordered from Joseph Wright (now the Metropolitan Carriage & Wagon Co. Ltd) of Birmingham. How or when it was to be paid for was yet another question.

Financial problems were in fact to be the over-riding consideration in the Somerset & Dorset's fourteen years of independent life. Apart from its obvious state of unpreparedness for fulfilling its commitments in 1862, it was grossly over-capitalised to the tune of £629,073 of which the Dorset Central shares amounted to £193,826 and £249,990 represented debentures. Heavy capital expenditure on the equipment required for the new line was not likely to be met by any adequate increase in receipts from the enlarged system.

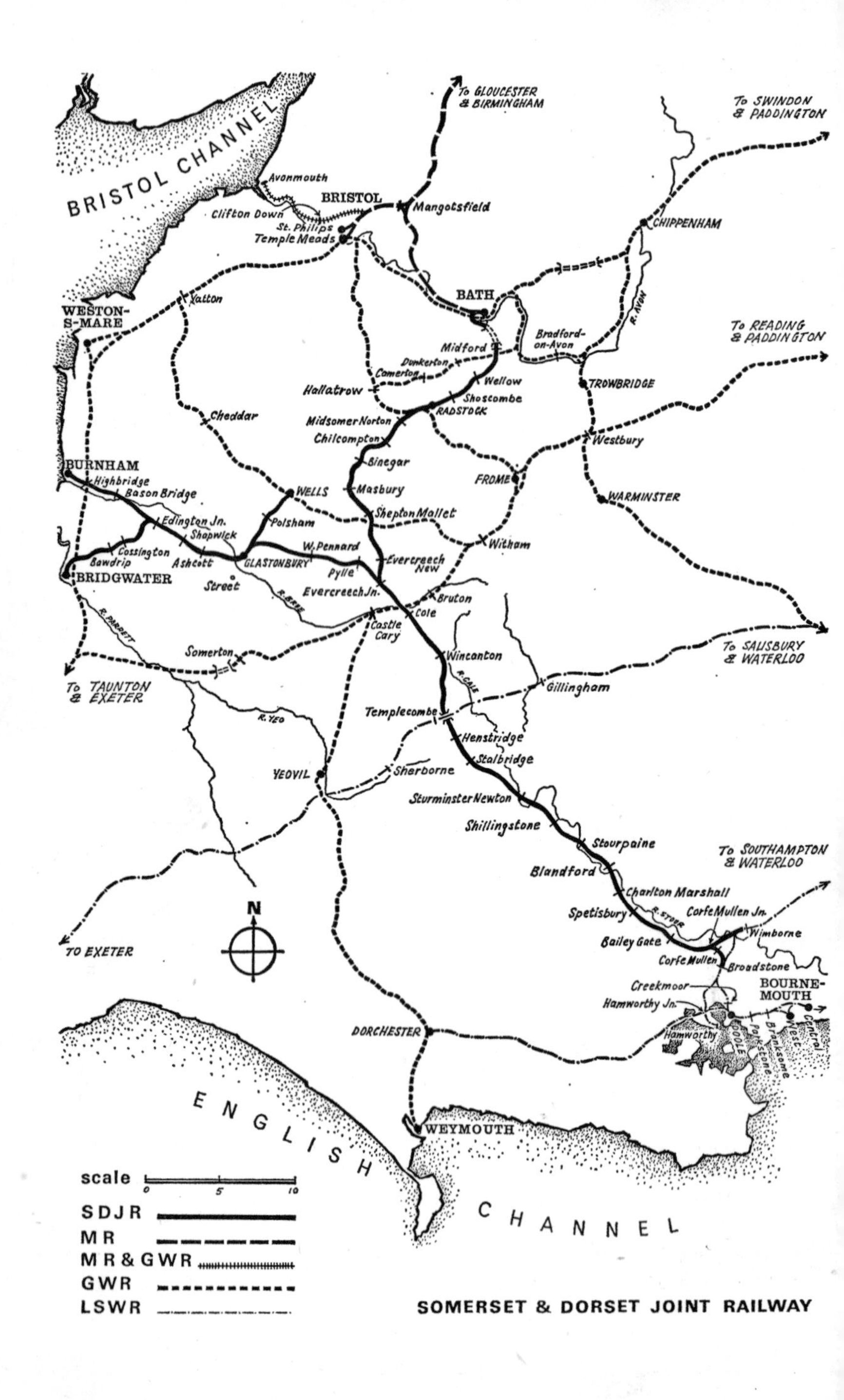

SOMERSET & DORSET JOINT RAILWAY

Already it would seem that the Somerset & Dorset had bitten off more than it could chew and was living beyond its means. In his history of the Salisbury & Yeovil Railway, Louis H. Ruegg mentions Templecombe as the point where

> the best paying line in the Kingdom is brought into connection (and contrast) with the worst. A short, direct line of 40 miles, unencumbered with branches, pays 14 per cent; a pretentious undertaking which sought to exchange the mineral wealth of South Wales for the products of France, has found the many additions to its originally modest aim to be so many clogs to success. . . When this was simply the Somerset Central, 'going from nowhere to nowhere' over a turf moor . . . it was worked by the Bristol & Exeter, paid 4 per cent, and sold at par. At the end of a short lease the Company were left to work their own line, and *in spite of, or as a consequence of, new enterprises,* thousands of pounds have been sunk, and the ordinary shareholders have been without a sixpence of dividend during many years.

The italicised phrases epitomise the Somerset & Dorset's dilemma: consolidation or expansion? Were they to develop the traffic on the system they had planned and all but completed, in the hope of eventually earning a modest dividend for their shareholders? Or were they to plunge on regardless, in the grandiose expectations of tapping new sources of traffic and linking themselves as a trunk line with systems that must have been far beyond the thoughts of the promoters when they first met at Hodge's Railway Hotel at Bridgwater less than a dozen years before?

In either direction enormous uncertainties and difficulties loomed large, yet there is no evidence in the directors' minutes to show that there were divided counsels or serious opposition to the policy of expansion which was followed. The Somerset & Dorset's fourteen years of independent existence fall into two phases: nine years (from 1862-71) of hectic planning and frustration, including four years of virtual bankruptcy while the company's affairs were in the hands of a Receiver; and a further five years (from 1871-75) full of equally frenzied activity, which nevertheless resulted in the fulfilment of the final scheme for the extension of the system, even at the price of complete financial prostration from which the company relapsed gratefully into the lease offered by the Midland and the LSW. The period of storm and stress was over.

The first meeting of the new board of directors took place on 4 October 1862 at the Virginia Ash Hotel at Henstridge, two miles south of Templecombe. For a moment the old and the new transport systems of southern England confronted one another, for the

Virginia Ash Hotel was a coaching inn at an historic intersection of the turnpike roads from London to Exeter and from Bristol to Poole; in a few months' time Templecombe station would begin to fulfil the same function and continued to do so for more than a century.

The appointment of a chairman was an unpleasant business for George Warry, but setting aside pleasure and keeping his duty in mind, he proposed Lord Rivers for the chair 'to the great annoyance of Danby Seymour who had set his heart upon it'. Rivers held the position until his death in 1866 when he was succeeded by the Deputy Chairman, George Warry.

The other nine directors represented the Somerset Central and the Dorset Central in more or less equal proportions, two of them —H. Danby Seymour and George Reed—having already sat on both boards. The Secretary was Robert Read and the Engineer in Chief (later Consulting Engineer), Charles Gregory, both continuing to

The S & D seal, which was still being used until c. 1905

carry out the duties which they had performed for the component companies before amalgamation. F. G. Slessor was Resident Engineer at Glastonbury, his appointment dating from the termination of the Bristol & Exeter's lease of the Somerset Central, while Robert Andrews had been appointed Locomotive Superintendent early in the year of the amalgamation.

The company's seal combined the seal of Dorchester and a representation of a very primitive train passing the town of Glastonbury, dominated by the tower of St John's Church with the famous Tor in the background. The head offices were at Glastonbury, occupying part of the Abbey Arms & Railway Hotel which

STATION SCENES

(8) *Highbridge train at Burnham hauled by one of the Cudworth double-framed 2—4—0s scrapped in 1897*

(9) *Blandford tableau* c. 1900 *including Fowler* 0—6—0 *goods engine and shunting horse*

AT HIGHBRIDGE WORKS

(10) *The erecting shop, showing 4—4—0 No. 15 under repair, also several Johnson 0—6—0s and one of the colliery shunters in the background*

(11) *Signal gang in action outside the works; the bearded figure is Signal Inspector Gill*

S & D PERSONALITIES: DIRECTORS AND OFFICERS

(12) *George Warry,* b. 1795, d. 1883

(13) *James Clark,* b. 1812, d. 1906

(14) *Alfred Whitaker, Locomotive Superintendent* 1889-1911

(15) *George Eyre, Traffic Superintendent,* 1902-21

SINGLE LINE WORKING

(16) *Tablet-exchanging by hand at Sturminster Newton in 1898; up train hauled by Johnson 4—4—0*

(17) *Testing the Whitaker apparatus at Stalbridge with an* SR *'West Country' Pacific in 1951; shedmaster Elliott of Bath*

James John Rocke, a local solicitor, had built near the station, the whole premises being eventually taken over by the Somerset & Dorset.

CONSOLIDATION IN THE SOUTH

The new company's first task was to complete the sixteen-mile section between Templecombe and Blandford. This it succeeded in opening on 31 August 1863, with intermediate stations at Henstridge, Stalbridge, Shillingstone and Sturminster Newton. One of the fascinations of the Somerset & Dorset system was the variety of scenery through which it passed, from the sea-levels of the mid-Somerset moors to the mountainous gradients of the bleak Mendip ridge on the Bath Extension. The Somerset Central's extension from Glastonbury to Cole had involved a steep climb across an outlying spur of Mendip to Evercreech, and on across the upper reaches of the Alham and the Brue. Between Cole and Wincanton the Dorset Central had crossed an almost imperceptible watershed from which streams flow north and west towards the Bristol Channel, and southwards into Christchurch Harbour on the English Channel.

There could hardly have been a more significant meeting place than Cole for the merging of two independent systems to form a Channel-to-Channel route. Wincanton stands upon the Cale, a tributary of the Stour, whose course the Dorset Central line followed all the way to Wimborne—first across the Blackmoor Vale, then through the gap cut by the Stour between Cranborne Chase and the Dorset Heights, and finally down the wider, shallower valley below Blandford. It was an undulating line, sometimes at river level, sometimes high on the hillside above it, always winding and rising and falling, with short stretches of 1 in 80 or 1 in 100 where it followed the contours as closely as possible for economy's sake.

From the traffic manager's point of view the focal point was Templecombe, and the extension of the line to Blandford aggravated operating difficulties there. The first station at Templecombe was opened on 7 May 1860 on the Salisbury & Yeovil Railway which was leased to the LSW, which worked the line until 1878 when it absorbed the smaller company. The Dorset Central's Act of 1857 had provided for a junction between the two lines: this took the form of a spur on the north side of the Salisbury & Yeovil line, diverging from the Dorset Central's Bruton line to join the Salisbury & Yeovil half a mile east of Templecombe station. The Salisbury &

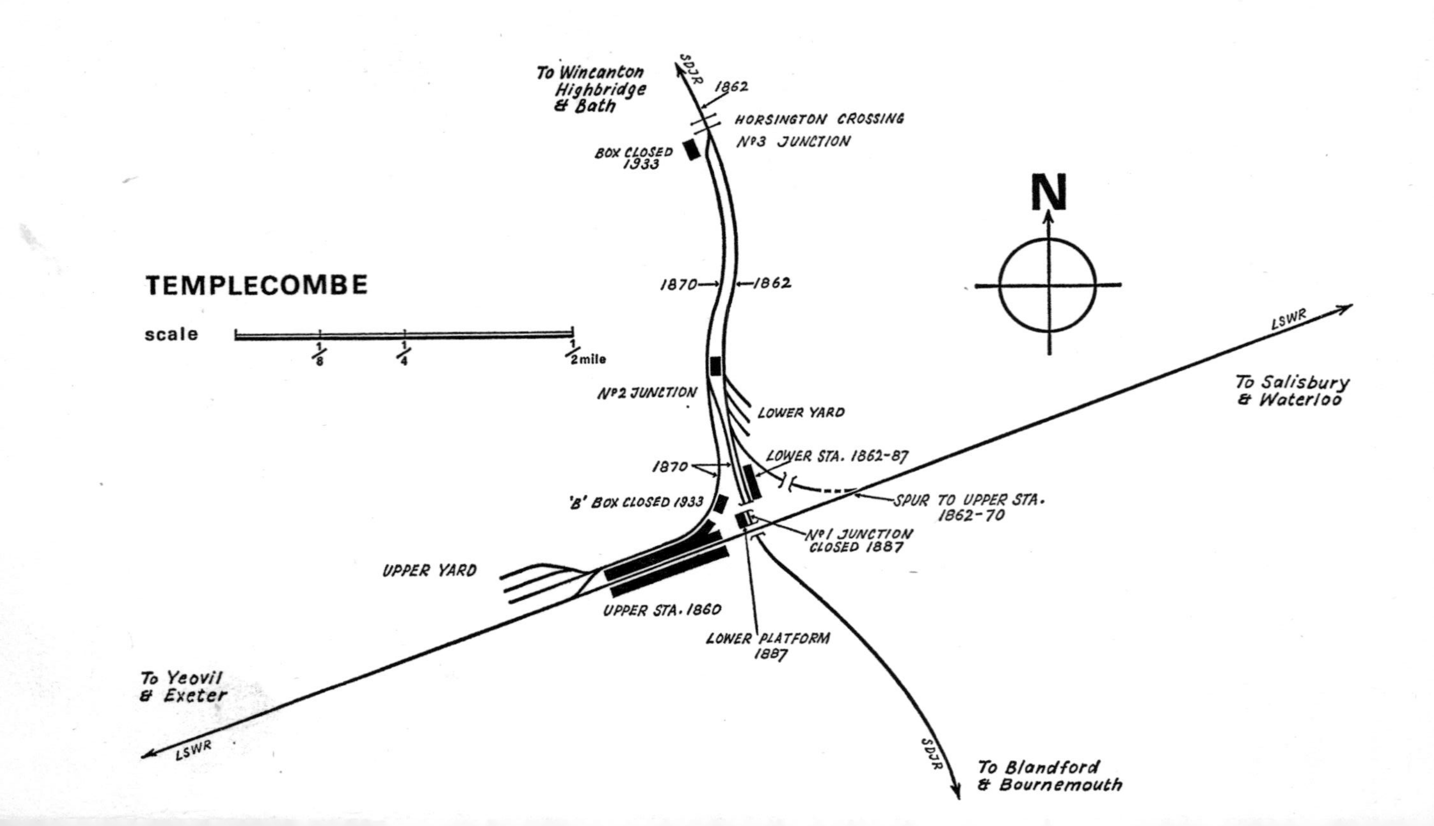
TEMPLECOMBE
scale
1/8
1/4
1/2 mile
N
To Wincanton Highbridge & Bath
SDJR
1862
HORSINGTON CROSSING
Nº3 JUNCTION
BOX CLOSED 1933
1870
1862
Nº2 JUNCTION
LOWER YARD
LOWER STA. 1862-87
1870
'B' BOX CLOSED 1933
SPUR TO UPPER STA. 1862-70
Nº1 JUNCTION CLOSED 1887
UPPER YARD
UPPER STA. 1860
LOWER PLATFORM 1887
LSWR
To Salisbury & Waterloo
To Yeovil & Exeter
LSWR
SDJR
To Blandford & Bournemouth

Yeovil agreed to lay an extra line from the junction to the station, to be used by Dorset Central trains as long as the Salisbury & Yeovil remained single: if it were doubled, the Dorset Central was to provide a third line.

When the line from Glastonbury was opened in February 1862, the Dorset Central provided its own station, eventually to be known as Templecombe Lower, and later still to be incorporated into the buildings of the locomotive department. The Blandford line reached this station by burrowing under the Salisbury & Yeovil line immediately to the east of the Upper station.

Between 1862 and 1870 the LSW for a time worked a shuttle service between the two stations (which were not more than a quarter of a mile apart, but on different levels), while some Somerset & Dorset trains also worked to the Salisbury & Yeovil station, travelling up the spur and then reversing to reach the Upper station. This was obviously not possible for trains to or from Blandford, when a double reversal would have been necessary to reach the Upper station, and with increasing traffic on both lines and the proposed doubling of the Salisbury & Yeovil line, a new solution had to be found.

The plan which was accepted was 'not recommended as being a perfectly good junction, but the best which the circumstances would permit of'. An Act of 16 July 1866 authorised the Salisbury & Yeovil to build a spur of sixty-seven chains from the Upper station to join the Somerset & Dorset line at No. 3 Junction, half a mile to the north of the Lower station; halfway along this spur was No. 2 Junction whence another spur, twenty-two chains long, led down *past* the Lower station to join the line to Blandford at No. 1 Junction (see plan on page 42).*

When these spurs were brought into use in March 1870, Somerset & Dorset trains began to use the northern face of the up Salisbury & Yeovil platform at the Upper station; the Lower station remained in use until 1887, but the original connecting spur was abandoned, though the earthworks are still visible with an unmistakable Dorset Central bridge, and part of the line survived as a siding leading out of the Somerset & Dorset's Lower Yard. Even with these improved arrangements, the facilities for the exchange of passenger and

* At a later date both these new spurs were transferred to the Somerset & Dorset apparently. They are so marked on Railway Clearing House diagrams, and the Templecombe Junction Railway (one mile ten chains) figures among the lines leased or worked by the Somerset & Dorset on the statistical returns made by the Joint Committee.

goods traffic remained very cumbersome (and to the uninitiated extremely bewildering) at what was the most important exchange point on the Somerset & Dorset line.

At the southern extremity of the line, Somerset & Dorset trains were to be involved in another reversal: the opening of the Templecombe-Blandford section meant that the Somerset & Dorset was now in a position to take over the working of the Blandford-Wimborne section from the LSW. A minute at about this time reflects the pleasantly cordial atmosphere which seems to have permanently prevailed between the two companies: 'the South Western Company and the Somerset & Dorset Company shall each toward the other act as friendly companies, and shall make and maintain friendly relations the one with the other'.

Much of the future history of the Somerset & Dorset is epitomised in that affirmation of goodwill. The friendly relations began at Wimborne, where Somerset & Dorset trains from Burnham were to use the LSW station, reverse there and then use the South Western line to reach Poole. At this time Wimborne was the most important railway centre in Dorset. It was Castleman, a Wimborne solicitor, who had been primarily responsible for the promotion of the Southampton & Dorchester Railway, familiarly known as 'Castleman's Corkscrew' because of the devious nature of the first part of the route by which it was proposed that the narrow gauge could be ultimately extended to Exeter.

The Southampton & Dorchester, authorised by an Act of 21 July 1845, had been opened on 1 June 1847, absorbed by the LSW in 1848, and the track doubled in 1863. From Hamworthy Junction (originally Poole Junction) there was a short branch to Poole—or in actual fact to Lower Hamworthy, on the northern shore of Poole Harbour, whence the town of Poole itself was reached across a toll bridge. From 1847 until 1872 this was Poole's station; the passenger service was withdrawn in 1896, since when it led a sort of posthumous existence as Hamworthy Goods. But it was at this point, lapped by the waters of Poole Harbour, that Somerset & Dorset trains completed their journey from coast to coast; and it was from Poole Quay that the Somerset & Dorset was determined to establish steam communication with Cherbourg.

In the summer of 1864 Robert Read had been to France to interview the manager of the Western Railway of France about the acceleration of the train service to Paris and the south in connection with the proposed cross-Channel steamer service, and the reduction of fares between Paris and Cherbourg and between Caen and

Cherbourg for through passengers. Early in 1865 he was at Glasgow examining S.S. *Albion* with a view to chartering her from P. L. Henderson of Liverpool for the Cherbourg service which it was hoped to run from 1 May. If possible a trial trip was to be run, and an invitation was to be issued to the Mayor and Town Council of Poole—perhaps a conciliatory gesture in view of the Somerset & Dorset's inability to share with the harbour trustees the expense of extending the ballast quay.

The service was maintained throughout the summers of 1865 and 1866. In June 1866, for example, *Albion* sailed from Poole on Mondays and Thursdays at 12.30 p.m., connecting with the 8.5 a.m. from Burnham which was due into Poole at 12.5 p.m., and taking six hours over the passage. But by August the directors were considering whether *Albion* was to be laid up during the six winter months, or chartered elsewhere, and at the general meeting in February 1867 it was announced that the service had been 'for the present suspended, the operation having hitherto resulted in a loss'.

Albion was by then registered at Hayle under new ownership, though *The Poole Pilot* for June 1867 expressed a hope that steam communication with Cherbourg would be resumed, a local company being in process of formation to buy the *Spicy* for this purpose. A previous local effort had been forestalled by the placing of *Albion* on the station. So ended a characteristically ambitious Somerset & Dorset maritime venture.

DIFFICULTIES AND DEBTS

The Poole-Cherbourg service was planned to run 'in connection with the service between the North, Bristol, South Wales and Poole'. This was certainly wishful thinking: Bristol and the North were still as remote as ever as far as the Somerset & Dorset was concerned. In February 1859 the Dorset Central shareholders had been told of the Somerset Central's decision to convert to narrow gauge, as a result of which it was expected that the Bristol & Exeter would lay narrow gauge over its line from Highbridge to Bristol. Three years later the Somerset Central was still prodding the Bristol & Exeter to the same course—perhaps a retaliatory measure for the compulsory laying of the broad gauge on the Bruton extension. By the time the amalgamation took place it was clear that the Bristol & Exeter was not going to play, and that other routes to Bristol and the north must be considered.

The difficulty was primarily geographical—and hence to some

extent financial: a combination of factors which had dished the South Midlands Union scheme in 1852. North-west of Wells the Mendip Hills rise like a great rampart above the moors to an average of 800 ft, effectively cutting off the central Somerset plain from the broken hill country to the south of Bristol. The turnpike road from Wells to Bristol plunged northwards across the ridge, but any proposed railway must find a way round.

The Bristol & Exeter main line had found a gap at Uphill, only a mile from the Bristol Channel; the only other possible gap was north of Axbridge, where the Bristol-Bridgwater turnpike road cut through another gap at Shute Shelve. This was the route proposed by the Somerset & Dorset in 1863 for an extension of the line from Wells through Cheddar and Axbridge to Yatton, with hopes of a further extension to Bristol in due course, by means of running powers, involving the laying of a third rail over the Bristol & Exeter main line from Yatton to Bristol. The Bristol & Exeter countered this threat with the proposal to build a line from Uphill to Glastonbury and Wells, striking into the very heart of the Somerset & Dorset's kingdom. In the face of this danger the Somerset & Dorset agreed to allow the Bristol & Exeter to take over the projected line from Wells to Yatton, and the western approach to Bristol was finally barred.

But already the eastern possibilities were being examined. Here the barrier of Mendip, though still formidable, was not impassable. The hills rise more gradually from the plain in a series of ridges and valleys, and beyond the main ridge at Beacon Hill lie fifteen miles of sprawling hill country, gashed by deep valleys of small rivers flowing north and east towards the Frome and the Avon. In the middle of this hill country lay the Somerset coalfield. Coal had been mined in this countryside since the Middle Ages, and many of the hillsides and valleys are marked by spoil-heaps from the shallow workings or forgotten shafts of the early miners.

By 1800 the coalfield centred on Radstock, with collieries dotted about hills and valleys in every direction. For centuries the coal had been carried by packhorses or carts, but in 1805 the Somersetshire Coal Canal had been opened along the Cam valley for ten miles, from a junction with the Kennet & Avon at the Dundas aqueduct to a terminal basin between Timsbury and Paulton, served by a number of tramways from surrounding collieries. From Midford a seven and a quarter-mile branch had been planned to Radstock, but never completed, and in 1815 a tramway was built along the unused towing path, also linked by tramways with outlying collieries.

By the middle of the nineteenth century the Somersetshire Coal Canal was the most prosperous canal in the south of England, paying its shareholders a comfortable dividend and as yet free from the menace of the railway. Not until 1854, the same year that saw the opening of the Somerset Central, did the railway reach Radstock: an eight and a quarter-mile broad-gauge branch from the Wilts, Somerset & Weymouth line at Frome, opened for mineral traffic only, on 14 November 1854. Even this invasion seems hardly to have affected the Somersetshire Coal Canal.

This then was the promised land towards which the Somerset & Dorset and other companies, both actual and potential, were casting longing eyes, and during the next few years there was a feverish spate of proposals and counter-proposals in which the Somerset & Dorset was directly or indirectly concerned, until the financial crisis of 1866 put an end to all such schemes, and it was only in 1873 that another railway at last reached the coalfield.

In 1862 the Somerset & Dorset directors were discussing the projected Somerset Coal Railway which was to run from Wincanton to the Radstock coalfield; in 1865 another separate company proposed a line from Bath to Radstock. All the other schemes seem to have involved the Bristol & North Somerset Railway whose narrow-gauge line from Bristol to Radstock had been authorised by an Act of 21 July 1863.

In the Parliamentary sessions of 1864-66 there were abortive schemes for the Somerset & Dorset to push north through Shepton Mallet to join the Bristol & North Somerset at Farrington Gurney, with a colliery branch to the Nettlebridge valley; for the amalgamation of the two companies, and for the takeover of the Bristol & North Somerset by the Somerset & Dorset. None of these schemes ever reached the Statute Book.

Perhaps the most interesting scheme was the Bristol & North Somerset (Southern Extension) Bill of 1866 which closely resembled a Somerset & Dorset proposal of the previous year; the proposed extension was to diverge from the Bristol-Radstock line near Farrington Gurney, climb past Chilcompton and Binegar to a 600 yd tunnel at Beacon Hill and, descending past Shepton Mallet (where there was to be a junction with the East Somerset Railway), to join the Somerset & Dorset line south of Evercreech. From Old Down, between Chilcompton and Binegar, a branch was to strike south-east down the Nettlebridge valley, following the course of the abandoned Dorset & Somerset Canal past Coleford to join the Radstock-Frome branch near the site of Mells Road station.

These proposals would have provided north Somerset with a very different pattern of railways, and it is fascinating to speculate on the possibility of a direct route from Bristol to Poole. The withdrawal of this Bill spelled the end of the Somerset & Dorset's hopes of reaching Bristol. In any event, the Bristol & North Somerset was finding it difficult to raise capital for its original line from Bristol to Radstock, which was not opened until 3 September 1873 (with the help of the GWR): in 1874 the mineral branch from Radstock to Frome was converted to narrow gauge, and on 5 July 1875 Bristol-Frome trains began to run through Radstock, a year after the Somerset & Dorset had reached the district on an entirely different route.

By 1866 the financial affairs of the Somerset & Dorset had reached a dreadful state. Since amalgamation, the line had been paying its way in so far as traffic receipts comfortably exceeded working expenses. Tonnage handled at Highbridge had doubled, but Burnham was clearly incapable of being developed into a port, while the Channel-to-Channel route served only scattered rural communities and no town, except Poole, with a population of more than 5,000.

This situation might have been tolerable if the Somerset & Dorset had been able to start in the clear; but it was always struggling to acquire (and pay for) an adequate amount of narrow-gauge rolling-stock to maintain its service. In October 1865, for instance, the directors were informed that traffic was being lost because of the inability to move it; large consignments had been refused because of the shortage of locomotives. Two more engines had in fact been ordered from George England in 1862, another four in 1863, and yet two more in 1865 at the cost of £7,000, though it is clear that the company was in no position to accept delivery of all the engines ordered.

In October 1865, George Reed had actually sold the company a second-hand engine, belonging to himself, for £1,450—'payment to be made by a bill at twelve months without interest' though, alas, in January 1867 interest began to be paid on yet another unsecured debt. George Reed was certainly dipping his hand deep into his own pocket to help the floundering company, for in the following year he was registered as the owner of a new steamer, named after himself, which had been acquired as an addition to the Somerset & Dorset fleet. In July 1866 arrangements were discussed for leasing two of the six engines ordered from the Vulcan Foundry because the company was unable to pay in cash. Earlier in the same year there were plans for an instalment system of payment for rolling-stock spread over a period of ten years.

The directors had rashly borrowed from the revenue account to pay for the new rolling-stock and equipment; these sums they were unable to repay (under the pressure of the little Railway Mania and the financial crisis of 1866). They were unable to raise fresh capital, though £100,000 in shares and £33,000 on loan had been authorised by their Act of 25 July 1864, and they were also unable to pay their debenture interest in June 1866. The Court of Chancery accordingly took charge of the company's affairs and Receivers were appointed. The half-yearly report presented on 27 February 1867 declared that, as on all other lines, traffic had suffered severely 'from the depression in trade prevailing throughout the year, and the interference with travelling caused by unfavourable weather, the prevalence of the cattle plague and cholera, and a commercial crisis of unparalleled magnitude and duration'.

The Court of Chancery was ruthless: some of the rolling-stock carried owner's plates to show that it no longer belonged to the company. A petition from the engine-drivers for a turntable at Templecombe to avoid having to run tender first to Highbridge was rejected; so were various proposals for dealing with the company's affairs, including schemes for capital rearrangement in 1868 and 1869. Meanwhile, the utmost possible economy in working expenditure was being effected, with a possible saving of up to £6,000 a year; the offices of locomotive and carriage superintendent and storekeeper were abolished as separate appointments, the departments being placed under the control of the Resident Engineer, F. G. Slessor. At last in 1870, the Receivers were discharged and the Court of Chancery allowed the company to raise £160,000 in debentures, making a total of £796,950 in debentures out of the total consolidated capital of £1,324,165: the four long years in the wilderness were over.

THE BATH EXTENSION

At this juncture the Somerset & Dorset took a deep breath and plunged forward into its most spectacular and costly extension. It was a courageous but fatal decision: courageous for the vision which replaced a struggling Channel-to-Channel line by the final link in a narrow-gauge route linking the North and the Midlands with the South Coast and the West of England; fatal in that it almost inevitably invited financial suicide and the death of the Somerset & Dorset as an independent company. There is no evidence to show how long the directors had been meditating this course: Bath is never mentioned specifically in the expansionist schemes of 1863-6, but the possible routes to Bristol were now blocked, and arrival of the Midland Railway in Bath on 4 August 1869 may have drawn their eyes in that direction.

The Midland line was a ten-mile branch from Mangotsfield on the Birmingham-Bristol main line. At first traffic used a temporary station, just across the river from the terminus at Queen Square, which was opened on 7 May 1870. The Somerset & Dorset accordingly proposed to build a single-line extension twenty-five miles fifty-nine chains in length, from a junction with the Burnham line, twenty-four chains north of Evercreech station, to a junction with the Midland, forty-one chains from Queen Square, the Midland granting running powers and full facilities for working over this last short section of line.

An Act of 21 August 1871 authorised the Somerset & Dorset to raise further capital —£360,000 in shares and £120,000 by mortgages or debentures. The contract with Messrs T. & C. Walker was for £352,000, but more than £400,000 was finally spent on the extension, apart from the cost of the additional rolling-stock, equipment and staff required. The 1871 Act also authorised the purchase of the Somersetshire Coal Canal tramway for £20,000. Since 1815 horses had been drawing eight or nine wagons, each holding 27 cwt of coal, along this tramway from Radstock to Midford, where the coal was loaded into boats on the Coal Canal.

The Somerset & Dorset was able to follow the line of the tramway for about six miles from Radstock to a point midway between Wellow and Midford, though the windings of the canal along the side of the valley precluded the use of the towing path, which can still be seen crossing and recrossing the line of the railway many times. The extensions of the tramway to collieries at Welton and Clandown were also acquired. The prospectus of 1872 claimed that the Coal Canal tramway had been moving more than 100,000 tons of coal a year.

The Somerset & Dorset had broken through into the coalfield with a vengeance, and a further Act of 5 August 1873 authorised the construction of a one and a half-mile branch to the Strap Pit of the Downside Colliery Company in the Nettlebridge valley. The capital authorised (£60,000 in shares and £20,000 in loans) was to be held distinct from the company's main capital, and shareholders were to benefit only from profits earned on the branch. Before these projects could materialise, the Somerset & Dorset was hamstrung by the expenses of the construction of the main line to Bath and had no wish to undertake further commitments, though it was not until 1878 that the Joint Committee formally abandoned the Nettlebridge scheme.

The Bath Extension was completed in the amazingly short period of two years. Three thousand men were employed on the works and there is a vivid picture of the construction of the line in *One Man's Road,* the autobiography of Arthur Waugh, whose father was a country doctor at Midsomer Norton: he recalls how the peace of the favourite walk which he took with his nurse was suddenly shattered by the coming of navvies, with the countryside scored with a long scarlet wound, and loud explosions as the rock was blasted away to make a cutting on the long bank up to Chilcompton. 'Several of our favourite trees were lying on the ground; the earth was turned up; boards, wheelbarrows, and the boots of rough loud-voiced men had beaten down the primroses into a pulp of red soil.' A swarm of navvies on the embankment shouted rude words after the perambulator, which made the nurse turn hurriedly for home with flaming cheeks.

It was no easy task to drive the Bath Extension over the Mendip range with a summit level of 811 ft above sea level at Masbury. The Consulting Engineer was W. H. Barlow, and the line shows signs of high engineering competence in extraordinarily difficult terrain: it winds almost continuously, with long stretches at the ruling gradient of 1 in 50, four tunnels totalling nearly 2,600 yd, and seven major viaducts. The Evercreech-Bath section in fact gives an entirely different impression from any other section of the Somerset & Dorset line, largely because of the grey limestone of which practically everything is built: stations, signalboxes, bridges and viaducts. It is still possible to identify many of the lineside quarries from which the stone was hewn.

Behind this feverish activity loomed the spectre of financial embarrassment, never far absent from the story of the Somerset & Dorset. Nobody knew this better than the Secretary, Robert Read. In March 1871 the directors reimbursed him to the extent of £500 'for extra services, loss of interest and expenses on advances to the Company' since 21 July 1866, i.e. during the period of the Receivership. Read generously disclaimed £200 of his salary and £200 expenses per annum. In the following year he received a remuneration of £1,000 for his services in securing the passing of the Bath Extension Act and for the risk he ran personally in guaranteeing the Parliamentary deposit: he was also offered a seat on the board, which he occupied as managing director until 1874, when his style reverted to general manager at a salary of £1,200 a year.

In April 1874 the contractors complained that as the company was unable to pay them in cash they had no alternative but to stop work and withdraw their men. The directors thereupon decided that all works 'not absolutely necessary for the opening of the line for traffic' should be suspended until they were able to raise fresh capital, and persuaded the contractors to accept new ordinary shares and debentures in part payment, and the balance in Lloyd's Bonds. In the end, work was going on day and night to get the line ready for the opening, for the company's faith and hope were pinned on the opening of the new extension which would finally solve all its financial worries and even reward the patience of its long-suffering shareholders.

20 July 1874 was a landmark in the history of the line. The first Somerset & Dorset train left Bath at 7.25 a.m. It carried few passengers, because very short notice of the opening had been given, the final Board of Trade inspection having only taken place on 17 July. At Wellow the church bells rang out; at Binegar a flag was flying and a large red banner proclaimed 'Success to the Railway'. But the thronging spectators at Evercreech and Wincanton so delayed the train that it contrived to reach Templecombe after the down train to Exeter had left.

> This is a bad beginning, commented the *Bath Chronicle*. May the Somerset & Dorset managers speedily mend their ways in the matter of punctuality or they will only too quickly find that would-be travellers will go by their longer but fairly punctual competitors, rather than by a route where times of arrival are uncertain and delays not improbable, albeit the mileage may be considerably less.

The directors were urged to do all they could to redeem the character of the line whose initials had already been facetiously interpreted as the 'Slow and Dirty Railway' (*Bath Chronicle and Herald*, 23 July 1874). Overnight, however, a completely new look had been given to the railway map of the West of England. Four trains a day each way were scheduled for the opening service, and two of them carried through carriages from Birmingham to Bournemouth: the Midland Railway had penetrated to the South Coast.

This had been made possible only through the Somerset & Dorset's 'friendly relations' with the LSW. When the Southampton & Dorchester line had been opened in 1847, there could never have been a thought of a branch to Bournemouth, which was then no more than a village. The first line to reach the growing town was a branch from Ringwood, which reached Christchurch on 13 November 1862 and Bournemouth East (later Bournemouth Central) on 14 March 1870. There had also been several abortive attempts to reach Bournemouth from the north, and at the same time to give the town of Poole a better service than that provided by the Hamworthy branch.

The first serious scheme appears in the plans deposited by the Dorset Central in 1859 though not included in its 1860 Act. These plans show a projected extension southwards from Wimborne, with a loop at Oakley to avoid reversal, through Broadstone and Poole, to a terminus somewhere near the site of the later Bournemouth West Junction—following very closely the final route of Somerset & Dorset trains from Broadstone onwards. After this, proposals proliferate. An 1860 Wimborne & Poole Railway was to follow almost the same line; the Poole Railway of 1860 proposed a dead-end branch from Broadstone with a tramway to the quay. In 1862 there was a proposal for a completely isolated line from Poole to Bournemouth, while the 1863 Poole, Bournemouth & Wimborne Railway proposed to link itself to the Southampton & Dorchester line at Hamworthy and Wimborne by means of an enormous loop with a branch going off vaguely towards Bournemouth.

We reach firm ground at last with the Poole & Bournemouth Railway which was incorporated under an Act of 26 May 1865. The deposited plans show that the original intention was to build a line running from a junction with the Southampton & Dorchester at Broadstone, down an incline of 1 in 60 and through Poole, to a terminus at Bournemouth West, a distance of seven and three-quarter miles, with a mile-long branch in Poole, 'terminating at or near the fish shambles on the public quay'. Comprehensive arrangements with the LSW and the Somerset & Dorset were also specified in the plans.

The Poole & Bournemouth Railway was clearly a protégé of the Somerset & Dorset, with Charles Waring as Chairman, and Robert Read as Secretary and later Managing Director. The authorised capital was £90,000. The section from Broadstone to Poole, however, was never actually authorised, being withdrawn at the Committee stage, but in the following year the LSW was authorised by an Act of 16 July 1866 to construct a four-mile branch from Broadstone, on a slightly different line and with a slightly easier gradient of 1 in 77, to link up with the branch to the quay and with the authorised line to Bournemouth, although instead of a terminus at Bournemouth West an extension was proposed to meet the line from Ringwood and Christchurch. This last proposal was not carried out, and several other minor adjustments in the two companies' plans were effected, with the result that the LSW finally built three and a half miles from New Poole Junction (i.e. Broadstone) to Poole, and the Poole & Bournemouth built the remaining three and three-quarter miles to Bournemouth West.

Under the LSW Act of 1866 the Poole & Bournemouth's authorised capital was reduced to £60,000, but the financial crisis of 1866 and the disastrous state of the Somerset & Dorset's own finances made it difficult to raise this capital, and two extensions of time had to be obtained for the completion of the works. On 2 December 1872 the LSW opened its line from Broadstone to Poole, and Somerset & Dorset trains from Burnham began to run into the new station instead of to Hamworthy, which thus became very much of a backwater. It was not until 15 June 1874 that the Poole & Bournemouth line was opened. This was worked from the outset by the LSW for £2,250 a year. It seems hardly likely that the Somerset & Dorset ever contemplated working it; it actually paid not more than £1,400 a year for rebate in gross receipts coming from, or destined for, the Poole & Bournemouth and carried on the Somerset & Dorset. The Poole & Bournemouth retained its nominal independence until absorbed by the LSW on 31 October 1882.

The arrival of the railway from the east and from the west in 1870 and 1874 gave Bournemouth all the impetus towards growth that it needed. 'The favourite watering place' referred to by the promoters of the Poole & Bournemouth in 1865 and whose population in 1851 had been 695, had nearly reached 6,000 in 1871 and 16,000 in 1881. The process was indubitably accelerated by the fact that from 20 July 1874 Somerset & Dorset trains were able to work through from Bath to Bournemouth West, and a new north to south trunk line had come into existence—and a narrow-gauge line at that—striking through the heart of the broad-gauge territory.

There was no doubt about the volume of potential traffic that was available; quite apart from excursion traffic to Bournemouth, there was an enormous influx of goods traffic over the new line, 107,529 tons being exchanged with the Midland at Bath in the first eleven months after the opening of the Extension, and 89,431 tons with the LSW at Templecombe. Against this was to be set the cost of new locomotives—six Fowler 0—6—0s and five 0—6—0 saddle tanks from Fox, Walker of Bristol, some of them in exchange for older and less powerful types.

The rolling-stock was inadequate and so was the track; there were not enough sidings or loops for crossing trains as directed by the crossing agent at Glastonbury; the service was undermanned by inadequately trained staff. Nor was the net revenue sufficient to provide proper maintenance: in the half-year following the opening of the Bath Extension (to 31 December 1874) it amounted to £5,840, and to 30 June 1875 to £4,347, of which £4,000 was earmarked to meet the interest on No. 1 debentures. There was no question of the payment of dividends on the ordinary shares, or on the Bath Extension shares which had been issued at a discount of up to 50 per cent, or on the preference shares, or on the majority of the debentures where arrears of interest were steadily accumulating.

The Somerset & Dorset had gambled everything on the Bath Extension—and lost, and it is tragic to think how close the line was to assured prosperity. In the circumstances there was little that the directors could do: the cupboard was bare, and there was little or no chance of any further reorganisation of capital; it was hardly feasible to allow the company's affairs to relapse into the Court of Chancery. The only possibility was to sell out—the question was to whom?

THE TAKE-OVER STRUGGLE

In a sense the take-over struggle for the Somerset & Dorset was the last major battle in the War of the Gauges. The Somerset & Dorset was now firmly linked with narrow-gauge systems at each extremity of its main line and, as far as the broad-gauge parties were concerned, the writing was on the wall. Within months of the opening of the Bath Extension, the Bristol & Exeter directors announced their intention of adding a third rail to all parts of their main line where the gauge was not already mixed; *The Railway News* even suggested that this was because heavy losses were already being incurred by the diversion of their northern traffic over the new line. Their 1875 Act authorised the alteration to mixed or narrow gauge and the abandonment of the broad gauge. But before this could be effected, the Bristol & Exeter had been amalgamated with the Great Western (1 August 1876), the amalgamation being finally precipitated by the take-over of the Somerset & Dorset, and representing a final stiffening of the defences of the broad-gauge party against the opening up of a rival narrow-gauge route between the North and West of England.

At the outset it was always on the cards that those supporting the broad gauge would get control of the Somerset & Dorset, and when it slipped from their grasp—whatever moral or legal objections might be adduced in deciding the issues—it was very largely the result of a tactical mistake on their part. MacDermot, as the historian of the Great Western Railway, might refer to the 'unpleasant incident' of the take-over of the Somerset & Dorset, but it was an incident that need never have occurred.

In May 1875 the Somerset & Dorset approached the Great Western which, after consultation with the Bristol & Exeter, announced itself to be ready to take over the line if terms could be agreed. By early August no progress had been made with the negotiations, but on Thursday 12 August the Great Western and the Bristol & Exeter made the fatal move of sending their managers to meet Scott, the LSW's Manager, at Waterloo, to inform him of their proposed terms for the take-over of the Somerset & Dorset, with the suggestion that the LSW might be interested in taking over the southern half of the line below Templecombe. Scott's reaction was swift and dramatic: he was unimpressed by the offer of the southern half of the line, and appalled to discover that the Somerset & Dorset had offered to sell out to the Great Western.

While the LSW board was officially considering the offer and negotiations were suspended, Scott was 'secretly very busy'.* He was immediately instructed to meet Allport, the Midland General Manager, at Birmingham, and over the weekend they together inspected the Somerset & Dorset line and examined its accounts. A Midland board meeting was followed by a meeting of deputations of Midland and LSW directors, and a definite offer for a long-term lease of the Somerset & Dorset by the two companies was sent to Robert Read. On Friday 20 August 1875 the Somerset & Dorset board met, only eight days after the first approach had been made to the LSW, rejected the terms offered by the Great Western and the Bristol & Exeter as 'not consistent with the interests of this company', and embraced the considerably better terms offered to Robert Read the previous evening by the Midland and the LSW for a 999-year lease from 1 November.

The week's drama was over, leaving the Great Western with a sense of bitter frustration, and a determination to prevent the agreement going through if it were humanly possible. It published its acrimonious correspondence with the LSW, accusing the latter of

* A full account of the complex moves of the different parties is to be found in MacDermot's *History of the Great Western Railway*, revised C. R. Clinker 1964, Vol ii, pp. 51-54.

breach of faith in making use of information which had been disclosed to it 'in an open and friendly manner' to reach what could only be described as a hostile agreement behind the GWR's back. The Midland was also arraigned for breach of an Agreement of 1863 by which it was bound not to extend beyond Bath and to agree with the GWR on the leasing or working of any lines in the district. It was a tangled issue between expediency and honour. No defence could be offered for the behaviour of the LSW, but the Railway Commissioners somewhat equivocally managed to absolve the Midland from the accusation of breach of agreement. The Great Western opposed the Bill for confirming the lease, but the chairman of the Parliamentary Committee set the good of the public at large against the suggestion that any company had not acted quite fair and above board, and the Act was obtained on 13 July 1876. The fate of the Somerset & Dorset line was settled for the next 71 years and nobody could really claim that the line would have been put to better use if it had fallen into the hands of the Great Western.

The lease came as a wonderful relief to the harassed directors of the Somerset & Dorset. Their half-yearly report issued in February 1875 referred to the many unavoidable difficulties that had combined to interfere with the efficient working of the Bath Extension 'in addition to those which are inseparable from the opening of a new line . . . the effects produced by an unusually hot autumn on the earthworks . . . the delay in the delivery of the engines specially ordered for working over the heavy gradients'. On 31 August they expressed their continued confidence in the ultimate development of the traffic: perhaps it was a case of hindsight when they confessed that they had for some time past entertained the conviction that their line 'could be developed more rapidly and worked more economically in the hands of some or one of the larger companies with whom it formed connections'.

The terms of the lease represented a very fair deal for the Somerset & Dorset: the rent was fixed at £43,056 for the first year, rising to £57,408 in the fourth year together with one-tenth of any sum by which the gross receipts exceeded £114,816 in any one year. This was sufficient to meet the interest on the 3½ per cent Bath Extension ordinary stock as well as all the debenture dividends. The 1876 Act also authorised the raising of £100,000 new share capital, together with a £33,333 loan from each of the leasing companies, which were placed on an absolutely equal footing in all respects as far as their obligations and liabilities under the Act were concerned. The bailiffs were out; the new tenants were in. The independent life of the Somerset & Dorset was over, but there was one vital link between the old order and the new. In November 1875 the directors had voted Robert Read £5,000 'for extraordinary services', and he was now installed as secretary and general manager of the Somerset & Dorset Joint Railway: he still had more than 15 years' service to give to the line which he had done so much to create.

Born in 1830, Read was the son of a Stroud schoolmaster: orphaned at the age of 15, he worked his way up in the railway world entirely unaided, joining the Somerset Central, as we have seen, at the age of 23. During the independent days of the Somerset & Dorset he lived with a large and high-spirited family at The Elms, Glastonbury, where a family group shows him surrounded by his three sons and seven daughters—a perfect mid-Victorian tableau. After the early death of his first wife he married again in 1880, and the only child of this marriage, Miss Muriel Read, has clear and vivid memories of her father who died in 1908. She recalls in particular her pride and excitement when they went to Cornwall for their holidays, sometimes in a directors' carriage which was put at their disposal, and every stationmaster down the line would come out and greet her father with delight. An old faded photograph shows a strong bearded Victorian with sparkling eyes and more than a touch of humour and humanity—a man who certainly aroused feelings of affection as well as esteem. *Res non verba* was his family motto, and Read's career embodies many of those qualities that contributed to the greatness of Victorian England: vision, courage, vigour, integrity, and utter devotion to duty.

CHAPTER 4

The Joint Line

URGENT REFORMS

'Before the Midland and the L & SW jointly took it over, the Somerset & Dorset Railway was about as crazy an undertaking as ever conducted business, at least as a nominal main line railway. . . The MR and the LSWR between them made of the Somerset & Dorset a model line.' Such is the verdict of C. Hamilton Ellis in his history of the Midland Railway, and it is a perfect summary of the period from 1875 to 1914. It was a period of gradual but ruthless reorganisation and consolidation upon the decidedly flimsy foundations laid by the old company. Louis H. Ruegg writing in 1878 might refer to 'that most unfortunate of railways'—and the most impecunious; by 1914 it was neither impecunious nor unfortunate, but the legend of incompetence still lurked beneath the sobriquet of 'Slow and Dirty', which was unfair to an efficient and progressive line.

Between the signing of the agreement for the leasing of the line from 1 November 1875 and its confirmation by the Act of 13 July 1876, there was very little that the Midland and the LSW could do. The line was worked under a provisional arrangement pending Parliamentary approval of the lease: their powers were strictly limited, and there was no question of embarking on the heavy expenditure which the line required or of materially altering the Somerset & Dorset arrangements. Within a month of their assuming full legal responsibility for the line, the shattering disaster at Radstock, in which 13 people were killed and 34 injured, focused public attention on the Somerset & Dorset line in a most unwelcome and tragic manner.

The accident itself is fully described in Chapter 7, but it was the glaring deficiencies in equipment and staff, as well as the appallingly haphazard operational methods which were revealed by the inquest and the inquiry, that brought home to the Joint Committee the liabilities it had inherited from the old company. On the other hand, it vehemently denied that it was justly answerable 'for the want of proper arrangements and of discipline' which were stated to have caused the accident; while it had spared no pains to improve the condition of the line and to ensure the safety of the public using it, it could not be expected to accept responsibility for the condition of the line as transferred to it by an Act of Parliament 25 days before: in fact it was expressly absolved from such responsibility in Captain Tyler's report on the accident.

All this is cogently affirmed in a letter from the Joint Committee (21 December 1876) replying to the allegation of 'reprehensible negligence' made by the Board of Trade on 22 November, and 'respectfully protesting against a grave and sweeping imputation of negligence which it feels strongly to be unmerited'. It also spoke out in defence of its predecessors: it was unable to ascertain that the condition of the line had ever previously been censured by the Board of Trade, and 'it is due to the officers of the Somerset and Dorset Co. to remark that they had worked the line in safety for many years previous to the transfer under the arrangements and upon the system then in force'. It did not disregard or underrate its responsibility 'to put and maintain the line in proper condition and to afford a safe and efficient public service thereon . . . but to complete all repairs and improvements will necessarily occupy time'.

It would certainly take time, but the committee had already made a start. Allport and Scott, the General Managers of the MR and the LSW, had made a tour of inspection on 30 September and 1 October in the company of Robert Read and B. S. Fisher, the S & D Locomotive Superintendent, S. W. Johnson, his counterpart from Derby, and the engineers of the two leasing companies. Their report, dated 7 October, made detailed recommendations for the future management of the Joint line. Of the culprits chiefly responsible for the Radstock disaster, the stationmasters at Wellow and Radstock had already been dismissed, and the crossing agent at Glastonbury was to follow them shortly. Glastonbury was anyhow castigated as a 'very inconvenient position for the principal offices', which were to be removed to Bath as soon as suitable accommodation was found.

This turned out to be 14 Green Park Buildings, to which the Somerset & Dorset offices were transferred in 1877, the superintendent of the line and the crossing agent being accommodated at Bath station, and the Glastonbury offices being made over to the resident engineer and his staff. The permanent way department was put under the control of the LSW engineer, and the locomotive department under the Midland locomotive superintendent, with the recommendation that heavy locomotive repairs should be undertaken at Bristol and renewals at Derby, while ordinary repairs should be undertaken at Highbridge, where the carriage and wagon department was to be maintained—a division of labour that was to be more or less permanent until 1930. More immediately, nine new engines were to be ordered, 0—4—4Ts of Midland design, the three Midland engines at present on hire to be returned, and the six Somerset & Dorset engines that were too light and unsuited to the Joint line to be taken over at a valuation by the lessees.

The Joint Committee was also to make 'such appointments as may be necessary to secure the safety of the line'. Of these by far the most crucial was the appointment of a superintendent of the line, who was to be responsible for its working, for the supervision of the staff, and for all train arrangements. This appointment went to Robert Armstrong Dykes, one of the outstanding personalities in the history of the Somerset & Dorset. Dykes came of a railway family, his father having been traffic superintendent of the Bristol & Exeter: he had himself worked for the Midland, and in 1876 he was manager of the Bourn & Lynn Joint Line of the Midland and Great Northern companies.

From 1876 until 1902 it was Dykes' task to put the Somerset & Dorset line in order. In an illustrated interview published in *The Railway Magazine* in March 1899, he gave an account of his stewardship: 'For some years I found I had a very uphill task before me, but by dint of unceasing labour on the part of Mr. Whitaker (Resident Locomotive Superintendent from 1889), Mr. Colson (Resident Engineer from 1876) and myself, and well backed by the owning companies, we have succeeded in placing our line on a par with any in the Kingdom'.

The first few years of the new regime were years of quiet consolidation, which came as something of a relief after the grandiose schemes and the recurring financial crises of the bad old independent days. The expansionist era was over; it was no longer a question of do-or-die. Instead, the Joint Committee buckled to its task of getting together and training a reliable staff, re-laying and improving its track, overhauling the signalling and telegraph systems in connection with the block working—Tyer's electric tablet system was eventually installed in 1886—and above all getting the trains moving with adequate rolling-stock and motive power. This meant not only local traffic, but also through coaches to Birmingham and, in 1880, to Bradford and Newcastle.

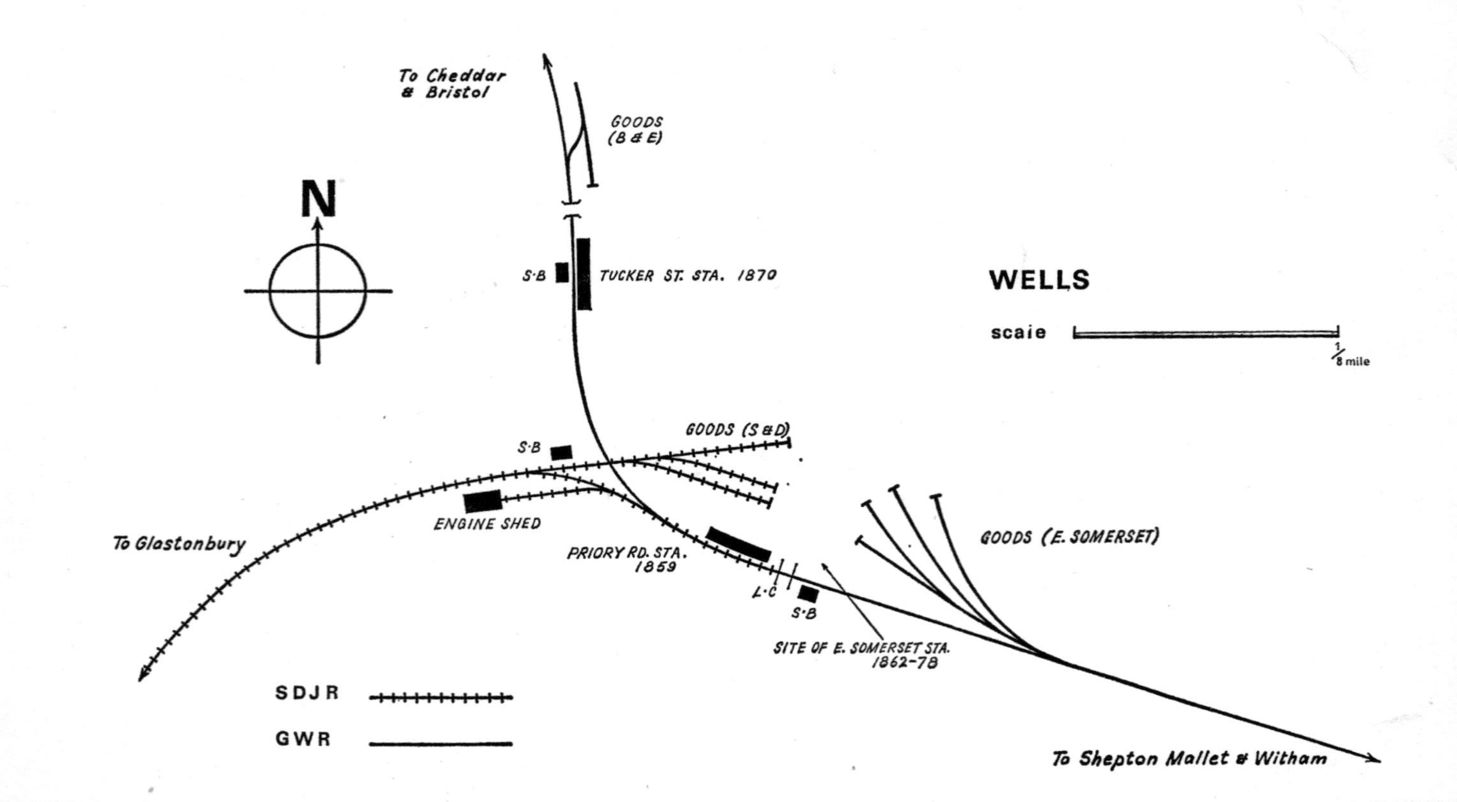

WELLS
scale
1/8 mile
N
To Cheddar & Bristol
GOODS (B & E)
S·B
TUCKER ST. STA. 1870
GOODS (S & D)
S·B
ENGINE SHED
To Glastonbury
PRIORY RD. STA. 1859
L·C
S·B
SITE OF E. SOMERSET STA. 1862-78
GOODS (E. SOMERSET)
To Shepton Mallet & Witham
SDJR
GWR

There was the ever-increasing exchange of goods traffic at Bath and Templecombe, and the development of traffic in the basic commodities of coal, stone and milk on which much of the prosperity of the line was to depend: it is noticeable how many sidings to collieries and quarries and other industrial sites date from the early decades of the Joint line. The net revenue doubled between 1876 and 1881, but it was also a period of cautious retrenchment. An Act of 16 April 1878 allowed the abandonment of the proposed Nettlebridge colliery branch authorised in 1873. The question of closing the stations at Masbury and Pylle was raised, though Pylle was handling a good deal of traffic from the new Lime siding. The charter of S.S. *Lincolnshire* was discontinued in October 1876, and when her successor *Terrier* was lost with all hands on 14 October 1877 on the Swansea-Highbridge run, she was apparently not replaced.

The only significant developments concerned the Wells branch. Before the building of the Bruton extension Wells had been the terminus of the Somerset Central line from Highbridge, which had reached Priory Road station in 1859. The East Somerset line from Witham had reached its own terminus in 1862 and, in 1870, the Bristol & Exeter line from Yatton reached Tucker Street station, thus providing Wells with three terminal stations belonging to three different companies and all within a few hundred yards of each other. The East Somerset and the Bristol & Exeter were broad-gauge lines; the Somerset Central line had originally been broad gauge, but the gauge had been mixed by 1862 and the broad-gauge rails removed by 1870.

By 1876 the GWR had absorbed both the East Somerset and the Bristol & Exeter, and the gauge on both their lines into Wells had been standardised. Connection between the two lines could be established only through the Somerset & Dorset yard and station; before conversion took place, the Somerset & Dorset agreed to allow broad-gauge trains to work through its property, using its metals for a distance of nine chains, but the Board of Trade refused to allow this on the grounds of the danger of broad-gauge passenger trains crossing narrow-gauge sidings on the level.

Not until all the lines had become standard gauge was the exchange of goods traffic begun, and on 1 January 1878 the GWR inaugurated through passenger working from Yatton to Witham. The old East Somerset station became the goods station, the name surviving in the East Somerset signalbox which controlled the level crossing at the east end of Priory Road station. It was not until

1 October 1934 that GWR passenger trains called at Priory Road, this practice continuing until the closure of the Somerset & Dorset station on 29 October 1951.

There was also a number of daily transfer trips between the two goods yards. The Somerset & Dorset's 1863 proposals for the Cheddar Valley and Yatton line—the scheme which they had surrendered to the Bristol & Exeter—had included a western spur to allow through running from Glastonbury to Bristol, and also an extension to the East Somerset station; a similar spur was also authorised by its 1873 Act, but this was never achieved.

PROGRESS IN THE 1880s

In the following decade two of the old Somerset & Dorset directors died after many years of service to the company—George Warry in 1883, and Charles Waring in 1887. Warry had served on the board from the earliest Somerset Central days; he had been chairman from 1855-62, and chairman of the Somerset & Dorset in 1866-7 and 1871-3. Born in 1795, he had practised as a barrister, had become chairman of the Bridgwater County Justices, and was the protagonist in the campaign for the establishment of the Somerset Constabulary. His diaries covering the period 1815-80, from which a number of quotations have been made, reveal a long life of devoted public service against the background of loving care for his estate at Shapwick, where he was Lord of the Manor for more than fifty years.

Charles Waring was a very different figure: he joined the board of the Somerset & Dorset in 1866 in its darkest days, and was chairman in 1867-71 and 1873-87. Waring Bros was a firm of contractors and, as such, members of the family held seats on many railway boards. As chairman of the Poole & Bournemouth Railway 1865-82, Waring got himself elected as MP for Poole in 1865 after a campaign of specious promises to electors who supported him, but was unseated in 1868 when it was clear that nothing had been done towards the construction of the line. *The Poole Pilot*, published monthly between 1867 and 1869, indulged in a campaign of vilification against Waring, labelling him as jackal, cad, bully, navvy, and so on; but there must have been more to him than that for him to have retained the confidence of his fellow directors for so many years.

The 1880s were a period of further quiet but steady progress and consolidation. In 1880 the committee turned down a proposal to

CARDIFF & BRISTOL CHANNEL STEAMSHIPS.

The Shortest and Cheapest Route to and from South Wales, the South-east, South and West of England, Southampton, Portsmouth, Isle of Wight, the Channel Islands, and France, via Southampton.

STEAM COMMUNICATION BETWEEN

BURNHAM AND CARDIFF.

☞ Passengers, Parcels and Goods are conveyed at Through Rates between **Cardiff** and all Stations on the **Somerset and Dorset Joint Railway, London, Portsmouth, Gosport, Southampton, Guernsey, Jersey, Lymington, Weymouth,** and all the principal Stations on the **London and South Western Railway.**

THIRD CLASS Tickets for **Cardiff** are issued from any Station between **Bournemouth, Poole,** and **Highbridge** inclusive, and from London and South Western Railway Stations; and from Cardiff, available by any Train leaving Burnham, after the arrival of the Packet.

THE FAST STEAMER

LADY MARY OR WYE,

Or other Steamer, is intended (Wind and Weather permitting, with or without a pilot, and with liberty to tow), during the month of

JULY, 1882,

To ply with Passengers and Merchandise, as follows:—

From CARDIFF to BURNHAM.

1	Saturday	3.45 p.m.
3	Monday	8.0 a.m.
4	Tuesday	7.30 „
5	Wednesday	7.0 „
6	Thursday	7.30 „
7	Friday	8.15 „
8	Saturday	9.15 „
10	Monday	10.30 a.m. & 2.45 p.m.
11	Tuesday	4.0 „
12	Wednesday	5.0 „
13	Thursday	6.0 „
14	Friday ...	4.45 „
15	Saturday	3.45 „
17	Monday	6.30 a.m. & 5.15 „
18	Tuesday	7.0 a.m.
19	Wednesday	9.30 „
20	Thursday	7.0 „
21	Friday	7.15 „
22	Saturday	8.0 „
24	Monday	8.30 a.m. & 12.30 p.m.
25	Tuesday	1.45 „
26	Wednesday	2.30 „
27	Thursday	2.30 „
28	Friday	1.45 „
29	Saturday	2.45 „
31	Monday	7.0 a.m.

Single Fares, After-Cabin 3s.6d. Fore-Cabin 2s.6d.
Return ditto ... ... 6s.0d. Ditto ... 4s.6d.
Return Tickets are available for 7 days.

From BURNHAM to CARDIFF.

1	Saturday	7.30 p.m.
3	Monday	6.0 „
4	Tuesday	7.30 „
5	Wednesday	10.30 a.m.
6	Thursday	11.0 „
7	Friday ...	11.45 „
8	Saturday	12.30 p.m.
10	Monday	12.30 „
11	Tuesday	12.30 „
12	Wednesday	2.0 „
13	Thursday	2.30 „
14	Friday	2.45 p.m. & 6.45 „
15	Saturday	7.30 „
17	Monday	8.45 a.m. & 7.30 „
18	Tuesday	7.0 „
19	Wednesday	6.30 „
20	Thursday	10.30 a.m.
21	Friday ...	10.45 „
22	Saturday	11.45 „
24	Monday	10.30 „
25	Tuesday	10.30 „
26	Wednesday	11.45 „
27	Thursday	12.30 p.m. & 4.45 p.m.
28	Friday ...	5.45 „
29	Saturday	6.30 „
31	Monday	7.0 „

Trains leave BURNHAM	ARRIVING AT Highbridge	Bridgwater	Taunton	Exeter	Glastonbury	Wells	T'Combe	Bournemouth	Salisbury	S'hampton	Portsmouth	Waterloo
at 8.5 a.m.	8.12 a.m.	8.48 a.m.	9.17 a.m.	10.48 a.m.	...	...	...	...	...	...	...	...
8.45 „	8.52 „	...	...	...	9.31 a.m.	9.55 a.m.	10.53 a.m.	2.7 p.m.	12.18 p.m.	1.37 p.m.	2.24 p.m.	2.25 p.m.
11.45 „	11.52 „	12.29 p.m.	12.55 p.m.	2.10 p.m.	12.44 p.m.	1.16 p.m.	1.55 p.m.	3.39 „	2.58 „	5.24 „	6.15 „	5.15 „
1.0 p.m.	1.8 p.m.	2.33 „	3.0 „	4.0 „	...	...	...	...	...	...	...	...
2.45 „	2.52 „	...	...	...	3.50 „	4.8 „	...	...	...	...	...	...
4.20 „	4.27 „	4.54 „	5.22 „	6.35 „	5.33 „	5.38 „	6.45 „	8.55 „	7.44 „	9.50 „	10.35 „	10.7 „

TRAINS LEAVE Waterloo	Portsmouth	S'hampton	Salisbury	Bournemouth	T'Combe	Wells	Glastonbury	Exeter	Taunton	Bridgwater	Highbridge	Arriving at BURNHAM
...	...	...	...	...	...	7.33 a.m.	7.39 a.m.	6 0 a.m.	7.35 a.m.	8.4 a.m.	8.32 a.m.	8.40 a.m.
...	...	...	8.15 a.m.	7.25 a.m.	9.26 a.m.	10.35 „	10.55 „	8.35 „	10.2 „	10.39 „	11 27 „	11.35 „
...	...	...	...	...	...	...	...	9.35 „	11.20 „	11.49 „	12 20 p.m.	12.27 p.m.
9.0 a.m.	8.0 a.m.	8.30 a.m.	11 15 „	10.5 „	12.3 p.m.	12.25 p.m.	12.55 p.m.	11.50 „	12.47 p.m.	1.15 p.m.	1.33 „	1.40 „
10.45 „	10.45 „	11.35 „	1.8 p.m.	11.45 „	2.50 „	3.35 „	3.50 „	...	...	...	4.38 „	4.45 „
11.45 „	12.35 p.m.	1.0 p.m.	2 43 „	2.10 p.m.	4.4 „	4.45 „	5.3 „	2.45 p.m.	4 45 „	5.12 „	5 38 „	5.45 „

All information as to freight, &c., may be obtained on application to Mr. JAMES HADDOW, Goods Manager, London and South Western Railway, Nine Elms, London; or Mr. W. B. MILLS, Waterloo Station; Mr. R. A. DYKES, Traffic Superintendent, Somerset and Dorset Railway, 14, Green Park, Bath; Mr. E. K. CORKE, Steam Packet Superintendent, Southampton; Mr. W. GAMMON, 31, Nicholas Lane, Lombard Street, London; Mr A. PEACE, West Quay, Bridgwater; Messrs. E. TAYLOR & Co., 69, Bute Street, Cardiff; and at the Offices of the Cardiff and Bristol Channel Steam Ship Co., Pier Head, Cardiff; also at any London and South Western or Somerset and Dorset Joint Railway Stations.

June, 1882. **BY ORDER.**

GOODALL, Steam Printer, 12, Westgate Buildings, Bath, and High Street, Glastonbury.

A poster for the S & D ferry service in 1882

promote an extension to Bridgwater, just as it later turned down proposals for building tramways to Street and Somerton. After various experiments with the cross-Channel ferry service from Burnham, in 1884 it fairly took the bit between its teeth and bought for £4,795 10s 0d *Sherbro*, a twin-funnelled, two-masted paddle steamer of 239 tons gross (built in 1870), and put her to work on the Burnham-Cardiff station. Posters proclaimed her as the 'New Fast Steamer', offering 'the shortest and cheapest route for goods & passengers to and from South Wales, the South and West of England Somersetshire Dorsetshire Southampton and France via Southampton'.

Sherbro sailed for four years under the Somerset & Dorset flag, sometimes making a loss and sometimes a modest profit, until sold in 1888 for £2,250. She was the last passenger-carrying vessel to be owned by the Somerset & Dorset, though she carried as much cargo as passenger traffic: cattle and dairy produce and fruit and vegetables which local people took across to sell at Cardiff market, returning the same day. After 1888, the Somerset & Dorset's maritime ventures were confined to Highbridge.

A much more important development was the building of the Wimborne avoiding line, or the western loop, as it was originally called. The continuous increase in traffic over the Somerset & Dorset line, especially the through traffic to and from Bournemouth, was underlining the nuisance of the reversal at Wimborne, involving the use of the LSW station and the two and a half-mile section to Broadstone, which was still carrying all the through traffic from Southampton to Dorchester and Weymouth. The LSW Act of 20 August 1883 authorised the construction of a western loop or cut-off, leaving the main line at Corfe Mullen Crossing, and climbing sharply at 1 in 80 out of the Stour valley over a heather-covered ridge to join the Southampton and Dorchester line just north of Broadstone (then still known as Poole New Junction).

The new line was just under three miles long, and when it was opened for goods traffic on 14 December 1885 it shortened the journey to Bournemouth by just about the same distance. The actual divergence took place at Bailey Gate, the two single lines to Wimborne and Broadstone running side by side for nearly two miles as far as Corfe Mullen Crossing until 1905, when double-line working was extended to a new junction at Corfe Mullen. Accommodation was provided for double track all the way to Broadstone, but it always remained a single-line section though proposals for doubling were made in 1925.

A certain mystery surrounds the opening of the new loop—known officially as the Poole & Bournemouth Junction Railway. When it was opened for goods traffic on 14 December 1885, the Board of Trade also sanctioned its opening for passenger traffic. (Officers' Minutes, 29 December 1885.) The working timetables show that it was only used by one goods train a day in each direction until 1 November 1886, when it was officially opened for passenger traffic and thereafter used by four fast trains a day in each direction (see page 68).

Shortly before the opening of the western loop to take the fast traffic, the condition of the line between Templecombe and Wimborne was called in question by Henry R. Farquharson, MP for Dorset West, in a letter of 11 August 1886 addressed to the Board of Trade:

> I am anxious to call your attention officially to the state of the Somerset and Dorset line between Templecombe and Wimborne. To thoroughly appreciate the condition of the line, someone should travel between the two stations I have named in a fast train, that is one that only stops at one or perhaps two of the intermediate stations. I have little doubt that such a traveller would never forget his journey: the curve going into Wimborne; the points at Shillingstone, Stalbridge, and Henstridge, would each one give him such a shock as he would never forget. It seems pretty generally agreed that some day a gigantic accident will happen.

Major Marindin immediately carried out an inspection for the Board of Trade, and his report allayed the most hysterical fears of the Member for Dorset West. 'The whole of this line (i.e. the Dorset Central),' he wrote, 'was originally made at as little cost as possible, and there are consequently incessant changes of gradient which do not conduce to smooth and comfortable travelling.' But six-sevenths of the line was laid with a good strong type of rail, none of it dating from before 1877, in first-rate order and well maintained, equal in fact to most main lines. In any event, there was a straight run through at Henstridge, and no discomfort entering the Stalbridge loop at 15 m.p.h. On the other hand there were uncomfortable lurches at Sturminster Newton and Shillingstone, and here and at Blandford a speed limit of 10 m.p.h. should be enforced, as excessive speed could cause discomfort. At Wimborne Junction there was appreciable danger, and a check rail was to be fitted as well as a speed limit of 10 m.p.h. The Bailey Gate-Wimborne section was to be brought up to the standard of the rest of the line, this section anyhow being due for re-laying shortly before the opening of the western loop.

This exchange gives a clear picture of the sort of difficulty under which the Joint Committee was labouring and of the efforts it had already made 'to improve the condition of the line and to ensure the safety of the public using it', as it had promised the Board of Trade in 1876. It also suggests that the Somerset & Dorset still had a bad name and that any smear was likely to stick. It is hard to judge how far such criticism was justified: E. L. Ahrons had some horrifying experiences to relate of journeys over the Somerset & Dorset, and Thomas Foster (1857-1946), a Radstock stonemason, whose diaries have survived, spent some weeks in December 1881 working at Chilcompton tunnel dressing stone. If the tunnel was being relined within seven years of its opening, it suggests that the original workmanship was defective.

This work cannot have had anything to do with the doubling of

POOLE & BOURNEMOUTH JUNCTION RAILWAY.

DIRECT ROUTE

TO BOURNEMOUTH.

This Line will be OPENED for Passenger Traffic on **NOVEMBER 1st,** *and several of the Trains between Bournemouth and Bath, the Midland Counties, and North of England and vice versa will be accelerated.*

Advertisement for the opening of the Corfe Mullen cut-off from the public timetable, November 1886

the main line through Chilcompton, which did not take place for several years. Further south this had already begun: the double line was opened from Evercreech Junction to Templecombe in 1884; the sections from Evercreech New to the Junction and from Radstock to Binegar were doubled in 1886, and another section from Shepton Mallet to Evercreech New in 1888, all these widenings being authorised by a series of LSW Acts obtained during the 1880s, which showed that things were now really moving.*

The most fundamental changes were brought about by the Midland Railway Acts of 24 June 1889 and 11 July 1891 under which Somerset & Dorset shareholders were permitted to exchange their holdings for Midland 3 per cent debenture stock. Of the £2,300,000 of Somerset & Dorset stock, more than £2 millions was surrendered on these terms, and to all intents and purposes the Somerset & Dorset had passed into the ownership of the two leasing companies.

The old board of directors was disbanded, including James Clark, the only survivor of the original Somerset Central board: he had attended the first meeting on 1 December 1851, and he was present at the last meeting on 3 April 1891. A new board, consisting of nominees of the Midland and LSW in equal numbers, was appointed as from 1 December 1891 and met for the first time at Waterloo on 3 February 1892. Robert Read, who had been serving as general manager and secretary for the leasing companies since 1875, was retired; the secretarial offices were removed, first to Derby, and after that jointly to Waterloo and Derby; and in a sense the Somerset & Dorset ceased to be a local line. Dykes continued to serve as traffic superintendent, and it was about this time that Alfred Whitaker, one of the most notable Somerset & Dorset personalities, arrived to take charge of the locomotive department, his predecessor W. H. French having died on 2 November 1889 as a result of an accident at Highbridge in which he was squeezed between the buffers of some goods wagons.

Robert Read had served the Somerset & Dorset for thirty-seven years: he arrived on the scene four months after the cutting of the first sod of the Somerset Central, and survived long enough to see the opening of what is generally known as the Bridgwater branch of the Somerset & Dorset Railway—which it was not. It is a nice touch that the Somerset & Dorset, which spent so much of its life in the hands of lessees, should finally lease and run what remained a nominally independent railway until after the Railways Act of 1921. This was the Bridgwater Railway, of which R. A. Read jr was a director, and his brother E. B. Read secretary from 1883 to 1922.

It took the Somerset & Dorset a long time to get to Bridgwater.

* Several of these dates conflict with those hitherto accepted. They are the dates given in the working timetables. The directors' report published on 25 February 1885 also refers to the Evercreech-Templecombe section as already open, while the Radstock-Binegar section was actually in use on 31 July 1885 when a fatal accident occurred at Binegar (see page 127).

The Somerset Central had rejected Bridgwater in favour of Highbridge as the terminus of the projected line from Glastonbury because of the cost of climbing over the Poldens: proposals for a branch from Shapwick had been defeated by the Bristol & Exeter in 1866 and again in 1875, while in 1880 the Joint Committee had declined another proposal for an extension of its line. Finally, an Act of 18 August 1882 authorised the Bridgewater (*sic*) Railway Company to construct a seven-mile line to Edington on the old Somerset Central line, five miles east of Highbridge.

The capital authorised was £135,000 with powers to borrow up to £45,000 on mortgage, but the LSW was to lease the line and work it in return for half the gross receipts, guaranteeing enough money over and above the Bridgwater company's share of the receipts to enable it to pay its dividends. Capital had been very shy, but a second Act (10 August 1888) allowed the now correctly-entitled Bridgwater Railway to issue £60,000 of its authorised capital in the form of 4½ per cent preference stock; the seven miles fifteen chains of single track were forthwith constructed, to be worked as a single block section with one intermediate station at Cossington; Edington Road became Edington Junction, and the branch was duly opened on 21 July 1890. In all but fact the line was part of the Somerset & Dorset system and was worked as such.

THE YEARS OF ACHIEVEMENT: 1890-1914

This final extension brought the Somerset & Dorset system up to 102 miles, with a further eleven miles of Midland and LSW metals over which running powers were exercised into Bath and Bournemouth. The quarter of a century that elapsed between this final expansion and reorganisation of the line, after fifteen years of very hard work and the outbreak of the first world war, was certainly the period of the greatest prosperity, efficiency and individuality. Although the line never completely lost its individual flavour and idiosyncrasies, after the first world war and grouping it passed more and more under the control of the two groups in which it was jointly vested, and rolling-stock and working practice became standardised. By 1900 both locomotives and carriage stock were painted in the famous Prussian blue livery, the top local officials had served the line for a number of years with the utmost keenness and devotion, and the motor-car was still in its infancy.

With the help of the Corfe Mullen cut-off and the continued doubling of the main line, timings were being improved and a wider range of through coaches was run. To handle these trains S. W. Johnson had introduced Derby-built 4—4—0s in 1891 to replace the 0—4—4Ts which had borne the brunt of the main-line work since 1877. The rolling-stock was built at Highbridge, where under Alfred Whitaker's surveillance the works were extended and largely rebuilt and re-equipped.

The sections from Binegar to Shepton Mallet and from Midford to Radstock were doubled between 1892 and 1894, and the Blandford-Corfe Mullen section between 1901 and 1905. This left three sections of single track (Bath Junction-Midford, Templecombe No. 2-Blandford, and Corfe Mullen Junction-Broadstone), twenty-six miles in all out of the sixty-three and three-quarter miles of main line between Bath and Broadstone, with a further three miles between Corfe Mullen and Wimborne. Eleven main-line signalboxes were thus still involved in the exchanging of tablets on the single-line sections, and it was to avoid the slowing of through trains to 10 m.p.h. during daylight and 4 m.p.h. after dark that Alfred Whitaker invented his automatic tablet-exchanging apparatus which was brought into operation in 1904.

This may have been regarded only as an interim measure, for in 1899 Dykes referred (in his interview with *The Railway Magazine*) to the Joint Committee's intention to double the whole of the main line. 'Each of the owning companies interests itself in putting all the traffic it can over the line, and fosters through traffic in every possible way'; and the tablet-exchanging apparatus helped enormously towards the expeditious handling of this through traffic. Dykes refers with pride to the ability of the Johnson 4—4—0s to handle eleven six-wheelers on the Bournemouth expresses, running the seventy-one and a half miles in 2h. 10m. with seven intermediate stops.

Second class was abolished on 1 July 1893. Sunday services were several times proposed, and always declined on the grounds that the probable traffic would not justify the expense. Proposals for stations on each side of Devonshire tunnel to serve the expanding suburbs of Bath, and at Single Hill, between Wellow and Radstock, were also declined.

A more interesting proposal, in view of the ultimate pattern of railways in North Somerset, was for a branch from Midford to Camerton. In 1895 the Somersetshire Coal Canal was offered for sale to the Somerset & Dorset, with a hint of blackmail in the veiled reference to 'the possible construction of light railways in the district'. Traffic on the canal had fallen away catastrophically since the arrival of the Somerset & Dorset in 1874 and the construction of the Hallatrow-Camerton branch of the Bristol & North Somerset, opened in 1882 to tap the collieries in the upper reaches of the Cam valley.

The Coal Canal had handled 157,000 tons of coal in 1864, but a mere 24,581 in 1884, and 11,400 in 1893, the year in which the company went into liquidation. The Somerset & Dorset, perhaps wisely, declined the offer: they would have had to fight the GWR at Camerton for coal traffic from the Camerton collieries, and Dunkerton was the only colliery further down the valley. In the end the canal was bought by the GWR which extended its Camerton branch along its bed, passing under the Somerset & Dorset viaduct at Midford on its way to Limpley Stoke. The branch was completed in 1910 and the passenger service ran for only seven years, though the Camerton-Limpley Stoke section remained open for mineral and freight traffic until 1951. As far as branch lines in North Somerset were concerned, the writing was already on the wall.

R. A. Dykes retired in 1902 and was succeeded as traffic superintendent by G. H. Eyre, whose period of service lasted until 1920, covering the arduous years of the first world war. Traffic continued to grow up to the outbreak of war, and in 1902 the offices at No. 14 Green Park expanded into No. 13 next door. Further improvements to the passenger service culminated in the introduction on 1 October 1910 of the forerunner of 'The Pines Express', a Manchester-Bournemouth restaurant-car train running all the year round.

Increased freight traffic is evidenced by the link-up with various industrial developments: from 1904 a 3 ft tramway connected the Oakhill Brewery with the Somerset & Dorset at Binegar; in 1909 Wilts United Dairies established its milk factory at Bason Bridge, and by 1914 a new signalbox had been built at Moorewood where the traffic from two large stone quarries and from a newly-opened colliery was handled. A detailed first-hand account of the line is to be found in a series of articles in *The Railway and Travel Monthly* between 1911 and 1914 by J. Thornton Burge, then stationmaster at Templecombe, illustrated by a number of very interesting contemporary photographs.

At Templecombe itself about 200 trains and engines passed No. 3 Junction in twenty-four hours; in 1910, 203,571 wagons were transferred between the Somerset & Dorset and the LSW, four or five specials a day being sometimes required to clear abnormal traffic working in from the north. The freight was heaviest by night, and between 8 p.m. and 2 a.m. trains were often blocked back several

CLIMBING MENDIP

(18) *Southbound freight on 1 in 50 gradient near Midsomer Norton; class* 7F 2—8—0, *ex*-SDJ *No.* 86, *with banker in rear*

(19) *Northbound summer express at Evercreech New;* 2P 4—4—0 *from Templecombe shed piloting* 9F 2—10—0. *Note the signal post made of old rails*

CLOSING SCENES

(20) 28 *March* 1965; *special train passing Glastonbury behind* 4F 0—6—0, *ex*-SDJ *No.* 60, *the last Somerset & Dorset engine to work over the line*

(21) 5 *March* 1966; *Great Western Society special at Radstock with Stanier* 8F 2—8—0 *No.* 48706—*showing new spur to the North Somerset line*

AT BATH

(22) *Afternoon calm at Queen Square—the main Somerset & Dorset departure platform*

(23) *The Somerset & Dorset engine shed in June 1965 with a recently retired* BR *class 5 4—6—0*

NORTH SOMERSET LANDSCAPES

(24) *'Bude' and 'Biggin Hill' head a special on 5 March 1966 across Midford viaduct above the abandoned* GWR *Cam Valley branch*

(25) *Writhlington colliery* c. 1900, *with main line in foreground and* SDJ 0—4—2 *saddle tank No. 25A shunting wagons with dumb buffers. Note electric repeater disc on signalbox*

sections, waiting their turn at the Upper Yard. Every day several milk trains were made up off the Somerset & Dorset, sometimes loaded to twenty-five to thirty vehicles. At Evercreech Junction 900 wagons were attached or detached daily, while 25,000 passengers a year used Stalbridge station.

Such details give the impression of a busy and prosperous concern; the profit margin was reasonable enough, though the larger revenue was continually offset by larger working expenses—in 1904, for instance, income was £209,404 and expenditure was £169,723; in 1913 income was £255,763 and expenditure £194,792. The Officers' Minutes show continual preoccupation with possible economies, while from Derby, S. W. Johnson fulminated against the appalling gradients and the heavy mileage involved in assisting and light running, which made the line so expensive to work. In the same breath he and Whitaker were asking for more and larger engines.

In 1901 there had been no additions to the locomotive stock since 1895, and three new 4—4—0s and five new 0—6—0s were ordered. By 1913, the small goods engines now available were castigated as quite unequal to the heavy goods traffic: eight of them were to be scrapped and replaced by six more powerful new engines—the Fowler 2—8—0s, the pride and glory of the line for the next fifty years.

During the years before the war, one doubtful asset was shed—the burden of Burnham Pier on which such grandiose hopes had been based nearly fifty years before. In 1899 its abandonment had been suggested, seeing that it was not used except by summer excursion steamers which paid 5s a time for the privilege. Although it was the direct means of bringing passenger traffic to the line, excursion trains being run in connection with the steamers, the Joint Committee was anxious to be rid of its obligations for the maintenance of the structure, the only alternative being its complete demolition in compliance with the demands of the Admiralty.

After several years of abortive negotiation, the pier was finally transferred to the local urban district council in 1905—the latter's powers being eventually acquired by the Burnham Pier Company in 1907, to which the Barry Railway was authorised to subscribe capital in the fleeting hopes of reviving the cross-Channel ferry services. As a passenger port Burnham was long since finished, though pleasure steamers continued to call at the pier from time to time during the season until about 1910. At Highbridge there was plenty of activity and the Joint Committee's vessels were fully occupied, though in 1903 the *Julia* was described as 'worn beyond repair'. Now forty years old, *Julia* had been acquired by the Somerset & Dorset Railway in 1873, and had spent most of her life carrying rails from Newport to Highbridge. In the year ending 31 May 1903, for instance, the *Julia* and the *Alpha* had between them brought over 7,960 tons of rails, while chartered vessels had brought a further 10,457 tons. There was clearly sufficient business in rails for another steamer of 150 tons besides the *Alpha*. A new *Julia* was therefore ordered, and in 1904 the old *Julia* was disposed of for £50, while at the same time the *Alpha* was lengthened to enable her to carry the longer rails now used by the LSWR.

The first world war brought even heavier traffic to the Somerset & Dorset line: holiday traffic disappeared and passenger train timings deteriorated, but there were hospital trains working up to Bath from the coast, and heavy trainloads of tanks, shrouded and secret, working south. C. Hamilton Ellis recalls the thrill of seeing a trainload of Mark V tanks, heavily sheeted, lumbering through the Dorset meadows towards the coast behind one of the new 2—8—0s: presumably not No. 85, which was on loan to the Midland and engaged on working coal traffic from Toton to Brent.

Early in 1915 the Admiralty established a pumping station at Corfe Mullen in connection with its new cordite factory at Holton Heath, and a siding was built to serve this. Later in the war another siding was built at Milldown, north of Blandford, to serve a German prisoner-of-war camp, and shortly before the Armistice there was talk of improving the facilities here and installing a block post owing to the increase of traffic in connection with the new Air Force depot at Blandford. The military authorities were then constructing a light railway about three miles long to the Air Force camp at a cost of £59,877, and the SDJ laid in a connection with this, immediately to the south of Blandford station, the Government bearing the cost of £1,707.

The line swung round north-eastwards and climbed the downs, where remains of earthworks and a concrete bridge are still visible, as well as the concrete platform 200 yd long at the camp station. Apart from troop trains, there was freight traffic, worked by a shunting engine from Wimborne which spent the day at Blandford, and also a daily passenger train from Bournemouth for the use of civilian personnel employed at the camp. The line was handed over to the Railway Executive in July 1919, and the camp was closed at the end of that year, but reopened at the request of the Ministry of Munitions in November 1920, for six months, for the removal of material. The Somerset & Dorset was to maintain the line and work the wagons at 10s a wagon with a minimum of twelve wagons a trip. The connection with the camp railway was finally removed in December 1928.

A large number of Somerset & Dorset men saw active service. Frank Redman, who began work at Highbridge in 1910, has shown me a photograph of himself and many of his comrades in uniform: he could recall each man's job and his subsequent career, but of some he said simply and movingly: 'He remained overseas'. From Highbridge works alone 101 men left to serve in the war: thirteen of these gave their lives for their country.

Crest used on the Joint line, combining the arms of Bath and the seal of Dorchester

CHAPTER 5

Grouping and Nationalisation

THE LMS AND SR TAKE-OVER

The 1920s were the last decade of real individuality on the Somerset & Dorset. There are still many survivors, both railwaymen and ordinary West Countrymen, who have vivid memories of the line before the first world war; but my own impressions of the line begin in the mid-twenties, when grouping had as yet hardly made any impact, and the famous blue livery, the dark green corduroy uniform, the signals and the timetables gave the impression that this was still very much an independent concern.

In actual fact, the Bridgwater Railway had been absorbed into the LSW from 1 January 1923, and from 1 July 1923 the Somerset & Dorset itself had become vested jointly in the London Midland & Scottish and the Southern Railway companies as created under the Railways Act of 1921. The Somerset & Dorset Railway Company was at the same time dissolved, and at long last the line became the legal property of the successors of the two companies which had been leasing it for forty-eight years.

For the time being at any rate there were to be few changes in the day-to-day administration of the line: the Resident Engineer at Glastonbury, W. E. Fox, and the Resident Locomotive Superintendent at Highbridge, R. C. Archbutt, continued to serve the Joint Committee; while at Bath, A. S. Redman had succeeded G. H. Eyre as Traffic Superintendent in 1920, and was himself succeeded in 1922 by G. H. Wheeler, the last to hold the office.

The last additions were made to the SDJ locomotive stock: three new Midland class 2 4—4—0s; five new Midland class 4 superheater 0—6—0s to replace five of the 'Scottie' type goods engines now forty years old*; a batch of 'Jinties'—the standard LMS six-coupled tanks—to replace the saddle tanks acquired in the 1870s for the Bath Extension; another five 2—8—0s, built this time by Robert

* The 'Scotties' were so called to distinguish them from the Fowler 0—6—0s; the first batch had been built by Neilson of Glasgow.

Stephenson & Company of which No. 86 appeared in the Railway Centenary Exhibition at Darlington in July 1925; and two Sentinel shunters for the Radstock colliery branches. In 1930 the Somerset & Dorset stud numbered eighty locomotives; there were ninety-two drivers and ninety-three firemen.

These new locomotives represented considerable capital expenditure at a time when working expenses were still rising and revenue was already beginning to fall. On 11 July 1920 the passenger service to Wimborne was withdrawn—latterly there had been only one train a day over the old main line, passengers for Wimborne normally changing at Broadstone Junction, while the closure of the Somerset & Dorset signalbox at Wimborne Junction and of the Bath Single Line Junction box were among the first economy moves of the post-grouping era.

Economies there would clearly have to be, for apart from the economic depression of the late 1920s, the railways were now facing the first onslaught of motor transport. Milk traffic in rural areas was particularly vulnerable, while increasing quantities of road stone were beginning to be moved by road and a number of smaller Somerset collieries were closed down. The rural bus was another competitor: to meet this threat five halts were opened between 1923 and 1929, the last being at Shoscombe & Single Hill where appeals for a station had been rejected on various occasions, even as late as 1922. The other halts were at Bawdrip, Charlton Marshall, Corfe Mullen and Stourpaine & Durweston.

The development of private motoring meant that fewer people were likely to use their local stations, though long distance and excursion traffic was well maintained. Revenue was no longer keeping pace with rising costs: in 1929, for instance, income was £375,794, but expenditure was £387,403.

This was the situation that led to the reforms of 1930, the first major reforms in administration since 1891, and indeed more drastic than anything that had happened since the take-over in 1875. On 1 July 1930 the separate management of the line was discontinued, the traffic superintendent's office at Green Park, Bath, was closed, and the traffic staff was transferred to the LMS which henceforward operated the line on behalf of the Joint Committee; the SR became responsible for all maintenance and civil engineering. The posts of locomotive superintendent and resident engineer disappeared, as did that of traffic superintendent, and if the Somerset & Dorset had a manager, it was now S. Sealy, the LMS district controller at Bath. Sealy's successors at Bath, designated assistant divisional superintendent, were S. A. Wilson (1944-54), S. A. Trigg (1954-5), and W. J. Payne (1955-8).

The results of these changes were immediately visible. The eighty locomotives had already been absorbed into LMS stock from 1 January 1930, and the rolling-stock was divided between the two owners. Since 1924 all goods engines had been painted unlined black, and passenger engines now followed suit. The famous blue livery disappeared from the scene, all carriage stock being painted standard Southern green. The works at Highbridge were run down from January and closed in May after an existence of sixty-eight years, and upwards of 300 men lost their jobs, a shattering blow to the little town during a period of nationwide economic depression. Many families uprooted themselves and moved to Derby or Lancing or even Swindon, but there was considerable unemployment, and the effect of the loss of earning power on the local economy was very marked.

In 1933 the Somerset & Dorset's shipping interests were wound up, and the two cargo vessels were disposed of, though Highbridge Wharf continued to be used by private shipping until about 1950. *Alpha* had been scrapped in 1925* and replaced by the much larger 195-ton *Radstock*; the latter was sold in 1934, but the thirty-year-old *Julia* was scrapped.

In the same year there were further economies by land: the Wimborne line was closed in June (the milk traffic having been discontinued in the previous year) except for the section from Corfe Mullen Junction to Carter's clay siding; and at Templecombe two Somerset & Dorset signalboxes (No. 3 Junction and B Box on the departure platform) were abolished, and the stationmaster at Templecombe Lower was dispensed with, the staff and the Lower Yard thereafter coming under the supervision of the SR stationmaster at Templecombe Upper.

If local traffic inevitably dwindled in the years before the second world war in the face of road competition, excursion and holiday traffic flourished. More and heavier through trains from the Midlands and the North were worked over the line in the summer months, including a number of Friday night trains whose arrivals at Bath in the early hours of Saturday morning were not recorded in the public timetables. Pigeon traffic also developed, and the appearance of Black Stanier LMS class 5 4—6—0s on 2 May 1938

* In 1920 *Alpha* had been sucked into the mud at No. 2 berth, Highbridge, and failing to rise with the tide was submerged, to the detriment of her cargo of 130 tons of flour.

marked the beginning of a new era, for Derby-built 4—4—0s had handled the expresses for forty-seven years.

THE 1939-45 WAR AND ITS AFTERMATH

When war broke out in 1939, the train service was at once drastically curtailed, and all the through expresses disappeared; so did the Black Staniers, and the influx of a batch of ex-LSW 4—4—0s and 0—4—4Ts marked a curious break with Derby tradition. Traffic was heavy throughout the war years, with the emphasis on freight, day and night, weekdays and Sundays. Millions of tons of equipment and war materials were lifted over Mendip by the famous class 7s, some of them already thirty years old, and the strategic importance of the line, offering one of the shortest routes between the industrial Midlands and North and the South Coast ports, was underlined by the numerous red brick pillboxes and concrete tank-blocks by which several sections were protected.

The supreme value of this cross-country link was realised in the months of preparation that led up to the invasion of Europe in June 1944. Little harm was suffered from enemy action: Templecombe station was bombed in September 1942, but railway property at Bath was virtually undamaged in the Baedeker raids earlier the same year. Although the camp railway was not reopened, much of the military traffic centred on Blandford, where a temporary Forces canteen operated on the up platform. The engineer's department at Glastonbury became a transit camp for American troops, and troop trains from Liverpool and other ports were dealt with there.

For some years after the war, passenger traffic was well maintained. Petrol rationing was still in force, the flood of private cars had not yet begun to flow along West Country roads, and vast crowds of Northerners and Midlanders were finding their way to the South and West to enjoy the holidays they had foregone during the war years. To meet this demand an extraordinary variety of engines was pressed into service for summer Saturdays, mainly obsolescent Midland types from Gloucester or Saltley or even Derby, as well as the class 7s.

The Transport Act of 6 August 1947 which resulted in the nationalisation of Britain's railway system from 1 January 1948 was ultimately responsible for the severance of the link with the Midland which had been the lifeline of the Somerset & Dorset for seventy-three years. Fifty years before, R. A. Dykes had seen that the prosperity of the line depended on the interest of the owning companies in putting all possible traffic on the line. After 1948 there were no 'owning companies', and the 'Joint' nature of the line, linked with three different Regions, led to a bewildering series of changes in the administration and operation while British Railways was attempting to put its house in order and tidy up the map. In the new order of things, one had a horrid feeling that the Somerset & Dorset was nobody's baby—least of all the baby of the Western Region in whose unwelcoming arms it was to find its ultimate repose.

From 2 February 1948 the Somerset & Dorset was assigned to the Southern Region of the Railway Executive under the British Transport Commission. It was commercially supervised by the district traffic superintendent at Southampton, to whom an assistant district operating superintendent of the London Midland Region, located at Bath, was responsible for the operation of the line. Bath itself was in the London Midland Region, which was still responsible for the motive power, carrying on the function of the former LMS Bristol motive power district (22 group) of which the sheds on the Joint line had formed part.

In January 1950 the regional boundary between the Western and Southern Regions was redrawn with the effect that everything northwards from Cole came under the Western Region commercially, though still operated by the Southern Region to which the locomotive stocked was loaned by the London Midland Region. The motive power depots (Bath, Radstock, Highbridge, Templecombe and Branksome) had already been transferred to the Southern Region in February 1950, and the stock of sixty-nine engines was transferred in 1953. Former SDJ engines, already renumbered by the LMS in 1930 and now appearing with British Railways livery and numbers, proceeded to acquire new shed code numbers in the 71 group as belonging to the Eastleigh motive power district.

On 1 February 1958 the regional boundary was again redrawn, this time between Templecombe and Henstridge: Templecombe station itself remained in the Southern Region, but the Western Region assumed control of the Somerset & Dorset line from Bath to Henstridge, taking over the stock of sixty-six engines at Bath, Radstock, Highbridge and Templecombe sheds and renumbering them in the 82 group.

The district offices at Bath were closed at the same time, though the control office remained open as a sub-office of Bristol Control until April 1962. Finally, in January 1963, the old LSW line from Salisbury to Exeter was transferred to the Western Region and the divisional boundary was once more redrawn between Shillingstone and Blandford; in September 1962 all through passenger trains from the North had been withdrawn, and the Somerset & Dorset had become a withered arm of the Western Region—a moribund and hopelessly uneconomic branch line. So far from putting all possible through traffic on the line, the management seemed only concerned to get rid of such traffic as remained.

On 1 January 1948 all this was very much in the future, and nobody could have foreseen the devastating effect of nationalisation on the Somerset & Dorset system. The first closures were obvious rationalisations—economies that might well have been made before the war. Templecombe Lower Yard was closed on 5 May 1950, all freight being worked to Templecombe Upper, though the Lower Yard still had to be used for berthing of empty stock, and for such workings as pigeon specials and engineers' trains.

The Wells branch was closed on 29 October 1951: during the last few years, an average of six passengers a day had used the line, and freight had dwindled from eighty to a hundred wagons a day to ten. The last train was fittingly hauled by an 0—4—4T No. 58086, formerly MR No. 1423, destined to be the last survivor of a type that had been introduced to the Joint line in 1877. On the same day the passenger service from Highbridge to Burnham was withdrawn, though excursion trains continued to work to Burnham until 8 September 1962. A year later, on 1 December 1952, the Bridgwater branch was closed for passenger traffic: four daily trains to and from Edington Junction had been carrying a mere handful of passengers. A daily freight train continued to run until 1 October 1954.

Against these gloomy occasions the centenary celebrations of 28 August 1954 rekindled for a moment something of the excitement that must have greeted the coming of the railway in 1854. This was the centenary of the first section of the Somerset Central from Glastonbury to Highbridge: in 1962 there would be no such junketings to celebrate the centenary of the Somerset & Dorset itself, for the sentence of death had already been pronounced.

In 1954 celebrations were organised by Messrs C. & J. Clark of Street and Messrs Clark, Son & Morland of Glastonbury, whose chairmen were both members of the family of James Clark, cofounder of both firms. The Mayor of Glastonbury, himself a great-grandson of James Clark, lent civic dignity to the occasion. More than 100 of the 250 living descendants of James Clark travelled by the special train, which carried between 600 and 700 passengers, most of them employees of the two firms with their wives and children. Some of them were in period costume, crinolined, top-hatted and bewhiskered. The sun shone, and what with a civic welcome at Burnham, tea in the Town Hall, and an afternoon at the seaside, it was a tremendous occasion for all. Especially for No. 43201, a class 3F 0—6—0 built at Derby in 1896 as No. 64 of the SDJ, which was festooned with bunting, carried a large commemorative disc on its smokebox, and proudly displayed its original number and the initials and crest of the Joint line. Driver Peck and Fireman Cook of Highbridge, black-bearded and bowler-hatted, drove No. 64 and twelve crowded corridor coaches in fine style along the line that Charles Gregory had laid so firmly and so well across the turf moor a hundred years before.

THE RUN-DOWN

In 1958, as we have seen, the Western Region virtually assumed control of the Somerset & Dorset; in March 1963 the Beeching Report was published, in which both the main line and the branch were marked down for closure. The end was in sight. By the time the Beeching Report was completed, enough traffic had been diverted from the line to make it utterly unviable. The process of running-down, and the ruthless stages by which the closure of the line was ultimately effected, left only sadness in the hearts of those who lived near it and had known it in its heyday—for them it had become a part of their lives; but real bitterness ate into the hearts of the railwaymen, many of whom had given a lifetime of service to 'the Dorset', and who fought to the end in the face of appalling difficulties and every sort of discouragement to provide for the needs of the local community.

The run-down started immediately: very soon after the Western Region had taken over, much of the beer traffic from Burton was re-routed *via* Taunton to the West of England. This had been one of the traditional traffics over the Somerset & Dorset ever since 1874, the 11 a.m. freight from Bath being known as 'the Burton' from time immemorial.

One by one the through freight trains ceased to run; ultimately even fertilisers from Avonmouth to Blandford were re-routed *via* Bath Spa, Westbury, Southampton and Bournemouth—135 miles from Bristol against sixty-five miles over 'the Dorset'. The Sunday trains to Bournemouth were withdrawn: they were said not to pay, though they were so well patronised that passengers from intermediate stations often had to stand.

On certain occasions Bank Holiday excursions were run only after strong local representations had been made. The weekend service of through trains from the north was gradually pared away; the overnight workings were withdrawn in 1962, and the death-blow was delivered with the announcement that 'The Pines Express' (and all through holiday traffic) was to be re-routed over the ex-GWR route *via* Oxford and Basingstoke. (Even this through working to Bournemouth was doomed to be withdrawn on 6 March 1967.) The last 'Pines' ran over the Somerset & Dorset on 8 September, single-headed by 2—10—0 No. 92220 *Evening Star* in immaculate condition: all down the line large numbers of people stood sadly to watch its passing.

By now a policy of cynical indifference seems to have prevailed: moribund Collett 0—6—0s were being drafted to work the branch, scrapped when they failed and cannibalised to keep others running; the class 9F 2—10—0s reappeared to work the non-existent holiday expresses in the summer of 1963 and loitered along with three-coach local sets and semi-fasts; the old timetable remained unaltered so that 'utterly meaningless connections continued to feed non-existent passengers into a ghost "Pines" ', as Kenneth Hudson put it in his broadcast programme *How to kill a railway* (23 December 1965).

On 7 September 1964 the night freight trains and the 2.40 a.m. mail from Bath to Bournemouth were withdrawn and the line closed at night for the first time since the 1870s. By now practically all through freight had been diverted elsewhere, until (apart from coal trains from Writhlington and Norton Hill) only a single daily train remained after the closure of Emborough quarries in June 1965.

Freight facilities had been withdrawn from most intermediate stations between 1963 and 1965; Midford, Wellow (one of the best patronised stations on the line) and Chilcompton were reduced to unstaffed halts. The station buildings had been unpainted for years; flowerbeds had run to wild; sidings were ripped up; signalboxes were gutted and demolished. Over all there was an atmosphere of dereliction and decay.

Nobody who has followed the fortunes of the Somerset & Dorset would claim that the line was likely to be a money-spinner in the mid-twentieth century any more than in the mid-nineteenth. The balance sheets for the 1930s had made it clear that ever-mounting losses must be expected even before the age of mass-motoring. Once British Railways had decided that the line was not commercially viable, the only reasonable policy was to close it swiftly and finally—as the Midland & Great Northern Joint line was closed: there could be no justification for a deliberate policy of running it down slowly over a number of years with no visible attempt to effect worthwhile economies or to attract possible traffic, and then to assert that the line did not pay. It was the handling of the closure, not the necessity for it, that made the issue of the Somerset & Dorset something of a *cause célèbre*.

On 2 August 1965 engineering works in connection with the Bournemouth electrification scheme required the temporary closure of Bournemouth West station, and Somerset & Dorset trains were either terminated at Branksome or diverted to Bournemouth Central. They never returned to Bournemouth West as the Minister of Transport in the meantime agreed to its closure on 4 October. This was the first Ministerial decision which directly affected the Somerset & Dorset main line.

The proposal to withdraw the passenger service over the whole system (and also from Bath to Mangotsfield), announced in June to take effect in September, had to be cancelled owing to the inevitable objections; the Transport Users' Consultative Committee met during October at Shepton Mallet and at Blandford to consider the objections which had been lodged. Thereafter there was silence. The Minister of Transport's decision was agonisingly delayed; morale rose and fell as rumours trickled along the grapevine.

In October 1964 the Tory Government was replaced by Labour, whose election manifesto stated that there would be no more major rail closures until national and regional plans for transport had been drawn up. Surely the withdrawal of passenger services over 104 miles of track from Mangotsfield to Bournemouth and from Evercreech Junction to Highbridge must be considered a 'major' closure? But the Minister's consent to the closure was announced on 10 September 1965; any hardship likely to arise would be alleviated by additional bus services, with particular reference to the needs of children attending schools at Bruton and Cole and of the inhabitants of Shoscombe. The decision caused violent protests.

A mass meeting of railwaymen at Templecombe, called by Norman Down and Ernie Cross of Binegar, accused the Western Region in the presence of two MPs and four prospective candidates, in front of television cameras and microphones, of 'cold-blooded, deliberate murder of the line, planned and carefully executed over a period of ten years, way before Dr Beeching's plan'. The local

Labour party appealed to the Prime Minister, denouncing the closure as a breach of faith. In December 1965 Tom Fraser was replaced as Minister of Transport by Barbara Castle, but the decision stood.

The last few months were played out on a note of macabre comedy and general exasperation: the Somerset & Dorset was destined to die in the full glare of publicity. Closure was announced for 3 January 1966, and several Farewell Specials were chartered for the final weekend. January 3 was D-Day for the Western Region, which was to announce that steam had been eliminated and the whole Region dieselised. Unwisely, the closure date was announced before the Western traffic commissioners met to license the new bus and coach services stipulated by the Minister.

A few days before their meeting, one of the road operators withdrew his application for a licence to operate one of the services because of staff shortage and other difficulties. It was clear that the closure was being rushed through regardless of the inadequate time allowed for making proper arrangements for the alternative services. British Railways countered this by announcing an 'interim emergency service' from 3 January, consisting of morning and evening trains each way on the branch, and four trains each way on the main line stopping at all stations (five south of Templecombe): no train left Bath between 8.15 a.m. and 4.25 p.m., to all intents and purposes there was no longer a through service to Bournemouth, and connections at Evercreech and Templecombe virtually ceased to exist. It was worse than the minimum bus services stipulated in the Minister's consent to closure! The official reason given was shortage of staff and the fear that an attempt to keep the full existing rail services running would break down. Under public pressure British Railways chartered a minibus to provide an additional service between Bath, Wellow and Shoscombe.

Meanwhile, railwaymen had taken things into their own hands. On 1 January one of the Farewell Specials was brought to a halt by signals at Binegar: it was six o'clock on a dark mid-winter evening, a few oil-lamps flickered on the windswept platform, and as the ten-coach train hauled by the spectacular combination of two 8F 2—8—0s drew to a halt the floodlights of press and BBC cameras revealed Ernie Cross, the signalman, standing in the six-foot way between the tracks. He handed the organisers of the rail tour a prepared statement protesting against the 'vicious attitude' of the Western Region in its refusal to provide an adequate service on the line. A fortnight later, claiming that there was enough rolling-stock and staff to run a proper service, Bath railwaymen refused to issue tickets on the chartered bus service from Shoscombe to Bath, and urged villagers to boycott the service. These were no frivolous gestures to win cheap notoriety, but acts of conscience by loyal and thinking railwaymen. When no official notice was taken of his action, Ernie Cross issued a full statement to the press ('Was my action really necessary?') with the outline of a plan for a more efficient and economical operation of the line, drawn up by men who had spent a lifetime in the service of the Somerset & Dorset. It was the railwaymen's gesture of no confidence in the management.

But the management was now only interested in closing the line. The 'interim emergency service 'lasted just two months. Norton Hill colliery conveniently closed on 12 February, the road services were duly licensed, closure was announced for 7 March 1966, and the preceding Saturday and Sunday witnessed the scenes that I have already described in the opening pages of this book. At present (March 1967) it is possible to travel from Glastonbury to Highbridge by bus at 5.26 a.m. and 5.27 p.m. on Mondays to Fridays, taking about an hour and a quarter over the journey as against the thirty-five-minute journey offered six times a day by the Somerset Central in 1854.

The 'express' coach service between Bath and Bournemouth takes 3h. 36m. over the journey of about seventy miles, and one thinks with pride of the 'Slow and Dirty', when the Johnson 4—4—0s got their expresses through to Bournemouth in 2h. 10m. with seven intermediate stops. But that was seventy years ago. Today a few miles of the Somerset & Dorset remain open for freight: a coal trip from Bath to the Co-op siding; coal from Writhlington over the North Somerset line to Bristol *via* the new spur at Radstock; milk from Bason Bridge to Highbridge, and also from Bailey Gate on the Blandford-Broadstone section which is used by a daily goods train from Poole as well as by special trains of Army vehicles. The rest of the Somerset & Dorset system is dead: all is quiet on the Western front.

CHAPTER 6

A Description of the Line

BATH TO EVERCREECH JUNCTION

Any description of the Somerset & Dorset main line must logically start at Bath. Except for through passengers from Bristol and the North, the approach to the Somerset & Dorset was likely to be along James Street West, or down Charles Street, towards the elegant Georgian facade of Queen Square station—a creditable design in Bath stone, and a dignified gateway to the town which it served: LMS and S & D STATION—as the legend proclaimed between the wars—though it had always been Midland property ever since its opening on 7 May 1870, even after the triumphant entry of the Somerset & Dorset on 20 July 1874.

To the south of the station entrance, in what was then the pleasant *cul-de-sac* of Green Park, stood the Somerset & Dorset offices—No. 14 Green Park Buildings from 1877 onwards, and No. 13 as well from 1902, an arrangement which lasted until the reorganisation of 1930. The premises were destroyed during the bombing of Bath in 1942, and the street itself now forms part of Bath's ring road. After nationalisation the station was rather more appropriately renamed Green Park.

Nevertheless, it remained Queen Square throughout the days of the Somerset & Dorset and a minor Victorian monument to the bitter end, where it always seemed to be Sunday afternoon—except on summer Saturdays, and for brief interludes while 'The Pines Express' came and went. Perhaps the most bizarre and frivolous moment in its history was the night of 9 June 1961 when it opened its doors to the Eleven o'clock Special—a dance organised as part of the Bath Festival—with a diesel shuttle service running over the Somerset & Dorset to a barbecue at Wellow, while performances of the Ealing Studios' comedy 'The Titfield Thunderbolt', which was filmed in the Cam valley and included glimpses of the Somerset & Dorset line at Midford, were screened in the waiting-room.

Usually the wooden platform echoed hollowly under the fine

single-span glass roof that covered the four tracks and the circulating area, and there was a pleasing air of spaciousness about the station: it suggested that the Midland always had hopes of extension southwards despite the 1863 agreement with the Great Western, for the size of the building was quite out of keeping with its ostensible function as the terminus of a ten-mile branch from Mangotsfield. Glass carriage-canopies at the front and side of the station greeted the traveller, who booked his ticket at a purely Victorian booking office with all its original fittings, while standing in the impressively lofty entrance hall which extended to the full height of the building with a coffered roof and ornamental plaster work.

Some of the large windows that looked out into the street and into the station belonged to offices or to accommodation latterly provided for refreshment-room staff. Large airy waiting rooms boasted Midland furniture, there were vintage lavatories, and at the north-west corner of the station was the stationmaster's office and a network of small rooms which incorporated the control office for the Somerset & Dorset line—replacing the original crossing agent at the Glastonbury offices in 1877. The control board was sited on the west wall of the room, and dealt with all train movements between Warmley and Corfe Mullen, including the branches.

Somerset & Dorset trains used either platform indiscriminately, though most of the through trains used the southern platform: this could take nine bogie coaches, and the northern platform eight. Neither of them was adequate for dealing with summer expresses which regularly consisted of twelve or even more coaches. At the platform end a girder bridge carried the line across the Avon, and away beyond that, pairs of Somerset & Dorset engines would back down to couple up, unidentifiably far beyond the eagle gaze of the keenest train-spotter.

Hereabouts was the site of the temporary terminus used by the Midland from 4 August 1869 to 7 May 1870, between the signalbox, a forty-one-lever box of standard Midland design, and the two engine sheds: a small, two-road, stone-built Midland shed (a sub-shed to Bristol, Barrow Road), and the far larger four-road Somerset & Dorset shed.

This was a surprising building, constructed of wood, with lattice windows and an open wooden-girdered roof—just how it survived for nearly a century without being burned to the ground is one of the minor mysteries of the S & D: 'Of course we've had fires, mind,' an old driver said to me, as if that were sufficient explanation. At best, about fifty engines were shedded here: there was a sharp little

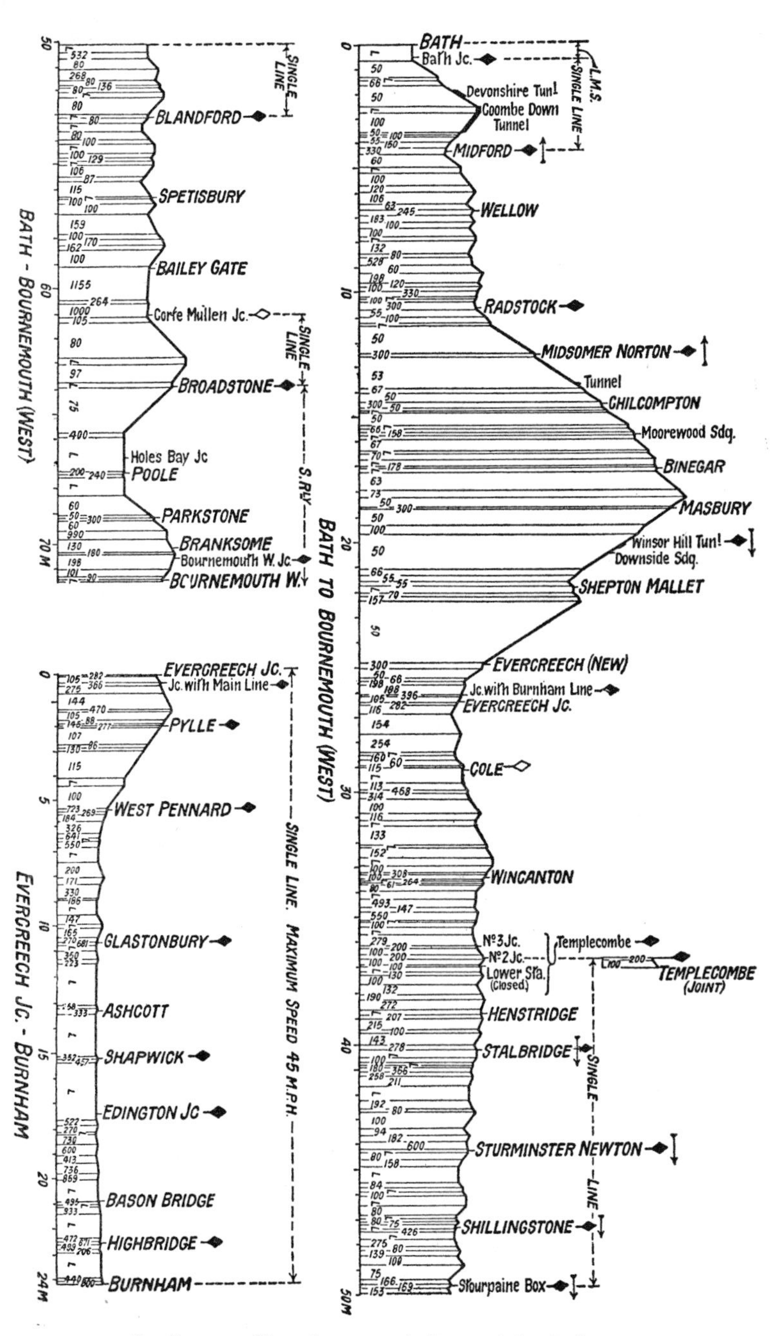

Gradient profiles—Somerset & Dorset Joint Railway

climb up to the level of the main line, and on this level there was a 60 ft turntable shared by the two companies. On each side of the line as far as Bath Junction were the marshalling yards—the Midland yard on the south side and the Dorset on the north.

At Bath Junction, half a mile from Queen Square, the Somerset & Dorset line swung away towards the south, looping around the suburb of Twerton and climbing towards the great rampart of Combe Down on a gradient of 1 in 50. In later years the train tablet for the single-line section to Midford was picked up at Bath Junction Box between the two diverging lines. For many years there was also a Somerset & Dorset box (Bath Single Line Junction Box) less than a hundred yards away at the north end of the viaduct over the Lower Bristol Road, where the single-line section actually began, and where the train tablet and, if necessary, the banking engine staff were picked up. Both this box and an earlier Midland Junction box were replaced by Bath Junction Box on 13 April 1924.

Banking engines assisted down freight trains through Devonshire tunnel and as far as the entrance to Combe Down tunnel at the summit of the incline and, having seen the rear brake vans pass into the tunnel, returned to Bath Junction to give up the banking engine staff, thirteen minutes running time being allowed for the double journey. They also worked two sidings between the junction and the summit: May's siding (up side), which served the brickyard (latterly Bath Victoria Brick & Tile Company) and was taken out in the 1950s; and the Co-op siding (down side) serving its coal depot and bakery in Melcombe Road. In each case the driver had to obtain the banking engine staff at Bath Junction as well as the key to the sidings, and propelled his wagons towards Combe Down. If he were banking a freight train, the wagons were placed between the banking engine and the brake van of the freight train and taken up to the summit, the work at the sidings being done on the return journey.

The Co-op siding was on a short level stretch before the climb was resumed at 1 in 66. Hereabouts on the up side once stood the Bath Ticket Platform, one mile thirty chains from Queen Square. This figures in working timetables for 1875 and 1876. Queen Square was an open station, and tickets were collected at Weston on the Mangotsfield line. The ticket platform served the same function for the Somerset & Dorset. The OS six-inch map for 1885 records the platform and some sort of signalbox or ground frame on the site, but on 5 November 1876 a new platform was brought into use at Bath Single Line Junction, enabling down trains to pass on the other line while tickets were being collected. The staff, consisting of signalmen, ticket collectors and telegraph clerks, were transferred to the new box, but this arrangement apparently lasted only until November 1883, after which there are no further details of staff appointments at Bath Ticket Platform which disappears from the working timetable, while a ticket collector had already been appointed at Midford.

The gradient steepened again to 1 in 50 before the line plunged into the 440 yd Devonshire tunnel which took its name from Devonshire Buildings on the Bath-Wells road; it emerged for a brief glimpse of the beautiful wooded Lyncombe Vale before again plunging into the darkness of Combe Down tunnel, 1,829 yd long, where the gradient changed to 1 in 100 down towards Midford.*

Both tunnels were notoriously foul and unpleasant to work: it was a heavily-occupied section of line with engines always labouring on the heavy grades, and on double-headed trains the footplate of the train engine could bear an unpleasing resemblance to Dante's Inferno. Combe Down tunnel, incidentally, was the longest tunnel in Britain without ventilation shafts. Although the clearances were narrow, the Somerset & Dorset legend of the Midland compound, sent down from Derby for trials and getting its outside cylinders firmly wedged in the portals of Combe Down, must be regarded as apocryphal. Nevertheless, it can only have been the engineering difficulties and the tremendous expense involved that militated against the doubling of the whole section from Bath Junction to Midford.

When the Midford-Radstock section was doubled in 1892-4, the deposited plans show that the original intention was to extend the double line to the southern end of the tunnel: even this would have involved much heavy engineering work along the hillside at Midford as well as a new signalbox at the mouth of the tunnel, though Tucking Mill viaduct was actually rebuilt to take a double line, and space had originally been left for a station to serve Combe Down.

From the tunnel mouth began one of the most beautiful stretches of scenery on the line, which first crossed the wooded Horsecombe Vale, past Midford Castle, built fantastically in the shape of the ace of clubs with attendant follies in its park, leaping the valley of

* There are slight discrepancies in the length of these tunnels as listed in various publications. I have taken my figures for all the tunnels on the Somerset & Dorset from the control board at Bath whose figures coincide with those on SR diagrams of the line.

the Cam on a lofty viaduct and then winding along green hillsides above the Wellow Brook, with almost continuous curves and frequent changes of gradient—an unspoiled piece of North Somerset country. The down goods yard at Midford, some distance on the Bath side of the station and still on the single-line section, was controlled by a ground frame; the station itself perched precariously on the steep hillside with its single platform on the up side built right against the rock. Unlike all the other stations on the Bath Extension the buildings were of simple wooden construction, with the suggestion that they were temporary buildings which would have to be demolished if and when the line was doubled. The signalbox, too, was unusual, with a flat roof: this was the result of a 'temporary' reconstruction after the damage caused by the accident of 29 July 1936 (see page 129).

Midford was one of the key boxes on the system, controlling the entry to the single-line section to Bath. A number of 'misses' on the Whitaker tablet-exchanging apparatus occurred here because of the alignment and excessive speeds. On two occasions at least the tablet was lost and never found, and on other occasions it was retrieved from nearby gardens or from the roof of the Hope & Anchor. Immediately beyond the signalbox the double-track section began, though the junction was latterly made at the south end of the viaduct. It was an eight-arch viaduct of brick and stone, 168 yd long, carrying the line across the Bath-Frome road, the Cam brook, the GWR Camerton-Limpley Stoke branch, and the Somersetshire Coal Canal which the branch superseded.

A short distance to the west of the viaduct, an arm of the canal was carried by a stone-built aqueduct of 1803 across the Cam brook: here were wharves, where the coal hauled along the tramway from Radstock was off-loaded into the canal boats. The line of the tramway which was abandoned in 1874 can still be traced, crossing the railway at the south end of the viaduct and curving round the hillside in the direction of Wellow, eventually joining the railway near the Midford outer home signal.

From here onwards it looped and wove its way alongside the Somerset & Dorset, crossing and recrossing it on different levels at least a dozen times before Radstock. On several occasions, immediately to the east of Wellow church, for example, and again at Shoscombe, its course loops right round the heads of little valleys on embankments. Apart from the well-preserved tunnel at Wellow, various stone boundary posts inscribed S.C.C.C. have been discovered, and at Shoscombe and elsewhere the square stone sleepers that carried the track are still visible. Just how the coal traffic was maintained between the date of the purchase of the tramway and the opening of the railway is uncertain, but the deposited plans accompanying the Somerset & Dorset's Act of 1871 show a number of diversions of the tramway—as well as interesting details such as the location of crossing-places and water troughs provided for the horses who worked the line.

Wellow was the first station on the line to show the standard design of station building used on the Bath Extension: a bay-windowed stationmaster's office, a combined booking hall and waiting room and a ladies' room—built in grey limestone with a slate roof, a pleasing design that reappeared with slight local variations all the way to Evercreech Junction. Wellow was always a well-patronised station for, until the withdrawal of the passenger service, buses reached the village only once a week, situated as it is at the bottom of breakneck hills in almost every direction.

It was from the station buildings on the up platform that a down excursion was ordered to proceed to Radstock to meet an up train in hideous head-on collision on the single track at Foxcote on 7 August 1876. At that date there was no intermediate station before Radstock, and it was fifty-five years after the opening of the line that the halt at Shoscombe & Single Hill was opened on 23 September 1929 with great celebrations by no less a person than George Lansbury MP.

The halt consisted of two Southern-style concrete platforms, and on the path up to the village was a tiny booking office and waiting room. Like Wellow the halt was always well used, as until 1966 no buses succeeded in penetrating the network of steep and narrow lanes that served a fair-sized community. The halt was notable for being staffed throughout its thirty-six years of existence by two women servants of the railway—the Misses Tapper, later Mrs Beeho and Mrs Chivers, the latter living in a railway bungalow built on the actual bed of the old canal, and by tradition replacing a row of shacks occupied by the navvies who cut the Somerset & Dorset line.

Beyond Shoscombe the first signs of the Somerset coalfield are visible: the abandoned dirt-batch of Foxcote colliery, and the sidings belonging to Writhlington. The signalbox here was known by various different names: Foxcote at the time of the 1876 accident, then Braysdown and Writhlington and, latterly, Writhlington pure and simple, though Radstock drivers would always speak of 'going out to Braysdown'. The Somerset & Dorset served all three collieries, with a short siding to the Writhlington pit-head: a tramway came down from Foxcote on the down side, and there was an inclined plane from Braysdown served by sidings on the up side. Of these only Writhlington was still at work in 1966, by which time all the Radstock collieries had also been closed.

Of those served by the Somerset & Dorset, Clandown and Middle Pit had closed between the wars, and Ludlow in 1954: until about 1900 some coal had also come down from Wellsway and Welton collieries on the tramway which had been built a hundred years before to feed the canal. Even more recently, spoil from Middle Pit was brought down by horse-drawn wagon through the S & D yard to the batch at Ludlow. Coal from Tyning was carried across the Somerset & Dorset by a tramway to the GWR yard: the very low arch of the Tyning Bridge (known affectionately to generations of Radstock enginemen as 'Marble Arch', and almost certainly the original arch spanning the Coal Canal tramway) precluded the use in this part of the yard of any locomotives except the three little colliery shunters Nos. 25A, 26A and 45A. These survived until 1929, when they were replaced by two Sentinel 0—4—0 shunters Nos. 101 and 102. These propelled wagons up the short incline to Ludlow, where they would be taken over by horses, and sometimes even taken on to the GWR, this being the only possible method of communication between the two lines, although for nearly a century they ran within a few yards of each other for about half a mile.

East Box controlled the goods yard, and the approach to the engine-shed, a two-road stone-built structure, surprisingly solid for a Somerset & Dorset engine-shed. The station buildings, of standard design, were on the up side, and the West Box controlled the level crossing on the Bath-Shepton Mallet road. This crossing (only yards from another crossing over the GWR) was to cause major traffic jams and many hours of frustration for motorists; in fact at peak holiday times road traffic constantly piled up for several miles in each direction. It is interesting to find that, as early as November 1874, three months after the opening of the line, there were complaints about the 'alleged detentions to the public road traffic'.

In 1875, the Board of Trade ordered a bridge to be built, and in 1877 it announced its intention of commencing legal proceedings to enforce the substitution of a bridge to replace both level crossings. But the Somerset & Dorset and the Bristol & North Somerset stood firm to resist the Board of Trade's order—and there the matter seems to have rested. In any event, the Somerset & Dorset had constructed a subway under its line—a murky and hazardous passage, wide enough for only a single vehicle, crossing the line of the old tramway on the level and flooded regularly after heavy rain.

Immediately beyond the crossing, the single-track Clandown branch diverged on the up side. This again was worked by the diminutive colliery shunters, which propelled their wagons to the gasworks siding, to Middle Pit sidings and to Clandown sidings at the foot of the rope-hauled incline which gave access to the colliery itself. The half-mile branch was laid on the line of a very early tramway which was constructed about 1800 as a feeder for the Somersetshire Coal Canal and appears on the 1817 OS map.

From Radstock, down trains attacked the seven and a half-mile climb to Masbury summit, practically every freight train calling for rear-end assistance here. The bank began with a stretch of 1 in 55, easing off for a bit, and then steepening to 1 in 50 all the way to Midsomer Norton: for about a half a mile three lines of railway ran side by side up the valley, the Somerset & Dorset climbing steadily above the GWR and the old Welton tramway, the latter being the property of the Somerset & Dorset as indicated by a notice that still stands on an otherwise undistinguished piece of Gladstone Street in Welton, where the line once ran to Welton Hill colliery.

The Somerset & Dorset crossed these lines on the North Somerset viaduct, known locally as the Five Arches: the plans deposited in 1870 reveal that a connecting spur was originally intended with the B & NS a short distance west of Radstock, and the failure to build this until 1966 must have involved many long and wasteful detours to enable wagons to reach their destinations on the other company's line. After the 'unpleasant episode' of 1875, so bitter were the relations between the companies that, during repairs to the viaduct in 1881, a stone-mason employed by the Somerset & Dorset was actually ordered not to work above the B & NS as thereby committing an act of trespass on its line.

Approaching Midsomer Norton, the line passed the large dirt-batches of Norton Hill colliery, served by a set of sidings on the down side: these were worked by main-line engines, by banking engines from Radstock, and by shunting engines belonging to the colliery: *Leonidas* and *Lord Salisbury*. Midsomer Norton station, inconveniently situated at the top of a long hill up from the town, boasted a station hand-bell stamped S & DR, one of the few relics from the 1862-75 era, and the most beautiful gardens on the northern half of the line, whose lovingly-tended lawns and flower-beds won first prizes under the SR and the WR each year from 1953 to 1960, thus maintaining a tradition dating from 1913 when the Joint Committee instituted awards for the best-kept station, and Midsomer Norton carried off the first prize of £4.

Another two miles of steady climbing through a twin-bore tunnel sixty-six yd long brought the line into Chilcompton station, high above the valley where the old part of the village lies: 'Chilcompton (for Downside)' as the public timetable announced before the motor age took over, special trains at the beginning and end of each school term being run to and from London *via* Templecombe until 1950. Here, too, there were water-towers, it being a regular watering-place for bankers returning to Radstock from the summit, and a siding off the down yard, serving a tip to which coal was brought by road from New Rock colliery half a mile away.

Moorewood sidings, where the line levelled out a little after a particularly gruelling stretch of 1 in 50 at Lynch Hill, were for long a busy industrial scene. Moorewood signalbox was the last box to be built on the Somerset & Dorset line. It was opened in 1914 to replace the ground frame, worked by a key from Binegar, which controlled the Old Down siding. This was on the up side, and had been opened in 1901 to serve the Emborough quarries which had begun to develop the site of an earlier brick and tile works, where fuller's earth and ochre had also been obtained.

In course of time three large stone-crushing plants were built here, while on the down side an aerial ropeway brought more stone from Clement Dalley's quarry at Cockhill. There was also the 2 ft gauge tramway, worked by diminutive 0—6—0 tanks, which off-loaded coal into main-line wagons from Moorewood colliery in the Nettlebridge valley. Both these workings terminated about 1930, but the down sidings continued to be used for storing wagons, and the signalbox remained open for one shift a day to work the Emborough stone traffic until 21 June 1965.

Between Moorewood and Binegar the line climbed again at 1 in 67 over a viaduct, past the huge quarries scooped out of the hillsides. Even on railway property there were signs of quarrying, as James Clark, walking the unfinished line in 1873, had noticed a bed of fine mountain limestone near Gurney Slade, and extra land had been acquired to work it. At Binegar, too, there were Read's stone sidings, with lime-kilns and crushing plants fed by an aerial rope-way from quarries at Gurney Slade. There was also a large stone shed in the down yard, belonging to the Oakhill Brewery, whose famous stout was brought to Binegar by a 2 ft 6 in. gauge railway

HIGHBRIDGE WHARF

(26) *The authorisation to collect tolls at the Wharf dated from 1827 when the Glastonbury Canal obtained its Act*

(27) *'S.S. Alpha'* (1879-1925) *unloading at Highbridge in* 1924

BRANCH LINE SCENES

(28) *Porter Mogg at Edington Junction with an* SCR *handbell of* 1862 *and the cap badge of the Somerset Joint Committee*

(29) *On Cossington bank in the* 1920s: 4—4—0 *No.* 70 *and* SDJ *rolling-stock during the last years of the famous blue livery*

worked by 0—4—0 tank locomotives called *Oakhill* and *Mendip*. This little line, opened in 1904, operated until the first world war from the effects of which the stout trade never recovered—and the rails were taken up in 1921.

Until 1914 Binegar must have been a busy enough little station by day—and by night too, for the signalbox worked round the clock, dealing with the bankers off up and down freights all through the night. Bankers on down trains picked up the banking engine staff marked 'Masbury Summit' from the tablet-exchanging apparatus, and having seen the rear brakevan pass over the summit, returned to Binegar on the wrong line. Early working timetables include both Masbury Summit and Cannard's Grave Summit.

Binegar also boasted what was perhaps the oldest piece of equipment still in regular use on the Somerset & Dorset—a station handbell that once belonged to the Somerset Central Railway. Between 1959 and 1966, calf traffic for Scotland was dealt with here, and one of the banking engine turns from Radstock involved 'doing the Binegar calf', i.e. attaching the vans to the rear of an up afternoon train.

The final approach to the summit involved a mile at 1 in 63 and 1 in 73; there was a summit level of about forty yd, 811 ft above sea level, and then the line fell away sharply through a deep cutting at 1 in 50 almost all the way to Shepton Mallet. Masbury station was quite different in design from the other stations on the Bath Extension: a grey stone building without an awning and containing merely a booking office and waiting room; close by on the platform was the stationmaster's house, with a bay window surmounted by a fanciful stone carving of a mediaeval castle, complete with crenellations and portcullis and the Gothic legend *Maesbury Castle*.

For some years after the first world war, under stationmasters Parsons and Light, chapel services were held in the waiting room on Sunday evenings to the accompaniment of a harmonium, the room being prepared by the porter on Saturday evenings as part of his duties. Masbury is hardly comparable with Garsdale, on the Settle & Carlisle line, where services were regularly held in the station for the isolated railway community, but it is a lonely spot with only a handful of houses within a radius of a mile or so. It was originally intended to call the station Dinder, which would have been more than somewhat misleading, as the village of Dinder was three miles away and 600 ft lower. The station was reduced to a halt in 1935, though the signalbox remained open by day to break the four and three-quarter-mile section between Binegar and Shepton Mallet. Between the wars a stone-crushing plant was installed by Mendipadam, a subsidiary of Emborough Stone Company, and during the second world war the sidings were extended to serve a large US Army camp.

Maesbury Castle is actually an Iron Age hill fort, 957 ft above sea level: from its ramparts a magnificent panorama of the railway could be enjoyed, from Moorewood to Winsor Hill, and even beyond Shepton Mallet to Cannard's Grave summit. Even from the railway on the hillside there was a breath-taking view to Quantock and Exmoor, with Countisbury Foreland stretching far out into the Bristol Channel, and in the foreground the towers of Wells Cathedral, and Glastonbury Tor rising out of the Isle of Avalon.

Just north of Winsor Hill the lofty Hamwood viaduct carried the line across a deep wooded ravine. Hamwood Quarry sidings (with the inevitable stone-crushing plant) were on the up side; Winsor Hill Quarry and sidings on the down side. The latter dated from 1875 when a Mr Beauchamp agreed to send large quantities of stone over the line. Between the up and down line at the north end of the tunnels, controlling the entrance to both lots of sidings, was Winsor Hill signalbox, the only signalbox on the line built entirely of stone. This was built in 1892, replacing an earlier box which operated when the sidings were first constructed. The two single-line tunnels were cut through solid rock, the original down tunnel measuring 242 yd and the up tunnel, added when the line was doubled in 1892, 132 yd.

During the construction of the original tunnel, four navvies were killed by a rockfall on 18 August 1873. They lie buried in the cemetery at Shepton Mallet under a monument fashioned from a portion of the rock which caused their death: William Francis aged 20, H. N. Rendal aged 30, John Smith aged 48, and William Nicholls aged 51. The simple inscription reads: 'For man also knoweth not his time'.

Immediately south of the tunnel was yet another siding which, from 1900 until 1940, served John Wainwright's Downside Quarry by means of a key obtained from Winsor Hill box to work the ground frame. The line then swept spectacularly round the town of Shepton Mallet, crossing the lofty Bath Road viaduct, part of which collapsed during a winter gale on 2 February 1946 and was rebuilt during the following summer, and the longer Charlton viaduct (317 yd), before reaching Charlton Road station.

From Charlton viaduct southwards, the gradient changed suddenly, and the line climbed for half a mile with stretches at 1 in 55 and 1 in 70 as far as Cannard's Grave summit. There were large yards on both sides of the line at Shepton Mallet: stone was quarried here, crushed on the spot, and sent up and down the line from the Committee's ballast siding; there was a tall water-tower, for most down freight trains took water here; and the offices of the signal inspector for the whole of the Joint line, together with a series of low one-storey wooden buildings in the down yard which housed the signal department until 1930.

To the south of the station, the line passed under the East Somerset line on its way from Witham to Shepton Mallet High Street, a mile from Charlton Road, and at Cannard's Grave summit the descent was resumed in a long cutting with six overbridges in the first mile, and a gradient of 1 in 50 all the way to Evercreech New, sweeping down the hillside in easy curves and across the graceful Prestleigh viaduct of eleven arches.

Evercreech New, conveniently placed on the edge of the large village, was a smaller station than most: considerable milk traffic was once handled here, as well as lime from the limeworks abutting on the line. By now the worst of the bank was over, and the gradients eased off gradually over the last mile and a half to Evercreech Junction, though one was very much aware that the northbound climb to Masbury began with the gradient of 1 in 105 at the end of the platform at the Junction.

It was always a surprise to find that the old Burnham line had the straight run in past the North Box, while the main line swung in on an enormous curve with a speed restriction of 25 m.p.h. Latterly, all trains, even 'The Pines', called at the Junction, but in Somerset & Dorset days some of the fastest trains did not stop. All freight trains called at the yards, many of them terminating or starting from there, both for the main line and for the branch. There was an up yard and a down yard at the North Junction, the latter being situated on the down side of the branch, where there was also a 56 ft turntable. Shunting continued here all night, these turns as well as the banking turns to Binegar being worked from Templecombe shed.

The Somerset Brick & Tile Works was served by a siding off the down main line, and there was another small goods yard at the station itself. There was an air of spaciousness about the station. The standard range of buildings was somewhat extended, there was a dignified stationmaster's house, and more substantial accommodation on the other platform in place of the usual wooden shelter.

The middle road, generally occupied by a waiting branch-line train, or on summer Saturdays by a string of pilot engines awaiting their turn over the Bath line, added to the sense of spaciousness.

It is surprising that no bay platform was ever built for starting the branch trains on the up side and eliminating many hours of draughty waiting between connections, though to the last the station staff provided a generous supply of reading material in the waiting rooms as well as flowers in their season, for the gardens too were well tended and deserved their many awards. The tall South Box controlled the level crossing on the A371 (referred to in working timetables as late as 1929 as 'the turnpike road') though there was a lower structure in use in the 1870s (see plate 7) before the doubling of the main line. There was also a Somerset Central station building dating from 1862, which was ultimately rebuilt and enlarged to form the stationmaster's house, being replaced by an unmistakable Somerset & Dorset building of 1874 vintage. Since the closure of the line, the former Railway Hotel has been renamed The Silent Whistle, the inn sign depicting a dilapidated signalbox and a WHISTLE notice beside a grass-grown track.

BURNHAM TO EVERCREECH JUNCTION

'The Branch' it became on 20 July 1874, and the Branch it remained for ever after—a slowly withering arm. From 'the Junction' one went *up the branch,* for down had once meant down from Highbridge to Glastonbury, off the Bristol & Exeter. A journey down the branch therefore began on the pier at Burnham, staring out across the mudflats of the Parrett estuary to the purple Quantocks and the dim Welsh coast. Embedded in the pier are lengths of rails, but it is difficult to envisage the *Leopard* and the *Sherboro* berthed there and trucks being hauled up and down the 1 in 23 gradient by wire ropes. For a time the rails were actually used for launching the lifeboat from the boathouse beside the railway station, but the lifeboat was taken away in 1930, about the same time as the promenade was extended southwards. At the pierhead stands the Queen's Hotel, but time has not obliterated the carved legend, The Reed Arms, commemorating the foremost citizen of Burnham, director of the Somerset & Dorset, to which he sold his own secondhand locomotive for £1,450 in the dark days of 1865.

Two hundred yards inland, the Somerset & Dorset Hotel faced across the road towards Burnham station. This was a dignified little building, its original single platform partly covered by an all-over roof, but a longer concrete 'excursion' platform had been added on the up side, and there was a short spur for engines to run round their trains at the seaward end of the station, where buffer-stops cut off the old extension to the pier. There was a small goods yard, a red-brick goods shed and a tiny signalbox at the end of the original platform, where the single track swung away southwards towards Highbridge, serving three brickyard sidings on the way, which were controlled by a key on the train staff.

It was little more than a mile to Highbridge Wharf on the up side. From 1854, for almost a century, this was a busy scene, with sidings and storage facilities provided by the railway for goods landed both from their own vessels and from private shipping: a toll board announced the Table of Tolls authorised by the Act of 7 & 8 Geo. IV, under which the Glastonbury Canal was constructed between 1829 and 1833, the gates of the sea-lock that gave access to the canal being buried under the car park at the east end of the wharf, though some of the stonework is still visible.

Highbridge C box, a delightful little structure with a wooden balustrade protected by an awning, controlled the junction of the Wharf line and Burnham branch as well as the busy crossing on the A38; next came Highbridge goods yard with another red-brick shed, then the tiny B box controlling the entrance to the goods yard and another road crossing, and then the crossing on the level of the Bristol & Exeter main line at the north end of the original Highbridge station. This was controlled by the main-line Highbridge West box, but a few yards away was yet another Somerset & Dorset box (A box) which worked in conjunction with the GWR box.

A box was closed by 1914 but the building remained on the end of No. 4 platform and was used as a guards' messroom. Transfer traffic was handled by way of a goods loop between B and C boxes, involving complicated reversals and awkward occupation of the GWR main line: in May 1965, after the Burnham branch and the Wharf lines had been taken up and B and C boxes closed, a direct connection was laid between the Somerset & Dorset line and the ex-GWR goods yard.

Highbridge station, with its seven platforms, always managed to look extraordinarily empty and desolate in latter years, though long ago, before the works closed and before the victory of the motor bus, when thirty trains a day were running in each direction on the Burnham line, it must have been busy enough. Two of the platforms belonged to the Bristol & Exeter whose original buildings still survive; adjoining them, and at an angle to them, were Nos. 4 and 5 which served the Burnham trains and from which the single track led across the GWR. No. 5 must originally have belonged to the Bristol & Exeter, for the Somerset Central paid them a rent of £10 a year 'for the privilege of landing passengers on their triangular platform at Highbridge'. After the closure of the Burnham section, all Somerset & Dorset passenger trains arrived at No. 5 and left from Nos. 2/3.

The Somerset Central station, opened in May 1862, was a terminal station approached from the Wells road, with an island platform on which stood the station building, a pleasing well-proportioned structure of red brick with stone facings. On the wall facing the town there was a bronze tablet commemorating the 101 railwaymen who left the locomotive, carriage and wagon works to serve in the 1914-18 war, of whom thirteen gave their lives. Designed and cast in the works, the tablet, which was dedicated on 8 May 1922 by the Bishop of Bath & Wells, was originally on the end of the messroom at the works, but was removed to the station in 1930 when the works closed, and in 1965 was again moved, this time to the Garden of Remembrance in the town.

Highbridge Loco, the most easterly as well as the largest of the four Somerset & Dorset signalboxes, controlled the entrance to the loco yard, with its turntable (49 ft 9 in) and two-road engine shed, as well as to the works. These lay on the south side of the line to Glastonbury and covered a considerable acreage on the north bank of the Brue. The first buildings, for the repair of locomotives and rolling-stock, were ready for use by February 1862, when the Bruton extension was opened and narrow-gauge working began over the Dorset Central as far as Templecombe. The works were at first on a very limited scale, but ample land was acquired and continual enlargements followed, providing a complete range of workshops for the rebuilding and repair of locomotives and for the building and repair of passenger carriages and wagons: erecting shop and foundry, spring shop and boiler shop, machine shop, paint shop, saw mill, stores and drawing office.*

After the closure in 1930, the works stood empty and desolate, except for a period of use for Government stores during the 1939-45 war. Most of the buildings survive, though the carriage and wagon department was burned down during the 1950s. The wooden paint shop was particularly impressive, with sturdy wooden columns and

* (See plan on page 103.) Before 1900 a certain amount of foundry work was carried out by two local firms, Wensley of Mark and Day of Mark Causeway.

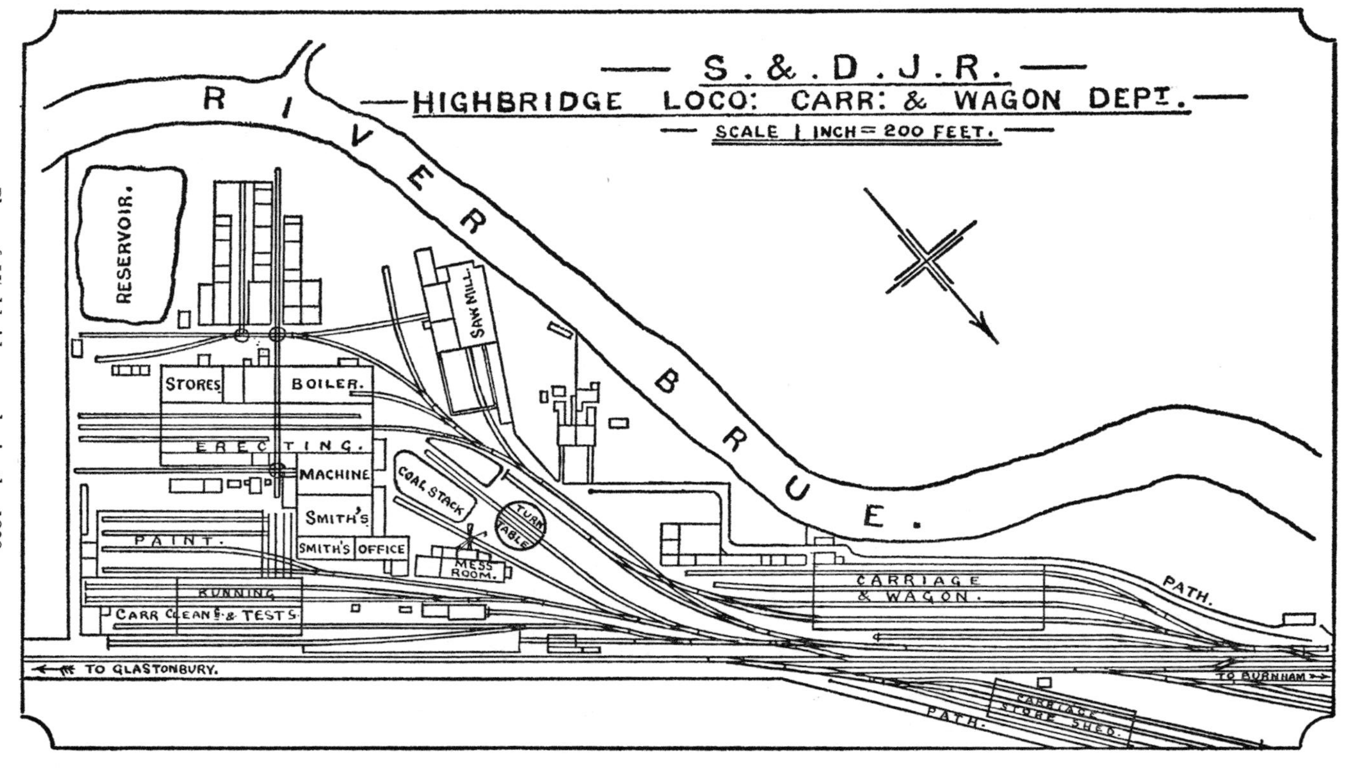

Plan of Highbridge works in the 1920s

girders which supported the roof; so was the red-brick erecting shop whose spacious whitewashed interior, with track still laid in the floor, echoed strangely in its emptiness. In the long line of lavatories a notice forbade the use of waste 'to avoid choking drainpipes and creating a nuisance': it was dated 29.6.92.

Although the equipment of Highbridge works was of a comprehensive nature, no locomotives were built new there except for three small tank engines. These were outside-cylinder saddle tanks specially designed to work on the Radstock colliery branches. No. 25A (0—4—2T) was built in 1885, Nos. 26A and 45A (both 0—4—0Ts) in 1895.

Normal work carried out included periodical overhauls, rebuilding by conversion of tender engines into tank engines and *vice versa*, and reboilering with larger boilers supplied from Derby, leaving Highbridge to adapt such details as boiler mountings to its own taste.

To judge by the distinctive appearance of the Johnson 4—4—0s when reboilered in the Edwardian era, it is clear that Highbridge took a certain degree of pleasure in departing from Midland conformity. This was typical of the personal atmosphere of the Somerset & Dorset. In the days when drivers had their own engines, they drove them to Highbridge for repair and collected them afterwards; with the works so handy, the locomotive sheds were equipped with the minimum of tools and machinery for repairs and were left badly off when Highbridge closed down in 1930.

Carriage construction was undertaken from an early date, even before the establishment of the Joint Committee, it is believed. At that time the coaches were painted chocolate brown. In the Joint days carriage construction followed the general pattern to be seen elsewhere in Great Britain, though because of the local nature of the service, it was entirely non-corridor stock. Design progressed through four-wheel and six-wheel vehicles to bogie carriages in 1898. The last of these were built in 1913 (see plates 50-52). By that time the through trains from the North were made up of Midland corridor stock, reinforced when necessary on the Somerset & Dorset itself by local non-corridor carriages. These latter were painted blue with gold lining to match the locomotives.

Once past the works and the site of a wartime US ordnance depot on the down side, the Somerset Central set off south-east on its twelve-mile journey across the moors to Glastonbury, keeping close company with the Brue as far as Bason Bridge. The station here was opened in 1856 with a single platform on the down side, and a group of low station buildings on the up side. Bason Bridge was never a block post, but the ground frame controlled the level crossing over the B3141, the first of fourteen manned crossings on the next twenty-one miles to Evercreech Junction; another ground frame controlled the sidings of a large milk factory established here in 1909 by Wilts United Dairies, whence milk trains travelled to London *via* Templecombe in Somerset & Dorset days, but since nationalisation *via* Highbridge and the Western Region.

From Bason Bridge to Edington was a lonely stretch of country with hardly a house in sight after Cripp's Corner, where the line crossed the Brue, and the canal diverged to the south, a country of rhines and drove roads, rich grazing for summer cattle but a waste of waters after winter rains. At Huntspill Crossing was the first of the neat red-brick crossing-keeper's houses, built as a result of complaints made in 1860 about the absence of suitable lodgings within reasonable distance of level crossings 'for the use of Policemen engaged there'. Such a cottage had already been built at Edington Road.

The station was opened in 1856 and served the Burtle area as well as Edington, which was a good two miles away on the Polden slopes. In 1890 it achieved higher status as Edington Junction on the opening of the Bridgwater branch, with a down platform as well as an island platform the outer face of which was used by the branch; but in 1952 the loop and the signalbox were removed, the down platform crumbled into ruin, and the little station finished its life as Edington Burtle, with a ground frame to guard the crossing.

At this point the South Drain and the canal reappeared on the south side of the line, but a mile or so further along, the South Drain passed under the railway, while the dried-up course of the canal remained visible on the south side all the way to Ashcott and beyond, the only notable feature being the ruins of the lock near the Shapwick down distant signal.

Shapwick was a block post and crossing place, the signalbox controlling the level crossing on the old Wedmore turnpike road; the wooden station building on the up platform seemed hardly to have changed since the morning in 1854 when George Warry rode over from Shapwick to watch the first train go down, but the station was actually destroyed by fire on 25 September 1900 as a result of the overheating of a stove pipe in the signalbox adjoining.

When the station was rebuilt, a better signalbox was built beyond the level crossing. The waiting room mysteriously contained a bench carved with the initials of the Tottenham & Hampstead

Junction Railway, whose life of independence ended in 1902 with a take-over by the Midland and Great Eastern Railways; one can only assume that the bench found its way in time to Derby and so down on to another Joint line. North of the station was a stationmaster's house of red brick dated 1861.

At Shapwick one is in the middle of the peat country, the peat beds stretching away on each side of the line, and the turves piled to dry in neat conical heaps, known as ruckles. Before the development of motor transport, much peat went away by rail from Shapwick and Ashcott: between them was Alexander's Siding (later serving the Eclipse Peat Company's works) where a 2 ft tramway crossed the Somerset & Dorset on the level—the site of the curious accident described in Chapter 7.

Ashcott (or Ashcott & Meare, to give its full title which does not seem to appear in any timetable after 1876) had a single platform on the down side, with a ground frame controlling the level crossing and a single siding, and a red-brick station building at road level. Almost at once the South Drain turned sharply south under the railway, where the stone abutments that once carried the canal over the Drain in its iron aqueduct are still visible. The canal bed then transferred to the north side of the line all the way to Glastonbury.

Ashcott curves always came as a surprise after long miles of straight track, and their radius of fifteen chains had led to the imposition of a 10 m.p.h. speed limit by the time the 1864 Rule Book was compiled. Between the wars, Petfu siding was built between Ashcott and Sharpham Crossing to serve another peat field.

At Aqueduct Crossing there was a glimpse of the stone abutments which carried the canal across the Brue though today the bed of the Brue is considerably higher than the dried-up canal. A good stretch of canal bed and towing path was visible beside the line before the latter curved away southwards towards Glastonbury.

The goods yard at Glastonbury was always a busy place by day, and handled a considerable amount of freight and parcels traffic to the very end. Glastonbury signalbox, one of the largest and most imposing on the whole system, had a distinct Midland air about it. The wooden station buildings, dating from early in this century, once included a bookstall on the up platform and even a refreshment room on the down platform. This was opened in 1899 by the Abbey Temperance Hotel Company which soon went bankrupt, after which the refreshment room was rented by a local baker, William Wadman, until 1932. The outer face of the down platform was used by the Wells branch train.

To the south of the station yard was The Pollards, a solidly ugly Victorian red-brick building with the arms of Glastonbury Abbey carved over the door. This was originally built by James John Rocke, a Glastonbury solicitor, in 1861 as The Abbey Arms & Railway Hotel, part of which was leased to the Somerset Central as offices, eventually becoming the offices of the Somerset & Dorset until 1877, and thereafter the district engineer's house.

A few weeks before the closure of the line in 1966, a ceiling was brought down while interior decoration was being undertaken, and this released a shower of old tickets, all dated between 1873 and 1876, including one issued to Shepton Mallet only a fortnight after the opening of the Bath Extension, and others issued for the annual excursion of the Highbridge locomotive and carriage department a week before the Radstock disaster of August 1876.

The engineer's workshops were on the north side, a quadrangle of one-storey wooden building comprising timber-sheds and stores, carpenters' shops, smiths', painters' and plumbers' shops. Nearby was a water-tower supplied from the stream which fed the canal basin, the canal having swung round from the north by means of a most extraordinary right-angle turn to cross the line of the railway and terminate at wharves now occupied by Snow's timber works.

Over Dye House Lane Crossing, Paradise Crossing and, appropriately enough, Cemetary Crossing (*sic*), the Wells branch and the Bruton extension forged north-east together round a curve with a nine and a half-chain radius and a speed limit of 5 m.p.h.; they ran as parallel single tracks for about a mile until the Bruton line swung away to the east to run dead straight for four miles through West Pennard. This was the first stone-built station on the line, two miles from its village, but situated on the Glastonbury-Shepton Mallet road and equidistant from West Pennard and Pilton; here, until 1964, there was a loop and a block post at the foot of the four-mile Pylle bank, which climbed up an extraordinarily beautiful wooded valley with a ruling gradient of 1 in 86 and several stretches at 1 in 100 or worse.

After Steanbow and Cockmill Crossings came Pylle Limeworks, half a mile short of Pylle station, on the up side; the siding was built in 1869 with a ground frame worked by tablet from Pylle station until 1912, and a disc and crossbar signal remained in use here for many years. Pylle station, another grey stone structure with a goods shed and stationmaster's house combined on the down side, ceased to be a blockpost when the loop was removed in 1929. From the summit, half a mile east of the station, the line curved gradually down over Elbow Corner Crossing, past the Evercreech down yard, to join the main line from Bath at Evercreech Junction North box, twenty-three miles seventy-five chains from the buffer stops at Burnham.

THE WELLS AND BRIDGWATER BRANCHES

Before the Bruton extension was built, the Wells branch was for three years, from 1859 to 1862, the eastern arm of the Somerset Central line from Highbridge. Where the Bruton line swung eastwards towards West Pennard, the Wells line carried straight on across the moor towards Wells, whose cathedral towers were visible against the background of the Mendip ridge. The two lines diverged at Wells Branch Junction until 2 December 1878, when the signalbox and junction were removed and a second track was laid from Glastonbury.

The gradients were negligible for the first three miles to Polsham, where there was a level crossing controlled from the station house, and a ground frame and siding worked by one down goods train daily. It is hard to see why a station was provided for the scattered hamlet of Polsham rather than for the much larger village of Coxley where there was anyhow a manned crossing.

Beyond Coxley the line climbed for a mile at 1 in 106 before curving to the east to reach the terminus at Wells. Just before the junction with the Cheddar Valley line there was the Somerset & Dorset signalbox, the branch being worked as a single block section five and a half miles long. On the up side was the small two-road engine shed and a delightful little pumping-house containing a waterwheel erected in 1861 by which the water tower was supplied. The fine stone-built goods shed was reached by crossing the GWR tracks on the level; the passenger station was also an imposing building, appropriate enough for a cathedral city, though being a shed-type structure with only a single platform on the down side nearest the town, it was always rather a gloomy place.

The Bridgwater branch was also worked as a single block section. It was built as a single line, though the original formation optimistically allowed for double track. Branch-line trains used the bay platform on the up side at Edington, and the single line swung away to the south almost immediately, over Chilton Drove Crossing and over the combined waters of the South Drain and the Glastonbury Canal. At Stone End there was another manned crossing, and shortly afterwards the line turned west and began to climb the

BURNHAM LINE.

The speed of the Trains on this Line must be limited to fifteen miles an hour between Burnham and the Auxiliary Signal at Highbridge Wharf, and to four miles an hour between that Signal and the Bristol and Exeter Line.

All Trains must stop at the Water Tank on the Burnham side of the Bristol and Exeter Line.

CURVE AT GLASTONBURY.

No Train must run over this curve at a higher speed than *eight miles* an hour in *approaching* this Station, or at more than *eight miles* an hour in *leaving* the Station.

WELLS BRANCH JUNCTION.

All Trains approaching this Junction from Wells, or from West Pennard, are to *stop* fifty yards short of the Points.

No Train, under any circumstance, must pass the Junction from either end, unless accompanied by the *Pilotman* appointed for that purpose, and who is distinguished by a broad red badge on the right arm.

Local hazards on the Somerset Central—from the s & Rule Book, 1864

Polden ridge, which involved a stretch of about a mile at 1 in 72. Near the foot of this bank was the entrance to Board's Siding, on the up side: when this was worked from Edington, the wagons were pushed in front of the engine with a brakevan at the Bridgwater end, the train returning to Edington when shunting was completed. The siding led up a long cutting parallel with the branch and only a few yards to the south, as far as a large quarry, which is now being used as a rubbish tip and in process of being obliterated—like the deep cutting approaching Cossington, now completely filled in.

Cossington station, with its single platform on the up side, lay to the north of the village, a pleasant grey stone building with stationmaster's house attached, on the edge of a pretty little wooded valley. The station might still be open, for the Bridgewater Railway Act of 1882 stipulated that at Cossington 'the Company shall construct and *for ever after maintain* . . . a fit and suitable stone or brick building with convenient approaches and proper goods sidings'. Cossington apparently continued to receive preferential treatment to judge by a delightful note in the Somerset & Dorset working timetables to the effect that

> All engines working Passenger Trains not running Funnel first must stop at Cossington whether marked to do so or not.

There was a ground frame and siding here, and after a final stretch at 1 in 108 the short summit level was reached in a deep cutting, crossed by the A39 which follows the line of the Roman road along the Polden ridge.

Over the summit the line fell sharply for more than a mile at 1 in 72 to cross the King's Sedgemoor Drain just beyond Bawdrip. Near the foot of the bank was Bawdrip Halt, opened in 1923, a concrete SR structure, situated on the up side and conveniently close to the village. Approaching Bridgwater there was a bridge under the A39 (removed since the closure), another manned crossing at Horsey lane, and then quite a hump at 1 in 72 to lift the line over the GWR and the A38 before it swung south to run into the terminus past a siding serving Board's brick and tile works, and over Castle Fields Crossing where the signalbox controlled the entrance to the station and yard.

Bridgwater station was quite unlike anything on the Somerset & Dorset, and one has to remind oneself that the independent Bridgwater Railway never in fact and in law belonged to the Somerset & Dorset. The station building, now serving as a British

Road Services depot, smacks of the LSW. Its six-bay facade of red and yellow brick looks south towards the town, and gave access to an island platform, part of which was covered by an awning roof. In the yard there was a red-brick goods shed, a red-brick single-road engine shed (though in later years no engine was stabled there overnight) and a 49 ft 8 in turntable. The branch line from Edington was seven miles fifteen chains long, but a forty-eight-chain extension diverged just north of Bridgwater station to serve the cattle dock, and curved right round in a semi-circle to reach the east bank of the Parrett. Its course can still be traced by sundry concrete posts of LSW or Southern vintage in tell-tale stretches of abandoned fencing—through a timber yard, past the site of Barham's brickyard, to certain rotting timbers in the mud-banks of the river. These are all that survive to mark the site of the Somerset & Dorset wharf, where freight was unloaded from ships until the time of the first world war, under the supervision of the wharfmaster whose red-brick dwellinghouse still stands a little inshore. In 1942, during the second world war, the track which had been used for storing wagons, was lifted for salvage, and when the line from Edington was finally closed in 1954 the goods yard still remained in use, served by a new spur from the former GWR Docks branch.

EVERCREECH JUNCTION TO TEMPLECOMBE

Looking southwards down the line from the footbridge at Evercreech Junction, one was immediately aware of a very different terrain from that observed on the Bath Extension: a green, elm-shadowed landscape across which the Somerset & Dorset pursued a very pleasant course, with undulating gradients and altogether easier curvature, though between Cole and Wincanton it climbed gradually to cross the watershed which separates the basins of the Somerset Brue and the Dorset Stour.

It was not without significance that hereabouts one was entering upon Dorset Central territory. The cottages at Lamyat Crossing and Bruton Road Crossing were obviously Somerset Central structures, but immediately to the south of the overbridge at Wyke Champflower was the point of junction between the two parent systems of the Somerset & Dorset. On the up side a derelict embankment curves away to join the Wilts, Somerset & Weymouth line coming up the valley from Castle Cary; the abortive junction which caused such prolonged heart-burnings in the 1860s and 1870s is visible just to the west of the Dorset Central bridge over the GWR.

I write 'the Dorset Central' bridge advisedly, because from this point onwards the architecture of the railway was very noticeably different in style and texture: the bridges over several minor roads, as well as those over the GWR and the River Brue, were built of a much yellower stone with distinctive red-brick arches unlike the Somerset Central's bridges which had plain stone arches. At Wyke junction there seems to have been some alteration in the layout, as there are the remains of a second curve at a lower level than the later line, and what is obviously a crossing-keeper's house at a point where a minor road was later diverted under the railway.

'Cole for Bruton' read the station nameboard, and as early as 1876 an omnibus from the Blue Ball Hotel, Bruton, met trains at Cole, just as later one from Castle Cary plied to and from Evercreech Junction. In later years the majority of passengers at Cole were schoolgirls travelling to and from Sunny Hill School and boys from Sexey's School, Bruton. The station itself was built to a Dorset Central design which, with its high gables and tall chimneys and the hipped roof in the waiting room and booking office, was recognisable all the way to Bailey Gate, whether built of stone as at Wincanton or Templecombe Lower, or of red brick from Stalbridge southwards. The signalbox at Cole also had nothing in common with the signalboxes further north: it was a squat wooden structure of unmistakable LSW inspiration.

South of Cole there are signs of lineside quarrying which must have provided the stone for the works on this section. The line swept past the lonely little churches of Pitcombe and Shepton Montague, with a glimpse of Redlynch House in its splendid park on the down side, and through a gap in the hills to the little valley of the Cale which gives Wincanton its name. Wincanton races at one time involved a good deal of horsebox traffic, as well as excursion trains from Highbridge and Bournemouth, though by the time the new course was laid out to the north of the town, most of the traffic came by road.

To the last, Wincanton retained most of its lower quadrant signals with wooden arms: the station was one of the first to be lit by gas on the line, the fittings having been ordered by the Dorset Central before the amalgamation of 1862. Wincanton has remained a small and compact market town (the population was 2,000 in 1831 as against 2,500 today), and the station and yard have hardly changed over the years except for the addition of the Cow & Gate siding in 1933. Southwards again, a more or less straight and level stretch of three miles, offering a chance of some brisk running,

ACCIDENTS

(30) *The scene of the accident at Foxcote, 7 August 1876*

(31) *Derailment at Burnham, Easter Monday 1914*

'SISTERS UNDER THE SKIN'

(32) *Johnson 0—6—0 No. 60 as rebuilt by Deeley taking the Wimborne line at Corfe Mullen in 1912*

(33) *Johnson 0—6—0 No. 76 (LMS No. 3260) in the South Drain near Ashcott, 26 August 1949*

brought one to the outskirts of the complex layout at Templecombe.

At Horsington Crossing stood the first Templecombe signalbox—No. 3 Junction, which controlled the approach to the Lower Yard, along the original line to the Dorset Central's Templecombe station and the spur to the Salisbury and Yeovil line. No. 3 was formerly a very busy signalbox, dealing at one time with about 200 train or locomotive movements a day; it was abolished in 1933, the junction points, and the down outer home and distant and up advanced starting signals being thereafter power-controlled from No. 2 Junction, half a mile to the south. By this point the main line had climbed well above the original line, at 1 in 100 as far as No. 2 Junction, and a further climb on a sharp curve gave a fine panoramic view of the buildings in the Lower Yard.

Until 1933 the approach to Templecombe station was controlled by the tiny Somerset & Dorset B box containing thirteen levers and situated just off the end of the platform used by Somerset & Dorset trains, but when this box was closed, all movements were controlled by the Southern Railway box on the main platform.

Although in effect a joint station, Templecombe was in fact entirely LSW property under the control of the LSW stationmaster, the Somerset & Dorset stationmaster controlling only the Lower Yard and B box. Somerset & Dorset passenger trains used the outer northern face of the up main-line platform, and through freight from the north and transfer trips from the Lower Yard worked through the platform road to reach the Upper Yard. Very full accounts of the handling of traffic at Templecombe at different periods were published by the then stationmaster J. Thornton Burge in *The Railway and Travel Monthly* for November 1911, and by the Rev R. B. Fellows in *The Railway Magazine* for December 1932.

In Somerset & Dorset days the Lower Yard was the scene of very varied activity: all up freight traffic was dealt with here, as well as such down freight as did not work direct into Templecombe Upper; transfer trips were organised, light engine movements, and empty stock workings, began and ended here. The buildings were of considerable interest. The two-road red-brick engine shed built in 1950 replaced an earlier wood and asbestos structure of Somerset & Dorset vintage; beyond this there was a 50 ft turntable, and an amalgam of buildings of different ages and heights used by the motive power department.

The central feature, containing the shedmaster's office—and until 1930 comprising the stationmaster's residence and office—was the original Dorset Central station building which had been added to at some period, an upper storey giving an entirely different appearance, though at each end of the building the dimensions and architectural features were identical with the buildings at Cole and Wincanton. At one time there was also a gasworks in the Lower Yard, the site of the gasholder being still visible close to the original Dorset Central goods shed, where the spur curved away to the east to join the Salisbury & Yeovil line: when the junction was abandoned in 1870, stop-blocks were put in position to form a useful dead-end siding for coal wagons and such like. An occupation bridge under this siding immediately to the east of the stop-blocks shows its Dorset Central origin in plain contrast with the red-brick LSW bridge a few yards to the south.

Of the original layout of the Dorset Central station no evidence remains: south of the locomotive department buildings there are the remains of an old platform later used as a cattle dock. The station continued to be used for a time after the building of the spur from No. 3 Junction to Templecombe Upper in 1870, but not after 16 January 1887. At this date Templecombe No. 1 box was abolished; this stood immediately to the north of the bridge under the LSW line, and controlled the entry into the Dorset Central station from the Blandford direction, as distinct from the new main line which climbed at 1 in 100 to No. 2 Junction (see plan on page 42).

TEMPLECOMBE TO BOURNEMOUTH

The southern half of the Somerset & Dorset line can be said to have begun at Templecombe No. 2: here the tablet was picked up for the first single-line section to Stalbridge, and once past the old station buildings, one was travelling on the sixteen miles of track planned by the Dorset Central in 1857 but not opened until 1863, a year after its amalgamation with the Somerset Central. Between the two bridges which took the line under the minor road, which gave access to the Lower Yard, and under the LSW line, was Templecombe Lower Platform. This was built on the up side in 1887 when passenger trains ceased using the old station: only a few trains stopped at the platform, but engine crews sometimes changed here on through trains which did not call at Templecombe Upper, and the last up train from Bournemouth decanted its passengers here until 3 January 1966.

For six or seven miles the line now ran more or less straight and more or less level (by Somerset & Dorset standards) all the way to Sturminster Newton, through pleasant and gently undulating open countryside. Before Stalbridge there were no fewer than six manned crossings, where most of the red-brick crossing-keepers' houses still survive: Common Lane, Park Lane, Plott Lane, Marsh Lane, South Mead, and Drews Lane. Plott Lane was controlled from Henstridge station which was the smallest station on the line: it was not a block post, but there was a ground frame incorporated in the

Whereas it has been a common practice for Enginemen on starting their Engines to incautiously open the Regulator, and so cause the wheels to fly round or slip, and thereby put an unnecessary and exceedingly injurious strain upon the Cranked Axle, and otherwise injure the Engine, as it is totally unnecssary and unworkman-like that an Engine should be allowed to slip, and is generally the result of indifference and inattention to the careful and proper working of the Engine, it is therefore necessary that Enginemen should notice carefully the state of the weather, and the load they have got to take before starting, that they may so regulate the weight upon the Driving-wheels of the Engine, as will as far as possible prevent such slipping, and consequent injury and detention.

From the 1864 Rule Book

station buildings on the up side—'a wooden lodge and platform and a short siding' as the Dorset Central directors had specified in 1862.

In April 1965 the last electric repeater, the oval wooden disc displayed for the attention of the telegraph lineman, was still in position on the outside wall of the 'wooden lodge', and I was able to rescue it from predatory souvenir-hunters for preservation at the Clapham Transport Museum. These discs measuring about 18 in x 12 in were painted white with a black cross, and called the attention of the travelling linemen to the state of the electrical apparatus in the box. There were also rectangular boards measuring about 20 in x 15 in which were displayed outside signalboxes to call signal linemen in case of need. Both these practices seem to have been discontinued about 1930 when the SR took over the signalling, though the hooks from which the boards were hung remained visible on the signalboxes, and indeed one or two of the electric repeaters were to be seen in position almost up to the time of closure.

Between Henstridge and Stalbridge the line crossed into Dorset under the first red-brick bridge so far encountered. Stalbridge was the first crossing-place on the single-line stretch to Blandford: up trains had a straight through run, as at all the other crossing-places, and the station buildings and yard were on the up side. A good solid red-brick signalbox controlled the level crossing over a minor road, and the red-brick station building was of standard Dorset Central design. On this southern half of the line the stations were conveniently placed close to the villages they served, and to the end there was a fair amount of local passenger traffic moving up and down the valley.

Just before Sturminster Newton the line crossed the Stour, the first of four such crossings within the next nine miles. At Sturminster the station buildings were again on the up side, and the platforms were staggered, with a level crossing for passengers. There was an LSW type wooden signalbox and the original red-brick goods shed in the down side yard. A good deal of cattle traffic was handled here in connection with the weekly market, and there was also a siding serving the milk factory belonging to the Milk Marketing Board: milk traffic was worked from here down to Wimborne until 1933.

There was no such concentration of traffic at Shillingstone which remained a perfect example of a rural station on the edge of its village. The buildings had been somewhat grandified and a platform canopy was provided—a feature missing at all the other Dorset Central stations except Blandford—in honour of royalty, King Edward VII using the station for his visits to Iwerne Minster House. This was perhaps the reason for the beautiful station garden here, which earned many awards in the competitions for 'best kept station'.

From Shillingstone to Blandford was one of the outstandingly beautiful sections of the line. The Stour cut through the chalk downs, the narrow, steep-sided valley being guarded at its northern entrance by the precipitous escarpments of Hambledon Hill and Hod Hill, and railway, road and river wound through the hills together.

Stourpaine crossing loop and signalbox were sited just beyond one of the river bridges which allowed for the double track that was never built. The loop was introduced into the layout early in this century and the signalbox was manned for ten hours daily, but between the wars through running was the normal practice, the down loop being used only when the box was switched in at times when heavy holiday traffic demanded the breaking up of the five and a half-mile block section between Sturminster and Blandford.

Stourpaine & Durweston Halt was half a mile further on, with a single concrete platform on the down side. The Dorset Central had considered a site for a station here in 1860, but nothing was done till 1928, when the halt was opened—and closed in 1956. The last two miles into Blandford involved some spectacular sweeping curves while the line climbed along the eastern side of the valley at 1 in 80 before descending, again at 1 in 80, through some heavy cutting just north of the station: a splendid view was obtained of Bryanston park and the mansion, 'bosom'd high in tufted trees', with the Stour looping round below the wooded cliff. Half a mile north of Blandford is the site of Milldown Crossing: the crossing-keeper's house still stands, and here was the last disc and crossbar signal, which was removed on 8 August 1902 when the crossing was replaced by a bridge. A ground frame controlled the approach to the siding serving the prisoner-of-war camp during the first world war.

Blandford—or Blandford Forum to give it the courtesy title which it acquired in 1953—was easily the most impressive station belonging to the Somerset & Dorset, with a splendid station building on the up platform, a subway, and a lofty signalbox dominating the scene on the down side. The original layout before the section to Bailey Gate was doubled in 1901 is shown in an old photograph, with much shorter platforms and a smaller signalbox on the up side. The new signalbox, which was opened in 1893, was struck by lightning and gutted by fire in a thunderstorm on 23 June 1906, but the signalman, Charles Whiting, escaped without harm.

The station building was of standard Dorset Central design on a somewhat grander scale than usual, red brick with stone facings.

Another old photograph in the stationmaster's office showed the whole of the staff clustered round one of the old Fowler 0—6—0s, not forgetting the shunting horses whose stables were in the goods yard on the down side (see plate 9). Close to the station is the Railway Inn, on whose sign appears a gay and spirited portrait, by Norman Seal, of the Somerset & Dorset's own *Bluebottle*. The sign had previously adorned the Railway Hotel at Glastonbury, which was much more appropriate, as the engine depicted—the first blue engine to appear on the line—had been acquired by the company in 1863 for working on the branch between Glastonbury and Wells.

Immediately to the south of the junction with the camp railway the line crossed the Stour for the last time: difficulty or expense involved in the building of this bridge seems to have delayed the arrival of the Dorset Central in Blandford itself, for the original terminus of the line from Wimborne was a temporary building at Blandford St Mary a mile to the south, beside a lane that led to the downs: this was described as 'unpretentious, and unsuitable for anything but the brief use which all Blandford residents must fervently wish' (*Sherborne Journal*, 8 November 1860).

For the next six miles or so to Bailey Gate the line kept close to the main road (A350), weaving and undulating along the hillside above it, through chalk cuttings and under mellow brick bridges, until it gradually descended to the level of the river in the valley bottom. Charlton Marshall was the setting of many of Dr T. F. Budden's photographs which so superbly capture the atmosphere of the old Somerset & Dorset: the halt with its two simple platforms was opened in 1928, and closed in 1956 at the same time as Spetisbury, though Spetisbury had originally been a station, ruins of whose buildings were visible long after trains had ceased to call there. It was never a permanent block post; the signals at one time were worked only for trains which called at the station—one of the signals being almost the last of the disc and crossbar type and surviving until 16 April 1901 (see plate 53).

Bailey Gate, with its basic Dorset Central building and its squat LSW type signalbox, served the village of Sturminster Marshall: in Dorset Central days it had actually been called Sturminster Marshall but in 1863 it was renamed (after the nearby turnpike gate) presumably to avoid confusion with Sturminster Newton. The main traffic handled here was milk, sidings being laid in 1919 to serve Carters & Dorset Modern Dairies (later absorbed into United Dairies), the milk first travelling to London *via* Wimborne, and after 1932 *via* Templecombe.

Down expresses roared through Bailey Gate on a falling gradient with easy curvature, and in a minute or so swept past two more signalboxes, each controlling a level crossing—Bailey Gate Crossing and Corfe Mullen: between them on the down side was Admiralty Siding. Shortly after grouping, plans were produced in 1925 to abolish both these crossings: an overbridge on the Wimborne-Dorchester main road (A31) would have eliminated Bailey Gate Crossing signalbox, and the diversion of a minor road at Corfe Mullen would have eliminated the crossing there. The signalbox would have remained, controlling the junction of the old main line to Wimborne and the cut-off to Broadstone. It also marked the end of the double-track section from Blandford, where trains picked up the tablet for the last block section over Somerset & Dorset metals, whichever line they took at the junction.

Plans were also made in 1925 for closing the Corfe Mullen-Wimborne section and for doubling the line to Broadstone. Passenger trains had already stopped running to Wimborne on 11 July 1920, but milk traffic continued until 28 February 1932 and freight until 17 June 1933. Curiously enough the 1925 plan for the closure of the Wimborne branch envisaged the removal of the track at the Corfe Mullen end, leaving a two-mile branch from Wimborne Junction to serve the clay pits at Carter's Siding; but in 1933 exactly the opposite course was taken: a mile of track was left in position from Corfe Mullen to Carter's Siding (sometimes used in later days for storage purposes), and the rest was removed.

This had the advantage of eliminating Lake Crossing which had not been manned since the withdrawal of the passenger service, and where the gates had latterly been operated by the train crew, for which seven minutes were allowed in the working timetable. The Wimborne branch was the only piece of the Somerset & Dorset over which I never travelled, and it was a curious experience to explore the abandoned formation thirty years after the last train had passed and, as I fought my way through the jungle that filled the waterlogged cuttings, to think that this had once been part of the Channel-to-Channel route. Through coaches from the North had travelled this way to Bournemouth until 1886, hundreds of thousands of milk churns from Dorset dairies had been carried this way to London, and innumerable freight trains had rumbled past Lake Crossing to be broken up and remarshalled in Wimborne yard.

From Corfe Mullen to Wimborne was about three and a quarter miles, of which the last twenty-three chains were over LSW metals from Wimborne Junction. The line ran pleasantly along the southern edge of the Stour valley, with easy gradients until the last half mile, when it climbed at 1 in 100/191 to meet the LSW. The Dorset Central red-brick bridges survive, but nothing is visible above ground of the Somerset & Dorset layout at the junction, except for a row of cottages. This was formerly a railwaymen's hostel, built in 1902 with sleeping accommodation for twelve, and closed soon after the withdrawal of the passenger service in 1920.

As well as the LSW signalbox which controlled the junction, there was also until April 1928 a Somerset & Dorset (Wimborne Loop) box sited near the point where the line branched into double track; there was also a water-tower, an engine shed accommodating five engines, and a 44 ft 9 in turntable, the site of which is barely decipherable in a coal-merchant's yard. It is almost impossible today to visualise this overgrown piece of waste land as having been a focal point in the Somerset & Dorset system for seventy years. Down trains continued past the junction—the LSW box was closed in 1933—and over a couple of splendid bridges, which carried the Southampton & Dorchester line across one of the drives to Canford Manor and across the Stour, to reach Wimborne station, where reversal was necessary in the case of trains proceeding to Bournemouth. The 1933 Appendix contains regulations for the banking of Somerset & Dorset freight trains up the one and a quarter-mile bank at 1 in 100 towards Broadstone; it is uncertain how often this was necessary, and anyhow by 1933 the branch had been closed.

The direct line from Corfe Mullen to Broadstone kept close to the old main line for the first half mile, but climbing sharply, mostly at 1 in 80, past Corfe Mullen village where the inhabitants had petitioned for a station in 1884, and belatedly been rewarded with a halt on the up side of the line—opened in 1928 and closed in 1956. A short summit level was followed by a 1 in 97 descent to the junction with the Southampton & Dorchester line at Broadstone, where in later days (as at Wimborne Junction) a concrete post marked the boundary between the Joint line and the Central Division of the SR.

Broadstone Junction (sixty-three and three-quarter miles from Bath) began life as New Poole Junction. It became Poole Junction in 1875, Poole Junction & Broadstone in 1883, Broadstone & New Poole Junction in 1887, Broadstone Junction in 1889, and Broadstone in 1929. (See R. H. Clark, *A Southern Region Chronology and Record*, Oakwood Press, 1964.) It always seemed rather forlorn in later days, but it once handled not only the Somerset & Dorset traffic and local trains from Salisbury and Brockenhurst, but also the full service from Waterloo to Dorchester and Weymouth until the opening of the Holes Bay curve in 1893. Before 1874, Somerset & Dorset trains used the original (western) platforms on their way to the Hamworthy station at Poole, but from 1874 onwards the new (eastern) platforms for the direct line to Poole and Bournemouth.

The remaining eight miles to Bournemouth West do not call for any detailed description. They were foreign territory where the Somerset & Dorset was only a visitor—a welcome visitor, and assured of a friendly reception—but it was very different to Bath where the Somerset & Dorset dominated the scene, though one must remember that the Somerset & Dorset had a large finger in the Poole & Bournemouth pie, even if inevitably it was the LSW which worked the line from Broadstone—down Somerset & Dorset trains reaching Bournemouth over the up LSW line. This line dropped down from Broadstone, more sharply than the Dorchester line, for about one and a half miles at 1 in 75, past Creekmoor Halt (opened in 1933) down to sea level along the shore of Holes Bay.

At Holes Bay Junction the new curve from Hamworthy Junction to give direct access from Poole to the Dorchester line, thus obviating the need for reversal at Broadstone, comes in from the west. Then comes Poole with its marshalling yard, three signalboxes, two narrow sharply-curved platforms at which all trains must stop, and two level crossings over busy streets. Between the ornamental lake in Poole Corporation's park and the tidal waters of the harbour the line swings inland to the east to tackle Parkstone bank, a mile or more at 1 in 60 or worse, continuing the climb as far as Branksome, banking assistance being available for freight trains from Poole to Branksome.

At Branksome Junction the London line diverged from the line to Bournemouth West, and inside the Branksome triangle was the Somerset & Dorset two-road engine shed—a wooden-framed asbestos building, dating from 1896, with its own coaling stage. The engine shed was demolished in 1965 in connection with the electrification of the Waterloo-Bournemouth line which involved the closure of Bournemouth West station and the diversion of most Somerset & Dorset trains to Bournemouth Central. For the previous ninety-one years all trains from Bath had worked into Bournemouth West, most of them apart from 'The Pines' and other long-distance expresses being dealt with at the two bay platforms on the up side. Opposite the station in Queen's Road stands the Midland Hotel, whose name epitomises the function of the Somerset & Dorset as far as Bournemouth was concerned.

CHAPTER 7

Obstruction—Danger!

THE RADSTOCK DISASTER

By far the best known incident in the history of the Somerset & Dorset is the Radstock disaster of 7 August 1876. It was Bank Holiday, and at about 11.20 p.m. a return excursion from Bath and an up relief train from Wimborne met in head-on collision on the single-line section near Foxcote signalbox.

The accident is still an abiding memory in the district. An old faded photograph, which belonged to the grand-daughter of one of the victims, shows the scene a day or two after the crash: piles of debris and sections of shattered coaches—eleven of the damaged vehicles were Midland stock—have been cleared away from the single track; four helmeted policemen stand on guard; a telegraph post and a signal wire post are visible, and in the background there is a hazy sense of August heat in the peaceful valley. (See plate 30.)

The more one reads about the accident—the reports of the inquest and the Board of Trade inquiry in contemporary newspapers run to many columns of minuscule print, while Captain Tyler's published report is in itself a considerable document—the greater the sense of confusion and conflict of evidence. Over all there hangs an air of tragic incompetence, and the failure of the human element, which has been responsible for so many railway accidents.

The Somerset & Dorset was officially worked by block telegraph combined with a system of crossing orders which, if properly organised, would have appeared to offer a fair substitute for the train staff.

> But, whatever the system of working, or the apparatus employed (as Captain Tyler observed in his summing-up), safety must more or less depend upon strict adherence to simple rules, and on the employment of responsible agents, carefully selected and closely watched. . . The risk of working must be materially increased when, as in the present instance, the regulations do not apply to the mode or the appliances of working; when the rules as regards the mode of telegraphing trains, or the use of crossing-orders or telegraph-passes, are not faithfully

> carried out; when there are too many telegraph-instruments on one wire; when signal-lamps cannot be lighted for want of oil; when special trains are run without printed notices, or even proper telegraphic advices; when wrangling takes place, and important messages are improperly checked from headquarters on the telegraph-instruments; and when the duties supposed to be performed by responsible stationmasters are allowed, in practice, to devolve upon telegraph-clerks of immature age or experience, employed for long hours, and taken away constantly to duties incompatible with their proper attention to the simple details prescribed with a view to safety. Railway traffic worked under such conditions cannot, whatever the system employed, be expected to be carried on without serious accidents.

There was little room in fact for surprise at the occurrence of the Radstock catastrophe. In the words of a contemporary newspaper, 'it mattered little whether the Somerset & Dorset line was supposed to be governed by one system or another, for as a matter of fact it was in a state of positive disorganisation'.

There was considerable congestion on the line that day. Sixteen excursion trains were scheduled, and Superintendent Difford, finding one of the down trains was overloaded in the morning, arranged for a relief train to leave Wimborne at 7.10 p.m. to follow the regular 6.10 p.m. from Bournemouth. Caleb Percy, the crossing agent at Glastonbury, notified all stations accordingly, and undertook to arrange crossings, though the driver admitted that he crossed six trains on the journey up without receiving a single written crossing order.

The train reached Radstock soon after 11 p.m. and, after an unsuccessful attempt to contact Glastonbury in view of the uncertainty of the whereabouts of a down train which was now an hour and a half overdue, Stationmaster Jarrett ordered the train to proceed to Foxcote. Here a signalbox had been opened on 24 May 1875 to serve the Braysdown colliery siding and to break the long block section to Wellow, which in itself constituted a breach of an undertaking given to the Board of Trade, allowing only one engine in steam at a time in the section between Radstock and Wellow. It was not in communication with Glastonbury, so that the sixteen-year-old signalman, Alfred Dando, had no knowledge of train movements except on his block telegraph instruments. In the moonlight the unlit Foxcote up distant signal was 'partly down' and Driver Bishop brought his train to a stand at the home signal.

After about five minutes' wait, the preceding train cleared Wellow, and Dando proceeded to put the up train on the block to Wellow, and showed a green light to the driver. At the inquest and the inquiry Dando stated unequivocally that he had never been given any notice that a down train was already on line from Wellow. Bishop had just got his heavy train of fourteen vehicles on the move again, and was travelling at about 8 m.p.h., when he saw the other train bearing down on him and just had time to close his regulator before the collision occurred.

The down train was the return working of an excursion from Radstock to Bath Regatta, booked to leave Bath at 9.15 p.m. It was due to return from Radstock to Bath at 9.55 p.m., picking up 300 members of the Bath Young Men's Liberal Association at Midford where they had been attending a fête. Earlier in the evening an abortive attempt had been made to cancel the down special when it was realised that there would be plenty of room in the up relief to take the Midford passengers.

Because of shortage of rolling-stock, it did not leave Bath until 10.43, and at about 11.14 it left Wellow without apparently having been put on the block to Foxcote, although a few minutes later the up train was accepted on the block before the down train could possibly have reached Foxcote, let alone the crossing place at Radstock. John Hamlin, the driver, had not asked for a crossing order as he was ignorant of the existence of the up special. Running down the gradient of 1 in 198 on the curve towards Foxcote, he was confronted by the home signal at danger—the unlit distant had again been 'nearly down to caution'—and had reduced speed to about 12 m.p.h. when he saw the light of the other train twenty-five yd away. When the crash came he had already got his engine into backward gear.

The sound of the crash was heard as far as five miles away on the still August night, and the continuous whistling of the engines added to the horror of the scene. Curiously enough the two engines almost kept the rails, and only the down engine had its wheels off the track. The engines were Nos. 5 and 7, both Fox, Walker 0—6—0STs. Driver Bishop of the up train specifically referred to his *tender* engine, which is confirmed in Captain Tyler's report, though elsewhere in it, Superintendent Difford stated that the train was hauled by a powerful *tank* engine, which explained its arrival at Radstock sooner than was expected. The tender engine would have been the England 2—4—0, renumbered 27 later in August; the new No. 7, delivered the previous month, had begun work on 1 August. LSW records refer to 'a very old tender locomotive' being involved in the accident, but it was two saddle tanks that arrived at Derby for repairs on 12 August 1876 ('injured at Radstock') at a cost of £685 and £743 respectively. The rolling-stock was less sturdily built than the engines, and the first six carriages of the down train were completely smashed; in these all the casualties occurred.

Twelve passengers as well as the guard of the down train were killed, and 28 passengers and six railway servants injured. All the passengers killed, including an eight-week-old baby with its mother, came from Radstock or from neighbouring villages. The bodies of the victims were laid out for identification in the granary of Paglinch Farm, a few hundred yards up the line, where the first part of the inquest was held. 'The bereaved children by the railroad collision,' George Tucker of Radstock wrote in his diary on 22 August, 'presented with a Bible each, those losing both parents 5s in addition.' The Joint Committee paid out nearly £9,000 in compensation, and generously gave jobs on the line to several children whose parents had been killed in the accident.

Captain Tyler's report laid the responsibility for the accident on many shoulders. Only Alfred Dando, confused and frightened as he was when arrested immediately after the accident, was justified in acting as he did. Superintendent Difford was criticised for the general laxity of discipline and for the discrepancy between the regulations and the practice on the line: Percy at Glastonbury and Jarrett at Radstock were censured for their failure to act correctly with reference to the crossing orders; but the ultimate responsibility was pinned on to the Wellow stationmaster, James Sleep, and the telegraph clerk, Arthur Hillard. The evidence given by these two was conflicting and unreliable; there were considerable discrepancies as to the time of the signals given and of train movements at Wellow, and Captain Tyler could only reach the conclusion that Sleep and Hillard had omitted to exchange any signals with Foxcote on sending off the down train.

In this proceeding Hillard was Sleep's agent: he was 15 years old, working fourteen hours a day at 7s 6d a week, and on the day of the accident he had been on duty for fifteen and a quarter hours, issuing and collecting tickets and keeping the accounts, as well as attending to his telegraph duties. From 6.30 p.m. until 11.15 he had sole charge of Wellow station, for after thirteen hours on duty Sleep had gone off to Midford, returning to Wellow on the down train which he proceeded to despatch on its fatal journey: he thus principally and directly contributed to the accident. In March 1877 he was charged with manslaughter at Taunton Assizes and sentenced to twelve months' imprisonment, after a recommendation to mercy in view of his excellent character for honesty and sobriety.

'MOVING ACCIDENTS BY FLOOD AND FIELD'

'It is perfectly marvellous,' wrote a newspaper reporter, 'that any railway not in the backwoods of the United States should be worked in the fashion of this unfortunate single line.' That was in 1876, but the Somerset & Dorset was not slow to mend its ways. Despite the appalling side-to-side motion of some of the old four-wheel coaches between Binegar and Evercreech where E. L. Ahrons more than once thought his days were going to end, and despite the frightful shaking-up somewhere between Blandford and Shillingstone which was to scare the wits out of the Member for Dorset West, the Somerset & Dorset was to become a very safe, and in many ways an exemplary, line: to such an extent that when George Eyre retired as traffic superintendent in 1920 he was congratulated on the fact that throughout his eighteen years' charge of the line which included the whole of the first world war, no fatal accident had occurred on it. In Alfred Whitaker's words: 'If ever a railway had been cursed and oppressed it was the old Somerset & Dorset, and it must be a keen satisfaction to Mr Eyre and all who helped him, to realise how the railway had improved from the terrible state in which it was in 1876'.

The Somerset & Dorset actually had a remarkable safety record. Apart from the Radstock tragedy, no major accident involving passengers is to be recorded in the 111 years of the line's existence. One or two somewhat peculiar accidents occurred, as might be expected of a line that had become a legend in its own lifetime. Some of these are well known, but a number of others, referred to in minute books or in local press reports, are interesting for the light which they throw on the conditions under which the line was worked at the time.

The first accident referred to in the company's minutes occurred on 10 June 1862, a few months after the Somerset Central had taken over the working of its own line from the Bristol & Exeter. An empty stock train from Templecombe was derailed near West Pennard: nobody was hurt, but damage was done to the station platform, to the line and to the coaches, whose wheels were found to be 1⅝ in out of gauge.

Another accident due to neglectful maintenance occurred on 5 October 1874 soon after the opening of the Bath Extension, and was caused by a subsidence in the centre of the new embankment. Soon after leaving Evercreech Junction, the fireman of an up train 'suddenly found the locomotive and tender jumping up and down': the engine went over the bridge and rolled down the embankment, killing the driver. At the inquest the coroner's jury recommended that the regulation about the inspection of the line before the first morning train should be included in the printed rules. 'The Line, since its opening,' observed the *Bath Chronicle* (8 October 1874), 'has not been considered any too safe by more than one competent judge, and signs have not been wanting of the line not having properly set.'

There was another derailment, on 26 February 1877, near Wincanton, in which the driver was killed. The engine involved was a Midland 0—4—4T No. 1262, and as a result this class was not allowed to work south of Evercreech till the road was re-laid, the LSW supplying six engines to meet the emergency.

Even in the 1880s, ten years after the Joint Committee had taken charge, all was not well with the track in the eyes of the MP for Dorset West, while E. L. Ahrons described the state of the rolling-stock and of the older parts of the permanent way as *extremely dubious,* to put it mildly. Slipshod methods of working also persisted as evidenced by two accidents at Binegar.

The first occurred on 31 July 1885, ironically enough the very day that the double line from Chilcompton had been brought into use after being passed by the Board of Trade inspector. Certain alterations in the interlocking gear in the signalbox were required by Colonel Rich, and while these were being carried out, the signalman, William Appelbee, moved the wrong lever and diverted an up express into collision with a goods train standing on the down line.

Guard Beakes—the oldest guard on the line with thirty years' service—and one of the passengers were killed and seven injured. Appelbee was tried for manslaughter, but acquitted. Interlocking gear had been removed without a man being appointed to watch the facing points, but apparently Appelbee had not been adequately instructed as to the exact situation when he moved the wrong lever and thus brought about the accident. It was the company's officials rather than the signalman who were guilty of negligence. It also transpired that the train was not provided with proper continuous brake power which would have enabled it to come to a stop from a speed of 27 m.p.h. within the available distance of 160 yd (see C. E. Stretton: *Safe Railway Working,* London, 1887, pp. 145-150).

Only a few months later, on 3 February 1886, two goods trains collided on the single line just south of Binegar at 2.45 a.m., one of the firemen being killed. A down goods was given a clear road, and even picked up the banking staff, although an up goods was already on the block. The signalman, John Cox, had apparently forgotten this train, the entries in his register being extremely confused, and the driver of the down train (who had incidentally been involved as fireman in the Radstock accident of 1876) had no business to proceed beyond Binegar without a crossing order, after failing to cross the up train as scheduled on the double line section between Chilcompton and Binegar.

Cox was sentenced to six months' hard labour, though Colonel Rich's report on behalf of the Board of Trade criticised as unsafe the handling of trains on the single-line portion of the Somerset & Dorset by the crossing agent at Bath, and recommended the adoption of the train staff or tablet system. In the same year the Board of Trade also animadverted on the continued running of mixed trains. (Until 1875 it had not been possible to separate mileage of passenger and goods trains in the official returns as so many of the trains were mixed.)

A derailment which might have had disastrous consequences occurred on Easter Monday 1914, when a crowded excursion train hauled by 0—4—4T No. 52 running bunker first jumped the points at the entrance to the excursion platform at Burnham. The engine and leading coaches were derailed, but remained upright and nobody was seriously hurt. (See plate 31.)

No passengers were involved in either of the unusual accidents which took place between the wars. One was sheer comedy, and on the cinema screen it might be condemned as improbable fiction. It is hilariously described in L. T. C. Rolt's *Red for Danger*. On 29 July 1936 an up freight over-ran the signals at Writhlington, and the crew of the 2—8—0 jumped from the footplate to avoid the impact of the collision with the 0—6—0T No. 7620 which was standing at the head of a rake of eight wagons which were in the course of being shunted at Braysdown colliery siding. The driver of the tank engine, also foreseeing a collision, had reversed his engine and opened the regulator, but realising that the 2—8—0 was now only moving very slowly, he jumped from his own footplate, clambered on to the footplate of the 2—8—0 and brought her to a stand:

> Here indeed was cause for self-congratulation! What presence of mind and resource in emergency! How chagrined her craven crew who had so prematurely abandoned ship! But, alas, never had pride so speedy

PRIMITIVES

(34) *No. 10, a 2—4—0 built by George England in 1863 with Fireman Nutt on the tender (cf p. 141)*

(35) *Vulcan Foundry 2—4—0 built for the* S & D *in 1866 (identical with Nos. 15 and 16) but never delivered*

(36) *Vulcan 2—4—0 No. 15 as rebuilt at Highbridge*

GOODS ENGINES

(37) *Stirling type 0—6—0 No. 20 built by Fowler of Leeds in 1874, in original condition*

(38) *Fowler 0—6—0 as rebuilt in 1906 with Deeley boiler and extended Ivatt type cab*

(39) *Small Johnson 0—6—0 class introduced in 1878; No. 46 was built by Vulcan Foundry in 1884*

> a fall. For as our hero had leaped from one side of his footplate, his fireman, a nervous youth, misunderstanding his motive for so doing, had jumped off the other side, and neither had closed the regulator. Triumph instantly turned to dismay when the intrepid driver looked up just in time to see his own engine rapidly disappearing backwards in the direction of Bath propelling the eight wagons before it.

Almost miraculously, No. 7620 had a clear road all the way to Bath, and made splendid time as far as Midford. Here she succeeded in getting rid of most of her wagons, littering the line with debris and partially demolishing the signalbox, while 'signals and telegraph poles fell like ninepins'. With unabated vigour she forged on, propelling in front of her the remains of one wagon with which she somehow managed to negotiate two single-line tunnels until she was herself derailed, near the site of the old ticket platform, before any further disaster and damage could occur at Bath Junction.

It was almost at this spot that tragedy had struck on 20 November 1929, when an up freight, hauled by 2—8—0 No. 89, then an almost new engine and still in SDJ livery, emerged from Combe Down tunnel and proceeded to gather speed as she hurtled down the bank with her train of thirty-seven wagons and a brakevan to inevitable derailment and destruction at the entrance to Bath goods yard. Driver Jennings was killed, as was Inspector Norman who was in charge of the goods yard, and so was Jack Loader, a young LMS clerk from Gloucester, who was unluckily taking a short cut through the yard on his way home from work.

Both fireman and guard said that the tunnel was exceptionally hot and smoky. After a short time the fireman, Maurice Pearce of Midsomer Norton, had to wrap a coat round his head and sit down, after which he remembered nothing. The report on the accident could only suggest that the enginemen were both overcome by smoke and fumes as the engine—which was said to have been steaming badly—laboured through the foul murk of Combe Down tunnel.

The last accident in which a Somerset & Dorset engine was involved took place in very different surroundings, on the dead level track of the original Somerset Central line. Shortly to the west of Ashcott station, a 2 ft line from the Eclipse Peat Company's factory to their peat-beds crosses the Somerset & Dorset on the level. One foggy morning, 26 August 1949, a light petrol locomotive hauling two peat-trucks stalled on the crossing. After attempting to uncouple the trucks and move his locomotive, the driver ran down the line to warn an approaching train, but was not seen owing to the fog.

The train, the 8.5 a.m. from Glastonbury, was a mixed train consisting of one passenger coach and a number of goods wagons, hauled by a class 3F 0—6—0 No. 3260 (formerly SDJ No. 76). The engine was derailed—the train crew leaping for safety—and plunged into the mud of the ten ft wide South Drain beside the line. There it might have stayed, for it was impossible to position a heavy crane to lift the engine without elaborate pile-driving to provide a firm base over the peat bog. A sort of amphibian salvage operation was however achieved, the drain was diverted round the engine and in the course of eight days, between 25 September and 2 October, No. 3260 was cut up into pieces weighing not more than four tons, which were lifted by a makeshift crane on a platform of old sleepers and removed to the scrap heap.

WEATHER PROBLEMS

In winter and foul weather the Somerset & Dorset main line can hardly have been much fun to work. Oddly enough, the first batch of 0—4—4Ts provided by Johnson were not fitted with cabs to give the train crews protection against Mendip wind and rain as they crawled slowly up the exposed hillsides to 811 ft above sea level. There were hazards even on the branch, but they were occasional Acts of God: at Burnham, for instance, on 10 September 1903, a gale blew down the starting signal, and the station was flooded, putting out the fire on the engine of the 8 p.m. passenger train which was embedded in sand and not liberated for several hours, while the tide had also overflowed the sidings at Highbridge. Another old photograph, taken at Glastonbury in 1907, shows the station flooded and the tracks completely submerged between the platforms.

The snow-fiend was the deadliest enemy, especially in the deep cuttings at Masbury and Cannard's Grave. On 26 December 1886 the line was blocked by snow, the same day as the *Richard & Emily* foundered in a gale on the Burnham-Swansea run. That was mid-winter weather, but on 30 March 1878 all traffic was brought to a standstill for a day until the line was reopened by a snow plough forced through by several engines.

The two epic winters were 1891 and 1963. The snowstorm which began in the afternoon of Monday 9 March 1891 continued unabating until the early hours of Wednesday 11 March. No passenger or goods trains ran on the Tuesday except on the Wells branch and two trains from Bridgwater to Templecombe and back: even here only one set of carriages was available, the rest of the stock being snowed up at various points on the line.

On the Burnham branch the early morning workmen's train had to be dug out despite the efforts of three engines, but when a train eventually got through to Burnham it was stranded on the return journey to Highbridge, and when two more engines sent to assist also became fast, further attempts were abandoned until mid-day on Wednesday.

On the main line a local service operated between Bath and Binegar, but a through service was only resumed between Bath and Templecombe late on Wednesday evening. Even so a renewal of the storm on Thursday night stopped the 2.50 a.m. down mail between Blandford and Bailey Gate on Friday morning, and full normal working was not achieved until the Saturday.

The heaviest drifting was near Shepton Mallet. A down goods was buried to the top of the engine funnel for twenty hours at Cannard's Grave, while an up goods was also fast in another drift near Bath Road viaduct on the single-line section to Binegar. The latter was eventually released by a breakdown train from Bath, but got stuck again in fresh drifts which were cleared only with the help of gangs of contractors' men engaged at the time on the doubling of this section of the main line. North of Winsor Hill tunnel there was now a drift three-quarters of a mile long and from nine to fifteen ft deep. The line to Binegar was not cleared until 6 p.m. on Wednesday to allow the up goods which had left Evercreech Junction at 9.35 p.m. on Monday to complete its journey to Bath.

These operations were under the direct control of Superintendent Dykes who had left Bath with a snow plough at 1.30 a.m. on Tuesday, and had completed the last four miles of his journey on foot through the blizzard to reach the stranded train. At one time eight engines were assembled at Shepton Mallet to carry on the fight. Dykes had four of them coupled together complete with plough and set off for Wimborne on the Wednesday morning: they spent an hour and a half blasting their way through a 400 yd drift at Cannard's Grave, from four to eight ft deep, but were not seriously delayed again until a mile north of Sturminster Newton. Here they stuck three-quarters of the way through a drift a hundred yd long and six ft deep, out of which they had to dig themselves before they could reach Blandford late in the afternoon. Here they met Alfred Whitaker with two Highbridge engines which had somehow fought their way down to Wimborne on Tuesday, spent the night there, and then became trapped in a new drift in Green Lane cutting near Bailey Gate, between 500 and 600 yd long and ten ft deep, which they did not negotiate until 4 p.m. on Wednesday afternoon.

The bare facts of the narrative do scant justice to the physical hardship and danger involved, and to the extraordinary courage and devotion to duty shown by all grades of Somerset & Dorset railwaymen in their tenacious efforts to keep their line open and the trains running. These qualities emerged again during the arctic winter of 1962-3, among the train crews, the permanent way gangs, and men like District Inspector Mann and Stationmaster Down of Binegar, who were on duty alternately for twelve hours at a time, in charge of the prolonged struggle which lasted for eight days, before the line was at last reopened for through traffic.

The first blizzard broke on Saturday night, 29 December. As there were no Sunday trains, it was arranged that a snow plough should be sent out from Bath late on Sunday night to clear the way for the 2.40 a.m. mail on Monday morning. The plough failed to break through an enormous drift at Winsor Hill and had to be hauled back to Binegar. The next three days saw continuous efforts with the plough and with gangs of men to get the down line open, the up line being completely blocked as much of the snow which was being cleared from the down line had to be thrown on to it in the deep cuttings.

An optimistic start was made in the early hours of Thursday morning 3 January with the decision to run the 2.40 a.m. mail and the 3.30 a.m. and 5.0 a.m. freights from Bath, with single-line working between Midsomer Norton and Shepton Mallet. The plough, which had been used up to midnight to keep the line clear, was sent back to Bath for servicing and coupled to the mail, but meanwhile further snow had fallen with considerable drifting and, after clearing Shepton Mallet with some difficulty at 6.3 a.m., the mail and the plough were finally trapped in an enormous drift between Shepton and Evercreech New. Conditions were now deteriorating rapidly and the 3.30 a.m. which had taken on the pilotman at Midsomer Norton failed between Masbury and Winsor Hill, the train crew finding refuge in a neighbouring farmhouse, while the pilotman fought his way down to Shepton Mallet on foot to clear the section and report to Control. Meanwhile the engine of the 5.0 a.m. had been taken into the section in search of the 3.30 a.m., but this in turn had to be abandoned in the same drift where, all unknown, the 3.30 a.m. was buried only a short distance ahead.

The train crew somehow struggled back to Masbury summit where they found yet another engine, which had been sent to look for them with a brakevan and twenty men, stuck fast in yet another drift and digging themselves out. The mail was 'lost' for the best part of the day, but the two engines were eventually uncoupled and got down to the Junction late in the afternoon, the train being retrieved next day under the direction of Stationmaster Stowe.

The 3.30 a.m. was finally removed from the section on the following Sunday, 6 January, by means of a combined operation: a breakdown train from Bath pulled the rear part of the train back to Binegar, while from the opposite direction three engines and a snow plough arrived to take the front part on the Evercreech Junction—and the line was clear. It was another week before double-line working was fully restored between Bath and Evercreech, a fortnight after the line had first become blocked. They were days which no railwayman would wish to relive.

CHAPTER 8

The Train Services

OPERATIONAL PROBLEMS

The Somerset & Dorset was a difficult and expensive line to run at the best of times. Basically, the operational difficulties resulted from the hard facts of history and geography. The system had grown piecemeal over a period of twenty years and under the aegis of three different companies, in the course of the process exchanging an east-west axis for a north-south axis whose terminal stations could be reached only by running powers over the lines of three other companies. The cumbersome reversal at Wimborne was ultimately eliminated, but the infuriatingly uneconomical manoeuvrings at Templecombe continued practically unchanged for more than a century after the Somerset & Dorset directors had agreed that their junction with the Salisbury & Yeovil line was not 'a perfectly good junction, but the best which the circumstances would permit of'.

In 1905 there were proposals to abandon the old main line south of No. 2 Junction and to construct a new loop line, two and three-quarter miles long, beyond the LSW station to rejoin the old line at Henstridge, and to concentrate all shunting at the Upper Yard. But this was estimated to cost £100,000, and the leasing companies rejected the proposal. Basic poverty always dogged the Somerset & Dorset: apart from the North Somerset coalfield, the line served only a sparsely-populated countryside dotted with a handful of small market towns; much of the passenger traffic was seasonal, and the heaviest freight traffic had to be hauled over the cruel gradients of the Bath Extension.

It was these twenty-six miles from Bath to Evercreech that were the real headache from the operational point of view. The many viaducts, the tunnels and the heavy earthworks were expensive to maintain; the almost continuous curves as well as the long stretches of 1 in 50 gradient limited the speed; the fastest expresses were allowed fifty minutes, but through freight required 1h. 45m. for the twenty-six miles. The single-line bottleneck between Bath Junction and Midford also interfered with the smooth flow of traffic, especially in the holiday season when a down train late off Bath could halt a stream of up expresses, blocked back as far as Radstock; while south of Templecombe holidaymakers bound for Bournemouth would find themselves marooned in the loop at Stalbridge or Shillingstone on account of the 3.40 p.m. from Bournemouth, which carried the afternoon mails for the North to connect with the 7.20 p.m. postal from Bristol to Newcastle and must not be delayed. The Joint Committee must have had cold feet about the doubling of the last twenty-three miles of its main line. At the beginning of the century Superintendent Dykes obviously expected it to be done within a few years, but the chance was missed, and after the first world war it was too late.

All this weighed heavily on the locomotive department. We have seen how S. W. Johnson complained about the expense incurred by the continual assisting and light running involved in working the line, though this was inevitable so long as the Midland policy of small engines persisted at Derby.

Even in later years—in fact even after the arrival of the 9F 2—10—0s in 1960—double-heading was the norm on the vast majority of expresses. A daily turn from Templecombe shed throughout the year involved piloting 'The Pines' in both directions between Evercreech Junction and Bath—as often as not a duty performed by 2P 4—4—0 No. 40634, the last SDJ express engine to remain on the Joint line.

Very early on summer Saturday mornings one would wake to hear pilots returning light to Bath after assisting overnight expresses over Mendip; later in the morning the centre road at the Junction would be filled with pilots waiting to take their turns on the northbound flow of holiday expresses. Waiting at Masbury summit, one never knew what strange combination might appear pounding up the bank: a couple of class 7 2—8—0s, a Jinty bunker-first piloting an Armstrong (all class 4F 0—6—0s were known as Armstrongs on the Somerset & Dorset since the day when Nos. 57-61 arrived from Scotswood works in 1922), a 3F 0—6—0 of Johnson vintage brought up from the branch to assist a West Country Pacific, or perhaps a 'foreigner', a Saltley 'Crab' or a Black Stanier from Willesden or Stoke, impressed 'to help out over the Dorset'.

On weekdays there were always the bankers at work at the rear end of practically every freight train all round the clock. When I first knew the line, they were still the Fox, Walker saddle tanks, already fifty years old, working up to Combe Down tunnel and from Radstock to Masbury summit. There was less banking in the up direction from Evercreech Junction, as more of the traffic consisted of empty mineral wagons; what banking was needed was usually done by 0—6—0s which worked as far as Binegar, and when they had uncoupled, the exchange of crows between the banker and the train engine would sound far away across the lonely hills on a still night.

To add a personal note, on 21 August 1937 I spent the day at Masbury summit, one of many such golden excursions on pre-war summer Saturdays. My record shows that in four and a half hours I saw twenty-one trains; three of them were locals, and of the expresses no fewer than twelve were double-headed. The north-bound expresses were destined for Nottingham and Lincoln, Sheffield and Bradford, Liverpool and Manchester, Manchester ('The Pines'), Derby, Sheffield and Bradford, and Birmingham.

All the south-bound expresses were destined for Bournemouth, except for one to Sidmouth and Exmouth. All these called at Evercreech Junction to give connections to and from the branch. All the twenty-three different engines which I saw belonged to two types—class 2P 4—4—0s and class 4F 0—6—0s—and only four of them were ex-SDJ engines. This was the Derby small engine policy with a vengeance: a 2P and a 4F together were expected to get twelve-coach trains up to the summit in each direction. I saw no freight trains. They would reappear in the cool of the evening, working through until the early hours of Sunday.

The pattern of the train services which I recorded that day—including the significant absence of freight on a summer Saturday—reflects the historical development of the Somerset & Dorset line. Apart from the weekend peak of holiday season traffic to Bournemouth, there were the regular through workings from the North, though after the second world war 'The Pines' and two semi-fasts from Bristol to Bournemouth were a mere shadow of the daily through services in 1914 or even 1939. There was less change in the pattern of the local services: slow indeed these were (but not necessarily dirty), though it is hard to see how much improvement could have been effected, what with the single-line bottlenecks, the fearsome gradients, and as many as twenty-nine intermediate stops between Bath and Bournemouth, quite apart from the double reversal at Templecombe.

The timetable can never have been easy to construct: heavy freight trains took a long time to clear the more mountainous sections of the line, local trains had to keep out of the way of the expresses for which they were acting as feeder services; and if down trains left Bath at reasonable times, they still had to make connections in each direction at Templecombe and also find a path over the heavily-occupied Broadstone-Poole-Bournemouth section. The vagaries of the Somerset & Dorset services were often ridiculed, but could generally be attributed to circumstances entirely outside their control. An express from the North getting into Bath late could disrupt the local services for hours. Even branch-line trains were involved in the hazard of crossing the GWR main line on the level at Highbridge.

THE PASSENGER SERVICE 1854-1914

In 1854 the Somerset Central offered a service of six trains a day each way (two on Sundays) between Highbridge and Glastonbury: thirty-five minutes were usually allowed for the twelve-mile journey, but two trains were booked in twenty-five minutes and another in thirty minutes. No crossings were involved and, with an easy turn-round, the service could be maintained by the Bristol & Exeter with a single engine and set of coaches.

By 1861 the line had been extended to Burnham and Wells, but was still worked by the Bristol & Exeter. Between Highbridge and Wells there were now seven trains a day each way (two on Sundays). Only two of these in each direction stopped at Bason Bridge and Ashcott; others missed Edington Road. The 6 a.m. from Wells stopped only at Glastonbury, and ran the seventeen and a half miles to Highbridge in thirty-five minutes; other trains took from thirty-eight to sixty minutes, and as four crossings occurred at Glastonbury, at least two sets of stock was required.

The Burnham extension was apparently regarded as a separate branch by the Bristol & Exeter, which worked the trains in connection with its own main-line trains rather than as providing a through service over the Somerset Central. In 1858 there were nine daily departures from Burnham, but only six arrivals, with two or three Sunday trains; in 1861 there were eleven in each direction and one or two on Sundays, and this service was maintained by the Somerset & Dorset when it started its narrow-gauge service. Meanwhile the LSW had been maintaining a service over the Dorset Central from Wimborne to Blandford: five trains a day each way (two on Sundays) taking thirty to thirty-five minutes for the ten-mile journey with two intermediate stops, and terminating at the temporary station at Blandford St Mary, one mile south of the present Blandford station. This was a shuttle service which rather surprisingly started and finished at Blandford, the engine presumably working light to and from Wimborne for overnight stabling.

On 3 February 1862 the Somerset Central, having added the third rail to its broad-gauge track and completed its extension from Glastonbury to Cole to meet the Dorset Central line from Templecombe, began to work its own narrow-gauge trains between Burnham and Wells and also to Templecombe, pending amalgamation with the Dorset Central later in the year. In 1863 there were five daily trains each way (two on Sundays) between Templecombe and Highbridge or Burnham, the first out and the last in at Templecombe using the Lower station, as did the Sunday trains. The others proceeded *via* the Lower station to the Upper.

There were also five through trains from Wells to Highbridge or Burnham. The best time for the thirty-five miles from Burnham to Templecombe was 1h. 42m. (1h. 25m. from Highbridge): this involved a wait at Highbridge and reversal to reach Templecombe Upper, and most trains took about two hours over the journey with ten intermediate stops. There were also the two broad-gauge Bristol & Exeter trains referred to in an earlier chapter: the daily passenger train from Bristol to Wells *via* Highbridge and the daily goods train (see page 35).

There was some discussion about the withdrawal of both these trains in 1866, but they continued to run until October 1868. Bristol & Exeter working timetables show that the goods train originally worked down to Wells and back to Glastonbury, and then continued to Evercreech, but after February 1864 it ceased working over the Bruton extension. In 1864-5 it left Bristol at 10.30 p.m. and performed its trip over the Somerset & Dorset in the early hours of the morning, but later left Bristol at the more civilised hour of 3.30 a.m.

The opening of the missing link between Templecombe and Blandford on 31 August 1863 at last enabled the Somerset & Dorset to operate its Channel-to-Channel service. There were four through trains a day each way from Burnham to the Hamworthy station at Poole (two on Sundays). The best time from Poole to Highbridge was 3h. 15m., and from Burnham to Poole 3h. 50m.; most trains required four hours for the seventy-mile journey, reversing at Wimborne, but calling at Templecombe Lower from which the LSW maintained a shuttle service to the Upper station until 1867. After then, almost all through trains used the Upper station only, at first by means of the old Dorset Central spur, but after 1870 by means of the new spur between No. 1 and No. 2 junctions. In the summer of 1864 a fifth train was added, there was a non-stop run from Highbridge to Glastonbury in twenty minutes, and one of the Sunday trains reached Poole in 3h. 20m. from Burnham.

The ferry service from Burnham to Cardiff also figures in the timetable, with 'the fine fast-sailing Clyde-built steamers *Defiance* and *Heather Bell*' performing the crossing once and sometimes twice daily. There were a number of local trains as well between Burnham and Highbridge, three each way from Burnham to Wells, six each way on the Wells branch, and four from Templecombe or Blandford to Wimborne. By 1874, after the years in the wilderness, the service had deteriorated: Sunday trains had disappeared, and there were altogether fewer trains. The three through trains now ran to the new Poole station, and the best times were 2h. 50m. (down) and 3h. 15m. (up).

The opening of the Bath Extension on 15 July 1874 brought a complete change of emphasis. At first the working timetables continued to show Burnham-Bournemouth as the main line, and a separate table for Bath-Evercreech Junction with a summary of the principal stations to Bournemouth. This was quite illogical, as there were no through trains on the old main line, but by May 1876 the layout of the timetables had been recast, the branch timetable carrying the summary of the principal stations south of the Junction. In July 1874 there were five trains each way over the branch, some of them working to and from Templecombe while an up train from Bournemouth was divided at Templecombe, the second portion forming a train to Burnham.

On the new main line there were four through trains to Bournemouth (two of them carrying through coaches from Birmingham) and one extra between Bath and Templecombe. These took between three and four hours over the seventy-four miles, except for the 12.35 p.m. down and the 10.20 a.m. up, which took 2h. 50m. and 2h. 40m. respectively, both running the thirty-seven miles of single line between Bath and Templecombe in seventy-five minutes.

In the next ten years some significant progress was made: by 1884 there were six through trains daily over the main line with two extra between Bath and Templecombe. The 2.30 p.m. down reached Bournemouth in 2h. 34m. with eight stops (and reversal at Wimborne) while the 9.15 a.m. up ran the thirty miles from Blandford to Shepton Mallet non-stop in fifty-six minutes. Since 1876 through coaches had been introduced from Bradford, Leeds

Dstnc frm B.Mouth.	STATIONS	11 arr p.m.	11 dep p.m.	12 arr pm	12 dep pm	13 arr pm	13 dep p.m	14 arr p m Exp Go	14 dep p m ress ods.	15 arr pm	15 dep pm	16 arr p.m.	16 dep p.m	17 arr p.m.	17 dep p m	18 arr p m	18 dep p m	19 arr p.m	19 ar p.m
	Bournemouth ...			...	2 10			...	3 0	...	...			...	4 15	...	6 10	...	8 3
2 40	Parkstone			2	16	...	...		3 7	...	...	...	...	...	4 22	...	6 17	...	8 3
4 22	Poole			...	2 21	...	...	3 15	3 35	...	...	.	...	4 30	4 40	...	6 24	8 46	8 5
7 60	Poole Junction			...	2 30	...	...	..	3 45	...	...	...	...	...	4 50	...	6 34	...	9
10 10	Wimborne		12 50	2 35	2 37			3 51	4 5	...	...			4 56	5 20	6 40	6 45	9 10	9
		...	...	Aftr Dwn	No 5 arr.							..	...	Aftr Dwn	No10 arr	Aftr Dwn	No13 arr	Aftr	No Dw
15 20	Bailey Gate	1 5	1 16	...	2 48			4	21	...	...	...	...		5 35	..	6 57	...	9
		Cros Dwn	No 5	Cros Dwn	No 9											Cros Dwn	No12		
18 5	Spetisbury	1	26	...	Sig.			4	30	...	...				5 44	...	7 4	...	9
21 28	Blandford	1 36	1 50	3 0	3 3			4 40	4 45	...	...	...	...	5 52	6 20	7 11	7 13	9 46	10
		...	...					Cros dn	No10					AfNo 13	12 & Dwn			Aftr Dwn	No arr
26 63	Shillingston	2	8	...	3 15			5	3	...	...	...	...	6 37	6 45	...	7 24	10	20
29 60	Sturminster Newton ...	2 17	2 30	...	3 23	...	...	5	12	..	...	...	...	6 55	7 5	...	7 31	10	30
		Cros Dwn	No 9					Cros Dwn	No12			...	...						
33 58	Stalbridge........	2	42	...	3 32	...	...	5	24	...	...	...	...	7 15	7 22	...	7 40	10	42
35 20	Henstridge	2	56	...	Sig.	...	...	5	29	...	.	...	...	7 28	7 33	...	7 45	10	4
37 13	T Combe Lower	2 55	...	..	...	..	...	5 35	...	..	...			...	...	7 51	7 53	10 55	..
37 49	T Combe No 2 J	...	..	3 41	3 43	...	...	...	...	...	...				...	7 55	8 4	..	
37 2	T Combe Upper	...	2 52	3 45	4 0	...	...	...	..	...	...	...	...	7 40	...	8 .6	8 7	...	1:
— —	T Combe No 2 J	...	..	4 2	4 3	...	...			...	...		...		...			...	...
— —	T Combe Lower	After Dwn	no 8 arr	..	.	...	3 20		5 42	...			6 10	—	7 30	Aftr Dwn	No16	..	...
				Af 10	Dnar	Aftr Dwr.	No 8	Aftr & 13	No12 Dwn			Aftr Dwn	No13 arr	Aftr Dwn	No15			Aftr	No Dw
40 56	Wincanton ..		3 0	...	4 10	3 30	3 40	5	50		...	6 20	6 35	7 38	7 45		8 15	10	39
						Cs 10	Dwn					Cs 15	Dwn	Cs 16	Dwn	AfNo	14Dn		
44 61	Cole for Bruton...	...	3 10	..	4 20	3 55	4 5	6	2			6 50	6 .5	..	7 56	...	8 25	10	52
47 40	Evercreech Jn.	3 17		4 26	4 28	4 15	4 40	6	10	..	..	7 5	7 45	cs No 8 5	14Dn ...	8 32	8 34	11 0	11
				Af 11 pass	Dn & 13Up	No12 Pass No11	Upto Aftr Dwn	Aftr Dwn	no 15 arr		Empty Engine to Radstock	Aftr Dwn	No16 arr			Cros Dwn	No17		
49 1	Evercreech	Empty	Engine	...	4 33	4	46	6	15			7	50			Sig		11	7
52 9	Shepton Mallett			4 42	4 44	5 1	5 15	6 25	6 27			8 5	8 20	...	...	8 50	8 53	11 21	11 2
						Cros Dwn	No13	Cs 14	Dwn			Cros dwn	No17						
	Winsor Quarry			...	...			...	...								Sig		
55 23	Masbury Statn.	...	3 30	—	Sig.	5 27	5 30	...	...	...	6 15	...	...	...	...			11 40	11 4
	" Sumt.	...	...	...	...	5	35	6 39	6 41	...	...	8 32	8 34	..	...	...	9 5	11	50
56 67	Binegar	...	3 35	4 55	4 58	...	...	6	46		6 20	8	39	...	...	...			
				Af13 Pass	dn & 10Up											Aftr Dwn	No18 arr		
59 36	Chilcompton ...	...	3 42	...	5 6	5 42	5 45	6	53		6 27	8 46	8 50	...			9 12	11	59
						Cros Dn	No14	Aftr Dwn	no 16 arr			Cros Dwn	No18						
61 34	MidsomrNorton	...	3 48		5 13	5	55	7	1		6 33	8	58	...	...	...	9 19	12	7
63 21	Radstock	3 53	...	5 18	5 20	6 5	6 38	7 8	7 10	6 38	7 45	9 5	9 30	...	...	9 25	9 27	12 15	12 2
				After Dwn	No14	Cros No16	Dwn			Aftr & 17	No16 Dwn	No18 pass	Upto			Pass Up	No16		
	Foxcote Siding			...	...	...	...	...	...	...	.	...	...	...	...	..		...	...
67 11	Wellow			...	5 29	6	50	7	29	8 0	8 15	9	45	...	...	...	9 35	12	33
								Aftr Dwn	No17 arr	Aftr Dwn	No18 arr			...					
69 42	Midford			..	5 35	6	57	7	35	8	23	10	3				9 40	12	41
72 42	Bath Ticket Plat			5 43	5 45	...	...	7	43	...	...	10 14	10 15	...	...	9 48	9 50	12 55	12
	" Goods			...	...	7 10	—	7 48		8 35	8 36	10 20	...	...	...	...	...	1 5	..
73 72	" Mid Statn.			5 50	...	...	...			8 40	...	—	.	...	...	9 55	...		

A page from the working timetable, August 1876. The relief to the 6.10 p.m. ex-Bournemouth was involved in the Radstock accident on 7 August and Sheffield as well as from York and Newcastle.

Ten years later, in 1894, the timetables show the effect of several important developments: the main line was now doubled between Midford and Templecombe; the Corfe Mullen cut-off was used by five of the seven through trains, Wimborne being served by connecting trains from Broadstone or Bailey Gate; and the Johnson 4—4—0s had arrived, with the result that the 2.25 p.m. down reached Bournemouth in 2h. 20m. with eight stops, while the 9.40 a.m. up reached Bath in 2h. 10m. with seven stops.

The opening of the Bridgwater Railway in 1890 resulted in Bradshaw printing Evercreech Junction-Bridgwater as the main branch and relegating Edington Junction-Burnham to a separate table. Again this was not strictly accurate, as most of the branch-line trains ran to Burnham. It was clearly designed as propaganda for two fast trains which ran between Bridgwater and Templecombe in connection with LSW expresses to Waterloo to compete with the GWR service to Paddington *via* Bristol. One of these trains covered the thirty-five miles from Templecombe to Bridgwater in sixty-six minutes, cold-shouldering Evercreech Junction, and stopping only at Glastonbury and Edington Junction.

By 1904, further improvements had taken place on the main line: doubling had been completed between Blandford and Corfe Mullen Junction, the Whitaker tablet-exchanging apparatus had been installed, and three more powerful 4—4—0s (Nos. 69-71) had arrived on the line. The 'Bournemouth Express' required only 2h. 2m. from Bath with three stops, running the forty and a half miles from Evercreech Junction to Poole in sixty-three minutes, while the 9.45 a.m. up 'North Express', which carried through coaches for Bradford and York, took 2h. 3m. to Bath with six stops. This was bettered in the summer service, with two expresses each way in 1h. 50m. and a relief train running on Mondays and Thursdays which took only 1h. 47m.—an all-time record for the Joint line—running the sixty-seven miles from Poole to Bath non-stop in ninety-six minutes. This was a really remarkable performance at nearly 42 m.p.h. There were also through coaches to Bristol St Philip's, the Midland Railway's own terminus for local services, Temple Meads being a joint station which it shared with the Great Western.

1914 represents the peak of the Somerset & Dorset's achievement as far as frequency and variety of daily services was concerned *throughout the year* on the main line. There were seven through trains in the down direction (six of them expresses or semi-fasts) and ten up, with five extra stopping trains on each half of the line:

SOUTH WESTERN AND MIDLAND RAILWAY COMPANIES'

Somerset and Dorset Joint Line.

1st Nov., 1886.	LOCAL AND THRO' TIME TABLES OF	1st Nov., 1886.

IMPROVED TRAIN SERVICE

IN CONNECTION WITH THE

MIDLAND & SOUTH WESTERN RAILWAYS.

Direct and Unbroken Route Without Change of Station or Break of Gauge between

THE NORTHERN & MIDLAND COUNTIES,

Liverpool, Manchester, Bradford, Leeds,

SHEFFIELD, DERBY, BIRMINGHAM,

WORCESTER, GLOUCESTER, CHELTENHAM,

BRISTOL, CLIFTON, BATH,

AND

BOURNEMOUTH, WEYMOUTH,

SOUTHAMPTON, PORTSMOUTH,

ISLE OF WIGHT,

SALISBURY, YEOVIL, EXETER,

NORTH AND SOUTH DEVON,

Shepton Mallett, Wells, Glastonbury, Highbridge, Burnham,

TEMPLECOMBE

Blandford, Wimborne, Poole, Dorchester, &c.

POOLE AND BOURNEMOUTH:

PRINTED BY WM. MATE AND SONS, HIGH STREET AND COMMERCIAL ROAD.

Cover of the public timetable, November 1886

four of the down locals ran *via* Wimborne, but only one in the up direction, which ran to Blandford to connect with the Manchester express. This latter was the forerunner of 'The Pines' introduced on 1 October 1910 with a restaurant car from Birmingham: 1h. 54m. from Bath to Bournemouth, and 2h. 10m. in the opposite direction but with six stops.* The 8.37 a.m. up ('North and Scotch Corridor Express') took only 1h. 50m. and carried a restaurant car to Derby (extended to Nottingham in the summer service). On the branch there were five down and seven up trips daily, some of them extended to Templecombe, with one or two extra local trips and a shuttle service of eighteen trains each way between Highbridge and Burnham.† The Bridgwater line had lost its 'expresses' and was now purely a branch line with six trains each way daily; on the Wells branch there were ten trains each way, one of them working through to Highbridge.

THE PASSENGER SERVICE 1914-66

The full express service was still running in December 1914, four months after the outbreak of war, but the through services were gradually reduced and only the service to Leeds and Bradford continued to run throughout the war. By 1920 only one passenger train a day was using the Wimborne line, and this was withdrawn in July. By 1924, a year after grouping, the post-war recovery had been more or less completed: as far as frequency of service was concerned, there were two daily North expresses (one of them to Nottingham and Lincoln), and four additional expresses in the summer service running on Fridays and Saturdays only. Only one of these expresses, the down Manchester train (which now carried a Liverpool portion), did the journey in under two hours.

A curious revival was a through train in each direction between Burnham and Bournemouth, taking 3h. 13m. down and 2h. 47m. up, timings which were almost identical with the 1874 timings to Poole (Hamworthy) *via* Wimborne. Another curiosity was that the Bridgwater branch now appeared by itself in Bradshaw under the

* In the summer of 1910 the GWR and the LSW put on a through train from Birkenhead to Bournemouth *via* Oxford. and in reply the LNW and MR put on their train from Manchester *via* Bath. 'The Pines Express' acquired its name in 1927, so called from the pine trees so plentiful in Bournemouth.

† For some years between the wars the shuttle service was worked by push-and-pull trains without a guard, introduced in 1927 on the Burnham branch and in the following year on the Wells branch.

LSW section of the SR, which might be correct in law, but was certainly mystifying to the ordinary traveller who indubitably recognised it as part of the Somerset & Dorset.

The 1934 timetable included a much larger number of relief expresses running at weekends only during the summer. Several trains ran daily to and from Clifton Down or Bristol St Philip's, and in the summer there was a daily express from Bristol Temple Meads to Bournemouth, taking 2h. 46m. down and 2h. 57m. up, with a similar 'excursion' working on Sundays. There were still two daily North expresses, with eight additional expresses on Saturdays only, all taking between 2h. and 2s. 15m. Overnight expresses also appeared in the public timetables, two in each direction running on Friday nights, the southbound trains having no booked stop between Birmingham and Broadstone, and the northbound trains leaving Bournemouth at 10.45 p.m. for Bradford, and at 11 p.m. for Manchester and Liverpool, with a through coach to Colne. All this came to an abrupt end on the outbreak of war in September 1939. By October the service was reduced to four trains each way on the main line, stopping at all stations and taking four to four and a half hours over the journey, with three or four trains daily on each of the branches.

When peace came in 1945, there was a gradual restoration of most of the pre-war services. The branch service was pruned—in 1951-2 Burnham, Wells and Bridgwater lost their passenger trains—but local trains on the main line showed little change, many of them running on schedules that can be traced back well into the previous century. 'The Pines' was restored in 1949, and now carried a Sheffield portion which ran as a separate train at summer weekends. In 1954 the down 'Pines' required 2h. 34m. with four stops, and the up train 2h. 11m. with five stops—identical with the best 1884 timing, and forty minutes slower than the 1914 timing of the same train. The 11.40 a.m. from Bournemouth was now no longer a North express: at first it ran to Gloucester (and at weekends, sometimes only in the summer, to Derby), but later to Bristol Temple Meads, returning as the 4.25 p.m. from Bath. It was a lightly-loaded train, often hauled by a 2P 4—4—0, on a schedule equal to that of 'The Pines'.

Holiday traffic reached its zenith in the summer months of the early 1950s. In 1954 there were ten down and twelve up regular expresses on summer Saturdays, as well as the Friday night trains from the North whose arrival times at Bath appeared in the LMR timetables, but not in the S & D table. (There were also two or three

TANK ENGINES

(40) *Fox, Walker 0—6—0 saddle tank No. 9, built in 1876*

(41) *No. 27A as rebuilt from England 2—4—0 No. 7 of 1861 and used for shunting at Highbridge until 1925*

0—4—4 TANKS

(42) *No. 13 built by Avonside Engine Co. in 1877 to Johnson's design, but fitted with cab (cf Plate 7)*

(43) *No. 30 as rebuilt with Deeley boiler*

(44) *No. 53, one of the Vulcan Foundry batch built in 1884*

Bristol-Bournemouth trains on summer Sundays, one of which for a time carried a restaurant car.)

On certain Saturdays, such as those immediately preceding August Bank Holiday, six or seven additional relief trains were needed, corresponding with the holiday weeks of Midland and North Country towns. The heaviest pressure on the northbound line came in the morning and, providing everything ran normally, this fitted in well with the heaviest southbound period, which came in the afternoon. By 10.30 a.m. four or five engines would be lined up in the centre road at Evercreech Junction, ready to assist northbound trains over the Mendips. These would be mostly 4—4—0s; but not infrequently there would be a class 4F 0—6—0 amongst them.

The succession of northbound expresses was as follows, bearing in mind that the actual 'minutes' of their departure from Evercreech might vary from season to season:

10.47 a.m. Bournemouth-Liverpool
11.04 a.m. 'The Pines Express' to Manchester
11.16 a.m. Leeds and Bradford express
11.50 a.m. Bournemouth-Cleethorpes
12.02 p.m. Bournemouth-Derby

The grouping of the regular trains, northbound in the mornings and southbound in the afternoon, eliminated most of the difficulties that could have arisen with the opposing traffic on the very steeply-graded single-line section between Bath Junction and Midford. But things could be very congested in the afternoon, when northbound relief trains were running. These were usually scheduled to leave Bournemouth in the early afternoon and some very tight scheduling was needed to fit them in among the succession of regular south-bound Saturday trains. On the Saturday before August Bank Holiday 1951, four additional northbound trains were scheduled, and the booked times at Midford for these and the regular trains were:

2.22 p.m. down from Cleethorpes
2.25 p.m. up to Birmingham*
2.40 p.m. down from Sheffield
2.41 p.m. up to Coventry*
3.00 p.m. down from Bradford
3.01 p.m. up to Walsall*
3.08 p.m. up to Rose Grove*
3.17 p.m. down stopping train
3.50 p.m. down 'Pines Express'

* relief trains

It will be seen that the line was being used to capacity, with two of the specials entering the single-line section one minute after the down trains had cleared in the reverse direction. Knowing what punctuality on British Railways could be like on a summer Saturday, it must be confessed that such scheduling was highly optimistic, and on the particular day in question the London Midland Region brought all four of the regular down expresses into Bath very late. This reacted heavily on the running of the northbound relief trains. The four down expresses passed Midford sixty-eight, twenty-seven, fifty-five and sixty-one minutes late respectively, while the lateness in the northbound relief group mounted to a maximum of fifty minutes by the time the special to Rose Grove had passed.

Such intense working was confined to about four or five Saturdays in each summer and, from the year 1955, with the rapidly-increasing amount of private motoring, the holiday peaks on the Somerset & Dorset line were tending to grow less. After the with-

Enginemen are required not to open the Cylinder Cocks or blow their Whistles whilst passing about the Stations on the Line, or at Highbridge, more than is necessary, as horses standing or at work there become so alarmed as to be dangerous.

From the 1864 Rule Book

drawal of all through trains on 10 September 1962, the local service was left unchanged, though the *raison d'être* of many of the trains had ceased to exist. The two semi-fasts (9.50 a.m. and 4.20 p.m. down, 11.46 a.m. and 3.40 p.m. up) worked to and from Bristol Temple Meads, as did one or two other trains. There were seven local trains each way over the northern half of the line, and six over the southern. (The first up train oddly enough started from Broadstone; the last [SO] terminated at Templecombe Lower Platform. There was also a return trip at 6.5 p.m. [SX] from Bath to Binegar.)

On the branch, there were five or six trains each way, two down trains working through to Templecombe. To the bitter end Highbridge drivers loyally assured me that the best service to London was 'over the Dorset', and before the rationalisation of the Bristol-

Paddington services there was a grain of truth in this, as it was possible to reach Waterloo in little more than four hours with only one change, which compared very favourably with many of the GWR timings *via* Bristol, the mileage being almost identical in each case.

This survey of the Somerset & Dorset timetables only underlines the sad deterioration of the through services on cross-country lines since 1914. Even in 1929 the working timetables show that the expresses from Bournemouth were carefully marshalled to provide through coaches to a much wider variety of destinations *daily throughout the year* than was the case later on. The 11.35 a.m., for instance, consisted of only four coaches, but these worked to York, Bradford and Lincoln. A number of unusual workings appear in the timetables over the years: Bradford to Plymouth (*via* Templecombe) in 1889-91; Bournemouth to Harrogate in 1904; Bournemouth to Worcester in 1907; Manchester to Swanage in 1922; and Nottingham to Sidmouth, Budleigh Salterton and Exmouth in 1929 (revived for a short time after the 1939-45 war, when it actually achieved a coast-to-coast run from Cleethorpes).

Prolonged research would doubtless uncover other short-lived experiments. The working timetables provide many interesting details of the workings of the SDJ carriages—local trips to Bristol and Gloucester, and further afield to Birmingham and beyond. A note in *The Railway Magazine* for April 1924 records the daily working of SDJ stock into Bradford at that time.

It is necessary to scotch the persistent legend that the absence of Sunday trains over the Somerset & Dorset was due to the sabbatarian principles of certain of the founding fathers. This is not true. From the outset Sunday trains ran on the Somerset Central and on the Dorset Central, and also from Burnham to Poole after the amalgamation. In October 1862 it was decided to discontinue Sunday trains during the winter, and during 1863 and 1864 the trains ran only during the summer, but by 1874 these had been withdrawn altogether and there was no Sunday service over the Bath Extension. Regular requests for a service were refused by the Joint Committee on purely economic grounds: there was unlikely to be any worthwhile through or local traffic. In the decade before the 1914-18 war, passengers were accommodated on the Sunday afternoon milk trains from Blandford to Templecombe and Bournemouth, but such Sunday trains as appeared in the summer timetables in later years were really no more than trains catering for excursion traffic and running to regular schedules.

Both before and after the 1914-18 war there was considerable local milk traffic from many stations, the trains for London being marshalled at Templecombe or Wimborne. The 1929 working timetable includes empty churn trains with numerous stops at wayside stations, but the concentration of milk on depots and factories and the introduction of rail tanks about 1930 altered the picture. After the closure of the line to Wimborne, trains ran from Bailey Gate and Bason Bridge to Templecombe on Sundays as well as on weekdays until the Western Region diverted the Bason Bridge traffic *via* Highbridge.

There was also considerable pigeon traffic during the summer months: Templecombe was a favourite release-point for fanciers from the Midlands and the North, from Derby, Birmingham and Worcester Pigeon Federations in particular, and a good deal of rolling-stock accumulated in the Lower Yard. The heaviest train I ever saw being worked over the Somerset & Dorset was a pigeon empty stock train from Templecombe to Worcester on 11 May 1963: this consisted of twenty-two vehicles weighing 582 tons and was hauled over Masbury summit by class 5 4—6—0 No. 73052, piloting class 4F 0—6—0 No. 44558 (ex-SDJ No. 58—game to the last) and banked at the rear by a Collett 0—6—0 No. 2219.

THE FREIGHT TRAFFIC

As with the majority of English railways which served as common carriers, freight traffic was the backbone of the Somerset & Dorset economy in the decades before the first world war. In 1913, for instance, when the total net income of the Joint Committee was £65,170, the gross receipts from freight were £149,303 compared with £105,998 from passenger traffic. The breakdown of these figures as published in the railway returns for that year gives the following details:

Tonnage and numbers of goods and livestock

	Total	Originating on system
General merchandise	411,803	103,327
Coal and coke	484,800	326,162
Other minerals	268,675	240,228
Livestock	141,883	96,544

By far the larger proportion of this was carried over the northern half of the line.

The run of working timetables (1875-1905) preserved among the British Transport Historical Records enable one to follow the growth of this traffic. In 1875 there were five daily goods trains over the old main line, of which three ran from Burnham to Templecombe and two to Wimborne. Already there were six daily trains on the Bath Extension, with a mineral train from Radstock, and from 1877 a stone train from Binegar or Winsor Hill. There was a hiatus of three to four hours in the middle of the night, but by 1878 the line was open all night between Bath and Templecombe.

In 1884 there were four trains a day on the branch, and twelve from Bath to Templecombe, and three from Templecombe to Wimborne, one of them a mixed train. In May 1888 the 2.30 a.m. express goods from Bath to Templecombe became the 2.50 a.m. express mail and goods to Bournemouth, which continued to run until 7 September 1964 (latterly as the 2.40 a.m.) and always as a mixed train. What with taking water at Chilcompton, crossing an up goods at Binegar, halting at Masbury summit, examination at Templecombe No. 2, and eight stops including the depositing of mail bags at Templecombe Lower Platform, it is little wonder that it required 5h. 5m. for the journey; in 1929 it still required 5h. 12m. How often have I woken in the early hours of the morning to listen to its long struggle up the Mendip gradients on greasy or frosty rails, calling for infinite patience and skill on the part of the Bath drivers.

By 1894 there were seventeen trains a day each way over the northern half of the line, the down trains comprising nine through goods to Templecombe, three to Evercreech Junction, four local goods and the Bournemouth mail. Night traffic was becoming intenser; five up trains left Templecombe between 12.10 a.m. and 3.45 a.m. In 1904 this had increased to ten between 10 p.m. and 4.45 a.m., while there were twenty-one down trains daily from Bath, and five coal and mineral trains from Radstock, Binegar or Winsor Hill.

In 1929 there was little change, except for even more coal and stone traffic, with corresponding trains of returning empties, and light engine movements to work the sidings—duties often performed by returning bankers. The night shift at Binegar involved passing thirteen through goods trains and dealing with the bankers off them in both directions. I once asked Percy Savage, the Midford signalman, if he was lonely on the night turns. 'There was never time to be lonely,' he said; 'you always had something on the block.'

There was plenty of night-life in the yards at Evercreech, but negligible activity south of Templecombe. The branch was always closed at night, and here the pattern had hardly changed: in 1929 there were five down trains from Highbridge and one from Bridgwater, of which three ran to Templecombe, but only three up trains, two of which started from Templecombe; there were also a few local trips and two daily trains each way on the Bridgwater and Wells branches, the latter involving transfer trips to the GWR East Somerset or Tucker Street goods yards.

EXCURSIONS

It is virtually impossible to give a comprehensive picture of excursion traffic over a period of a hundred years. Excursion traffic is occasional and ephemeral by nature. It is a pure accident that posters have survived for some of the excursions which ran on Black August Monday 1876; that I found a copy of the excursion supplement to the working timetables for the summer of 1898; or that I retained copies of the handbills for some of the last excursions over the main line to Bournemouth.

From the first days of the Somerset Central there were excursions to the seaside at Burnham, with cross-Channel trips to Cardiff, while Welshmen were offered cheap fares to visit Glastonbury and Wells. In 1882, for example, there were excursions on *The Lady Mary* or *Wye* from Cardiff to Glastonbury and Wells for 3s (see page 65), and on 27 July 1885 trains from Templecombe and Shepton Mallet were run to connect with *Sherbro* which sailed to Cardiff at 7.30 a.m.: 3s 6d return (4s 6d for saloon or bridge).

The attractions of Burnham must always have faded a little in comparison with the flesh-pots of the south coast. (In May 1868 the Somerset & Dorset offered a weekly excursion from Poole to Burnham for 1s 6d return. The editor of *The Poole Pilot* was sceptical about the attractions of Burnham but said, 'If a long ride for a little money is desired, it is here available.') In 1864 the directors had discussed the arrangements for the summer excursion and tourist traffic, including tourist tickets from Bristol to Poole and Wareham (for Bournemouth and Swanage respectively), and on August Monday 1876, as we have seen, sixteen extra trains were run over the line.

The 1898 supplement includes overnight workings from Birmingham to Bournemouth, leaving Bath at 3 a.m. on Monday mornings; also Cook's excursions from Birmingham to Bournemouth and the West of England *via* Templecombe, leaving Bath at 4.10 a.m. From 1901 these specials were included in the ordinary Working Time Book, to run when required. The SDJ public timetables for the early years of this century were thirty-six-page books, measuring 8½ in x 5½ in, and full of fascinating details; they show a wide range of excursion bookings and facilities: 11s return to London from stations between Bath and Wincanton; 18s to Guernsey or Jersey *via* Southampton (a period return up to fifteen days); bookings to Weston-super-Mare and Clevedon *via* Highbridge and to Swanage and Weymouth *via* Broadstone.

There were day returns to Burnham from Wells and Glastonbury

SATURDAY AFTERNOON EXCURSIONS

TO THE

Mendip Hills,

CHILCOMPTON (for DOWNSIDE ABBEY),
MASBURY (for WELLS CATHEDRAL,) &c.

EVERY SATURDAY during JULY, AUGUST & SEPTEMBER,
A Cheap Excursion Train will leave BATH (Mid. station) at **1.30** p.m. for

STATIONS.	RETURN FARE. Third Class.	STATIONS.	RETURN FARE. Third Class.
RADSTOCK ... Midsomer Norton and Welton ... Chilcompton ...	1s. 3d.	SHEPTON MALLET Evercreech New ... Evercreech Junction ...	1s. 9d.
Binegar ... Masbury ...	1s. 6d.		

The SCENERY OF THE MENDIPS is remarkably Picturesque. WELLS. with its MAGNIFICENT CATHEDRAL, is Three miles only from Masbury Station, and the Road between the two points commands extensive and varied Views of the surrounding country.
THESE TICKETS will be available for return by any ORDINARY TRAIN on date of issue only.

A suggestion from the summer timetable, 1902

for 1s 3d, and by 'Fast Excursion Train' to Bournemouth for 3s 6d from Bath, as well as half-day rambles on Mendip with a horse-brake from Wells to meet the excursionists at Masbury. Cheap fares are quoted to Lyme Regis, Seaton and Sidmouth, and circular trips from Bath to Wells, returning *via* Bristol and the GWR, or to Glastonbury returning *via* Highbridge and Weston-super-Mare with breaks of journey, e.g. at Cheddar, for 3s or 3s 6d.

Between the wars there were excursions to Clifton Down including admission to the zoo, to Bridgwater Fair, from Burnham and Wells to Bournemouth, and from Bath to Weymouth, among countless others. From 1945 both the Sunday and Bank Holiday excursions concentrated exclusively on Bournemouth including through workings over the branch from Weston-super-Mare as late as 1962. For the Whit Monday excursions in 1965 Bath enthusiasts had polished up two class 5 4—6—0s, and Nos. 73051 and 73054 had their final fling resplendent in their green livery; only a few days later I saw 73054 condemned and derelict at the back of the Bath engine shed. The last excursion of all left Bath at 8.45 a.m. on Bank Holiday, 30 August 1965, and returned from Bournemouth Central at 7.45 p.m. hauled by another class 5 No. 73001.

EPILOGUE

One of the most valuable services provided by the nineteenth century railway system of this country was the cheap excursion to the seaside. This was a facility offered for more than a century, first by the Somerset Central, and later by the Somerset & Dorset. George Tucker (1822-1910) was a colliery blacksmith at Radstock. His diary for the 1870s has survived, and gives a glimpse of the use which local bodies made of the recently-opened railways: in July 1875 the Reform Bible class went to Bournemouth, while the Wesleyans went to Weymouth over the GWR *via* Yeovil as did the enginemen, bailiffs and mechanics from Writhlington pits, while 1,700 union miners went to Bournemouth on another excursion.

A short holiday of Tucker's with his wife is of even greater significance. 'August 13, 1877. Left home by the S and D line for London via Templecombe at 7.50 arriving at the Waterloo S 1.40.' The Tuckers went on to relations near Rye, with a day trip to Hastings thrown in. 'August 18, 1877. Took our seats in a train for Templecombe at 11.50 joining the Somerset & Dorset train 4.45, arriving home at 6 quite safe (thanks to a kind providence) but tired.' The holiday cost £5 0s 2½d, and it is this sort of detailed evidence that shows how wide were the horizons which the railway, when eventually it penetrated into North Somerset, opened up for ordinary country people.

By its nature the Somerset & Dorset was never likely to be a money-spinner. While a description of the line written sixty years ago referred to its history as 'almost as exciting as romance', and Kenneth Hudson has spoken of the 'miracle' of its survival for 111 years, the sad truth remains that its ultimate closure was inevitable under any scheme of rationalisation of the British railway system in which economic viability was to be the ultimate criterion. In this light it could only be seen as an unprofitable duplicate route to the South and West.

The original schemes of the parent companies belonged to the lean years of the 1850s and to the succeeding outburst of activity which collapsed in 1866, and as Michael Robbins has written in *The Railway Age*, lines built since 1870 are mostly suspect as economic propositions, and probably always should have been. But the economists must not be allowed the final word. One recalls John Bright's splendid assertion that railways have rendered more services, and received less gratitude, than any other institution in the land; and I should like to think that the vast majority of those who knew the line whether they are railwaymen, or travellers, or merely amateurs in the true sense of the word, will remember the Somerset & Dorset with gratitude and with affection.

CHAPTER 9

Locomotives

(by O. S. NOCK)

THE FOUR PERIODS

The locomotive history of the Somerset & Dorset can be divided into four quite clearly defined periods:
1 Early days, before the Joint ownership, up to 1875.
2 The Johnson era, extending from 1875 to the early 1900s.
3 The Fowler era, corresponding to Sir Henry's tenure of office as chief mechanical engineer of the Midland Railway and of the LMS.
4 The last phases, when the blue engine livery disappeared, and various standard types arrived from other lines, ranging from Stanier 'Black Fives' to the BR 9F 2—10—0s.

Periods 1 and 2 are rendered very complicated to follow in every detail because many of the engines that were introduced in those periods were rebuilt—and renumbered—several times and assumed some of the outward characteristics of the later periods. There was also a brief intermission, between Periods 2 and 3, when evidence of the Deeley regime at Derby became apparent on the Somerset & Dorset. There was indeed one small class of 4—4—0 introduced at the very end of the Johnson era that proved a prototype for some extensive rebuilding of 4—4—0 locomotives on the Midland Railway itself. In the space at our disposal in this book it is not possible to trace out the history of every locomotive, many of which went through individual stages of rebuilding different from all others in the stock. But readers may be referred to the very complete chronology of Somerset & Dorset locomotives down to the introduction of the Stanier 'Black Fives' that appeared in *The Locomotive* between January 1938 and April 1941, compiled by P. C. Dewhurst.

THE PRIMITIVES

The 'primitives', if one may call them so belonging to Period 1, can be considered to fall into six groups, as follows:
(i) The 2—4—0 tender engines built by G. England & Co.: Nos. 1

to 7 in 1861, 9 and 10 in 1863, and 12 to 15 in 1864.
(ii) The Vulcan Foundry 2—4—0 tender engines Nos. 19 and 20 (later renumbered 15 and 16—see plates 35 and 36), of 1866.
(iii) The England outside-framed 2—4—0 tender engines Nos. 17 and 18, of 1865.
(iv) The 0—6—0 tender engines Nos. 19 to 24, built by Fowler & Co. of Leeds, and delivered in 1874.
(v) The 0—6—0 saddle tank engines built by Fox, Walker & Co. of Bristol, in 1874, and taking S & D numbers 1 to 5.
(vi) A group of curious though picturesque locomotives: No. 8, an England 2—4—0 saddle tank built in 1861 for the Burnham branch, which survived as No. 28A till 1928; No. 11, another England 2—4—0 tank, bought in 1863 for the Wells branch and generally known as *Bluebottle*, which was sold to the Admiralty in 1870 for use at Sheerness Dockyard; and yet another England 2—4—0 tender engine acquired from George Reed in 1865 (see page 48).

It will be appreciated that down to the year 1874 when the line over the Mendips from Evercreech Junction to Bath was completed, the Somerset & Dorset was relying almost entirely on 2—4—0 tender engines. To avoid quoting innumerable figures, the relevant dimensions are set out in a series of tables in this chapter, from which it will be seen that the England 2—4—0s of the 1861, 1863 and 1864 batches were of slightly varying dimensions, but tiny things withal. There should have been six of the Vulcan 2—4—0s of 1866. These were of the same general type as the Englands, but considerably larger, with 17 in x 22 in cylinders. Because of financial difficulties the S & D could take delivery of only two of these engines, and Vulcan disposed of the other four to the Alsace-Lorraine Railways. As one of the accompanying illustrations shows, one of these latter engines was photographed at the builder's works, inscribed 'S & DR' and 'No. 23'.

The third group of 2—4—0s, which came from G. England & Company, arrived on the S & D through difficulties of a different kind. They were of Cudworth design, built in large quanties for the South Eastern Railway, and embodying all his specialities, including his special coal-burning firebox. These two engines were rejected by the South Eastern because of late delivery, and having been left on their makers' hands they were sold to the Somerset & Dorset and duly arrived in all their characteristic South Eastern finery.

These 2—4—0s of the 1861-6 period are interesting as much for themselves as for the manner in which some of them were rebuilt. Of the 1861 engines four, Nos. 1, 3, 4 and 5, were 'traded in' to Fox,

Walker & Company in part payment for the new saddle tanks of 1874, and two of the old 2—4—0s, Nos. 1 and 5, went to the Bishops Castle Railway. But it was Nos. 6 and 7 of that first batch that underwent such transformations. As Nos. 26 and 27, later 26A and 27A, both were rebuilt as side tank engines, and 27A in her final form, with a Johnson boiler and contemporary Midland boiler mountings, became one of the prettiest little shunting engines one could imagine. As such, shunting at Highbridge Wharf, she survived until 1925. The later England engines, Nos. 9-10 and 12-15, were sold out of S & D Joint stock in 1878: Nos. 9, 10 and 14 to the Midland, and Nos. 12, 13 and 15 to the LSW, although by then they had all been renumbered.

The subsequent history of the two larger Vulcan 2—4—0s, and of the Cudworth outside-framed 2—4—0s, Nos. 17 and 18, provides an interesting sidelight on the engineering carried out at Highbridge Works during the time that B. S. Fisher was locomotive superintendent. He had come to Highbridge from the Taff Vale Railway in 1874, and very quickly took advantage of the association with the Midland Railway from the time of Joint ownership in 1875. The rebuilding of the Vulcan and Cudworth 2—4—0s produced a quartet of very dainty little engines.

The Vulcans were given straight running plates and typical Johnson boiler mountings, though the smallness of the coupled wheels, 5 ft 0 in, precluded any Highbridge adaptation of the flowing curves of the Johnson splashers developed to such an artistic extent at Derby. That was to come later on the S & D. Only the chimney remained slightly alien to Midland traditions. The Cudworths, although less extensively rebuilt from the mechanical point of view, underwent a positive metamorphosis externally, and looked like a couple of Kirtley 6 ft 2—4—0s, as rebuilt by Johnson, and now preserved in the form of the beautiful 158A. Closer examination of the S & D engines, eventually Nos. 17A and 45, reveals the considerable differences, particularly in the very large leading wheels, of 4 ft 6 in diameter. The two Vulcan rebuilds lasted until 1913-4, but the Cudworths both went to the scrapheap in 1897.

The six 0—6—0 goods engines (Nos. 19-24) built by Fowler in 1874, and having 17½ in x 24 in cylinders, and 4 ft 6 in coupled wheels, were introduced to work trains over the very heavy gradients of the new line between Evercreech Junction and Bath. They had a strong likeness to some 0—6—0 goods engines Fowler had built for the Great Northern Railway in 1867-8. Indeed, the first two of the S & D engines had domeless boilers into the bargain, which with the cut-away cab made them look even more like a Stirling product. They were excellent engines, and underwent two successive rebuildings. The first, with Johnson-type boilers, in 1892-3, left the Stirling cabs unchanged; but in the second rebuilding, with Deeley boilers, the cabs were also modified, but still retained a very strong Doncaster flavour, changing their style from that of Stirling to that of H. A. Ivatt. These engines were not withdrawn until 1928, and thus had a life of 55 years.

We come next to the Fox, Walker saddle tanks of 1874 (Nos. 1-5), to which a further batch were added in 1876 (Nos. 6-9). These had a nominal tractive effort roughly equal to the Fowler goods of 1874, having 17½ in x 24 in cylinders, and coupled wheels 4 ft 0 in diameter. These nine locomotives were subjected perhaps to more stages of rebuilding than any others of the early classes of the S & D.

Their similarity to the Fowler goods naturally made them most useful in heavy grade working, and when additional main-line engine power was needed, it was only natural to consider converting some of them to tender engines. No. 1 was so treated in 1888, and remained thus for 20 years, after which she was reconverted to a saddle tank, and remained thus for a further twenty-seven years! No. 8 was more drastically rebuilt as a side tank engine, with 4 ft 6 in diameter coupled wheels, in 1889, and in 1908 she was again rebuilt, with Deeley boiler, and converted into a tender engine; as such she remained in service until 1928.

It will thus be appreciated that the majority of the old engines which survived into the period of Joint ownership of the line became thoroughly Midlandised, either to Johnson or Deeley precepts. The handsome blue livery dates from 1886, after a brief period in Midland red, following the adoption of that colour at Derby in 1883. Before that, a dark green had been used from the outset until 1875. Then with the advent of Joint ownership the standard Midland light green was used until 1883.

THE JOHNSON ERA

It is now necessary to consider the Johnson engines built specially for the line, which were of three classes: 0—4—4 passenger tanks, 0—6—0 goods, and 4—4—0 main-line passenger. The 0—4—4 tank engines came first, in 1877: there were nine of them (Nos. 10-14 and 29-32), designed at Derby, and built by the Avonside Engine Company of Bristol. They followed closely in the style of Johnson's own 0—4—4 tanks which he had introduced on the Midland Railway in 1875; but why, in the year of grace 1877, the Somerset & Dorset variety was built with no greater protection for the enginemen than plain weather boards, front and back, is indeed a mystery. Johnson's first introduction of the type had been in 1873, when he was on the Great Eastern, and these engines had nothing more than weather boards. The Midland 0—4—4 tanks of 1875 had cabs.

The Somerset & Dorset examples were designed not for local traffic but for the main-line trains between Bath and Wimborne, and the use of a front-coupled engine for such duties caused considerable comment among those engineers who felt that some form of leading wheels, bogie or otherwise, was necessary in front of the driving wheels of a passenger engine engaged in express running.

Johnson's own 0—4—4 tanks on the Midland were regularly used on express trains between Leeds and Bradford with complete success, and Stroudley's famous advocacy of front-coupled drivers and the practical exposition of his ideas in the ever-famous 'Gladstone' class on the Brighton Railway came a few years after Johnson's introduction of 0—4—4 tank engines for fast passenger working. The nine Avonside engines of 1877 were reinforced by four more of similar design but with cabs, from the Vulcan Foundry in 1884 (Nos. 52-55).

The accompanying illustrations show some of these thirteen engines in various stages of rebuilding, one of the most unusual being that depicted by engine No. 53, one of the Vulcans, as rebuilt with a two-ring boiler barrel and the dome carried on the forward ring. In later years some of these engines were again rebuilt with Fowler boilers having Belpaire fireboxes. They were taken off the main-line trains in 1891 when Johnson's 4—4—0 passenger engines were introduced and were then transferred to local working particularly on the Highbridge and Burnham line. The original Somerset & Dorset 0—4—4 tanks had mostly been scrapped by the 1930s, but the usefulness of the type was emphasised by replacement of these engines by similar ones from the Midland line, and some of these latter, including some with Johnson boilers, were still at work at Highbridge in the 1950s.

The Johnson 0—6—0 goods engines were of two classes: one specially designed for the Joint line, with 17 in x 24 in cylinders and 4 ft 6 in coupled wheels, and the second, a class of ten engines identical, except for minor details, with Johnson's standard main-line goods engines on the Midland Railway. These latter had 18 in x 26 in cylinders, and 5 ft 2½ in diameter coupled wheels. The smaller class were delivered to the S & D in two groups, the first from Neilson & Company in 1878 (Nos. 33-38), and the remainder from the Vulcan Foundry in 1879 to 1890 (Nos. 39-44, 25-28, 46-51 and 56-61). There were 28 of them in all.

The larger engines had the distinction of being the only fully-standard Midland engines of Johnson design supplied to the Joint line. The first five, Nos. 62-66, were built at Derby and delivered in 1896, but the remaining five were part of an order for 60 engines of the class placed with Neilson by the Midland Railway. The last five were allocated to the S & D; but by some oversight, although they were correctly lettered S.D.J.R. and numbered 72 to 76, they were painted Midland red, and arrived at Highbridge thus. These beautiful engines, powerful and effective to an extent far beyond their slender and elegant appearance, were the very last of a line of 891 Johnson 0—6—0s supplied to the Midland, the M & GN Joint, and to the Somerset & Dorset. They, and the smaller S & D 0—6—0s of 1878, went through the usual processes of rebuilding. Some are illustrated elsewhere in this book.

We now come to the interesting family of 4—4—0 locomotives, which until 1914 were designed specially for the line, and rebuilt subsequently to suit its particular requirements. The handsome Johnson 4—4—0s, of which the first four were built at Derby in 1891, can be described as small-wheeled variants of the standard Midland express engines of the day, with 5 ft 9 in coupled wheels. They were a relatively small variant, with cylinders 18 in x 24 in diameter, a total evaporative heating surface of 1,202 sq ft and a grate area of only 16 sq ft. Four more were supplied in 1896-7, and the running number of the eight engines of this class were 14 to 18, 45, 67 and 68.

The stages of rebuilding applied successively to these engines transformed their appearance, and the second reboilering in 1907-11 gave them a distinctive appearance quite unlike any other British locomotive of the day. In 1926-7 two of them were rebuilt, a third time, with Fowler boilers and Belpaire fireboxes, and from having a character all their own they acquired a pseudo-Midland look. Four of these engines, including the two Belpaires, came into LMS stock in 1930; but they had all been scrapped by 1932.

In 1903 a new design of express passenger locomotive was introduced which proved a prototype for the Midland Railway itself. Earlier that year, in keeping with his policy of building engines with much larger boilers than previously, Johnson had put the '2736' class of 0—6—0 goods engines to work. This had a boiler of the same diameter as that of the new 'Belpaire' 4—4—0 express engines, but a round-topped firebox. The new goods engines had a new style of chimney, tapering outward from the base.

It was announced at the time that *all* the hundreds of Johnson standard 0—6—0 engines would eventually receive the new boilers, and it was doubtless in this spirit of standardisation that the three new SDJ 4—4—0s were built in the autumn of 1903. They had the same boiler as the Midland '2736' class 0—6—0 goods, 6 ft 0 in diameter coupled wheels, and 18 in x 26 in cylinders. They were numbered 69, 70 and 71, and had a neat and compact appearance, as well as being a notable addition to the Somerset & Dorset stock.

It is sometimes thought that these engines originated as part of the Midland policy of rebuilding the older Johnson 4—4—0s with larger boilers. This is not so. The S & D engines Nos. 69, 70 and 71 *anticipated* the first rebuilding of Midland 6 ft 6 in 4—4—0s. It was not until the late spring of 1904, more than six months after the completion of the S & D engines, that the first Midland 6 ft 6 in 4—4—0, No. 85, was rebuilt at Derby, to conform exactly in appearance to the S & D prototype except in the matter of wheel diameter. By way of historical documentation, No. 71 of the Somerset & Dorset was first illustrated in *The Locomotive* in March 1904, while the first illustration of one of the rebuilt 6 ft 6 in 4—4—0s of the Midland itself, in this latter case engine No. 14, did not appear until August 1906!

It is important to appreciate that the Somerset & Dorset engines, although having lineaments more usually associated with Deeley, were entirely of Johnson design. Despite their good design they had a very short life, like many of their counterparts on the Midland itself. Nos. 70 and 71 were scrapped in 1914, and No. 69 in 1919, to be replaced by 7 ft superheater 4—4—0s of the Fowler '483' class standardised on the Midland Railway.

DEELEY AND FOWLER

In 1907, under Deeley's supervision, two more 4—4—0s were supplied, of similar general style to the Johnson engines of 1903, but having the Derby characteristics of the day, including the Deeley arrangement of tubes in the boiler. Although these engines had the same power characteristics as Nos. 69-71, they had a much longer life, and were rebuilt in 1921-6 with new boilers with Belpaire fireboxes. The two engines were originally SDJ Nos. 77 and 78, and as LMS Nos. 320 and 321 they survived until 1931 and 1938 respectively. In 1914 the large-boilered Johnson 4—4—0s 70 and 71

THE 4—4—0S

(45) *Johnson 4—4—0 No. 18 as originally built at Derby in 1891*

(46) *No. 68 of the same class as rebuilt with large Deeley boiler introduced in 1907*

(47) *No. 70, one of the large-boilered Johnson class built at Derby in 1903*

THE LAST S & D DESIGNS

(48) *Large-boilered Deeley 4—4—0 No. 77 as built at Derby in 1907*

(49) *No. 80, the first of the famous Fowler 2—8—0 class, as built at Derby in 1914, with tender cab*

were replaced by two standard Midland 7 ft superheater 4—4—0s, taking the same numbers. These engines, with their 20½ x 26 in cylinders, were by far the most powerful yet placed on Somerset & Dorset metals; but in passing one may pause to reflect upon the wisdom of using coupled wheels of no less than 7 ft 0 in diameter over such a severely-graded route.

These engines were followed by three more, Nos. 67, 68 and 69, in 1920-21. When first introduced, the load limit for these engines was fixed at 212 tons—an extraordinary figure over the Mendip gradients, seeing that 180 tons was the limit for the same engines over the Derby-Manchester, and Settle and Carlisle, lines of the Midland Railway. This load was subsequently reduced to 190 tons, but increased again to 200 tons when the new standard LMS 6 ft 9 in 2P 4—4—0s were drafted to the Somerset & Dorset line. After the taking over of the locomotive stock by the LMS in 1930 the five 7 ft engines were transferred to the Midland line.

Up to the year 1914 three locomotive classes had been designed at Derby specially for the Somerset & Dorset line. All were adaptations of standard Midland practice, exemplified in the 17 in Johnson 0—6—0s, the small-wheeled 4—4—0s, and the three large-boilered 4—4—0s of 1903. But in 1914 there appeared an entirely new design, quite unlike anything on the Midland Railway. This was the Fowler heavy freight 2—8—0. In producing this large engine for a subsidiary line Derby drawing office and works broke fresh ground in a number of ways:

(i) its first two-cylinder engine with the cylinders outside;
(ii) first use of Walschaert's valve gear;
(iii) the highest tractive effort, yet, of any Derby engine.

With 21 in x 28 in cylinders, and coupled wheels 4 ft 7½ in diameter the nominal tractive effort at 85 per cent boiler pressure was high, amounting to 35,932 lb. The total adhesion weight on the four axles was only 56 tons, and with a factor of adhesion of only 3.5 it might have been expected that the engines would be prone to much slipping. On the contrary they proved very sure-footed, and when the line was desperately short of engines at summer weekends in the early 1950s these old 2—8—0s were pressed into passenger service. They were far more reliable on the banks than the capricious Bulleid Pacifics, and were rostered to haul ten corridor bogie coaches unassisted over Masbury summit, as against eight by the Southern 4—6—2s. They were extremely successful engines, and the six built in 1914, Nos. 80-85, had a life of almost fifty years. They were originally fitted with tender-cabs, and although these were removed about 1920, they continued to work tender first on up trains until adequate turntables were installed at Evercreech Junction and Bath in 1934.

In 1922 the freight locomotive stud of the line was augmented by five standard Fowler 0—6—0 goods engines, built new by Armstrong Whitworth & Company and numbered 57-61; but the most notable addition was that of five more 2—8—0s, with larger boilers than those of the Derby engines of 1914. The new engines were built by Robert Stephenson & Company in 1925 and were numbered 86-90. These were the same in every respect as the original 2—8—0s except in the boiler which had a combined heating surface of 1,845 sq ft, against 1,681 sq ft, and the adhesion weight was 59½ tons. Like the original engines they proved very successful and virtually lasted out the life of the railway itself.

In 1929 came the last additions to the SDJ locomotive stock: seven 0—6—0 tanks built by W. G. Bagnall Limited of Stafford, of standard LMS class 3F design, Nos. 19-25, two of which were actually the last S & D engines to survive as BR Nos. 47313 and 47314, and two 0—4—0 Sentinel shunting engines (Nos. 101 and 102) which replaced the three diminutive saddle tanks used on the Radstock colliery branches, one of which is illustrated in plate 25.

Before closing this necessarily brief account of the Somerset & Dorset locomotives, mention must be made of the power classification which, although based on Midland practice, did not necessarily have the same class numbers as the corresponding engines on the Midland itself. The superheater 4—4—0 passenger engines, both 6 ft 9 in and 7 ft, were class 3; the Fowler Midland type 0—6—0s were class 4 both for passenger and goods; while the 2—8—0s were class 5. When the stock was taken over by the LMS the 4—4—0s reverted to class 2P, but the 2—8—0s became class 7F.

The total locomotive stock of the line taken over by the LMS was eighty, of which only thirty-three could be classed as in any way modern. These latter were:

7 standard LMS 0—6—0 shunting tanks
5 class 2 7 ft 4—4—0s
3 class 2 6 ft 9 in 4—4—0s
5 class 4 0—6—0 standard LMS goods
11 SDJ 2—8—0s
2 Sentinel 0—4—0 shunters

Most of the older engines were withdrawn soon after 1930, except for the Johnson class 3 0—6—0s, the last of which, SDJ No. 72 built in 1902, survived until 1962 as BR No. 43216.

THE LAST DECADES

The period from 1930 to 1966 was notable only for the introduction of an extraordinary variety of standard types from other lines which were allocated for working the S & D. LMS types included Stanier 'Black Fives' and class 8F 2—8—0s, while Ivatt was represented by his class 4 2—6—0s and class 2 2—6—2 tanks. Bulleid 'West Country' Pacifics arrived in 1951, and from 1954 onwards there was a stream of BR standard types ranging from class 3 2—6—2 tanks through class 4 and class 5 4—6—0s to the 9F 2—10—0s which made their debut in 1960.

Under the Western Region, Collett 0—6—0s and ex-GWR pannier tanks worked on the northern half of the main line and on the branch, while late in 1963 the last new type to appear were the BR class 4 2—6—4 tanks which were working most of the main-line passenger trains at the time of the closure. For more details of the workings during the last decades readers may be referred to the article by D. W. Winkworth in *The Railway Magazine* for February 1966 on SDJ motive power since 1930, which also recounts the demise of the various classes of Somerset & Dorset locomotives.

SOMERSET & DORSET: THE PRIMITIVES

:e	Maker	Type	Cylinders		Coupled wheel dia.	Total h.s.	Grate area	Boiler pressure
			dia. in	stroke in	ft in	sq ft	sq ft	p.s.i.
1	G. England & Co.	2—4—0	15	18	5 0	?	?	Probly. 115
3	,,	2—4—0	16	18	5 0	849	14	115
6	Vulcan Foundry	2—4—0	17	22	5 0	1117	17	120
	as rebuilt	2—4—0†	17	22	5 0	1109	14.5	140
5	G. England & Co.	2—4—0*	16	24	6 0	984	21	130
	as rebuilt	2—4—0†	16½	24	6 0	1101	14.5	140
4	Fowler & Co.	0—6—0	17½	24	4 6	1084	15.8	140
4	Fox, Walker & Co.	0—6—0T§	17½	24	4 0	1142.5	14.1	150
	rebuilt 1888	0—6—0‡	17	24	4 0	1147	14.5	140

† Johnson style
* Cudworth SER design
§ Saddle tank
‡ Tender engine

SOMERSET & DORSET LOCOMOTIVES: THE JOHNSON CLASSES

Date	Maker	Type	Cylinders		Coupled wheel dia.		Total h.s. sq ft	Grate area sq ft	Bo pre p.
			dia. in	stroke in	ft	in			
1877	Avonside Engine Co. and Vulcan Foundry	0—4—4T	17	24	5	3	1201	14.6	1
1878	Neilson & Co. and Vulcan Foundry	0—6—0	17	24	4	6	1123.5	14.75	1
1891	M.R. Derby	4—4—0	18	24	5	9	1202	16	1
—	Rebuilt with Deeley boiler	4—4—0	18	24	5	9	1370	21.1	1
1896	M.R. Derby and Neilson & Co.	0—6—0	18	26	5	2½	1261	17.5	1
1903	M.R. Derby	4—4—0	18	26	6	0	1428	21.1	1

SOMERSET & DORSET LOCOMOTIVES: THE DEELEY & FOWLER CLAS

Date	Maker	Type	Cylinders		Coupled wheel dia.		Total h.s. sq ft	Grate area sq ft	Bo pre p
			dia. in	stroke in	ft	in			
1907	M.R. Derby	4—4—0	18	26	6	0	1347	21.1	[illegible]
1914	M.R. Derby	2—8—0	21	28	4	7½	1681*	28.4	[illegible]
1914	M.R. Derby	4—4—0	20½	26	7	0	1510*	21.1	[illegible]
1922†	Armstrong Whitworth & Co.	0—6—0	20	26	5	3	1420.5*	21.1	[illegible]
1925	Robt. Stephenson & Co.	2—8—0	21	28	4	7½	1845*	28.4	[illegible]
1928†	LMS Derby	4—4—0	19	26	6	9	1420.5*	21.1	[illegible]
1929†	W. G. Bagnall Ltd	0—6—0T	18	26	4	7	1074.5	16	[illegible]

† LMS standard designs
* including superheater

CHAPTER 10

Train Working and Locomotive Performance

(by O. S. NOCK)

EARLY DAYS

In its early days, before Joint ownership, the Somerset & Dorset seems to have been operated in the most casual and irresponsible way. In his classic series of articles in *The Railway Magazine*, 'Locomotive and train working in the latter part of the nineteenth century', E. L. Ahrons made merry over its shortcomings. He wrote:

> There was, connecting with a Midland train from the north, a so-called fast train, which was due to leave Bath about afternoon-tea time, and was supposed to reach Wimborne somewhere about supper time.
>
> I do not know the exact timetable times, but the above timing of the train was quite good enough for the Somerset & Dorset arrangements of that day, and if the train had only stuck to tea and supper times all would have been well. It managed the tea-time start fairly well, but got out of hand at Evercreech, where something on the single line coming from the opposite direction caused a very long delay. At Templecombe the clock, and the meal-times too, had utterly gone by the board. I know something of the sort must have happened because I remember wanting my supper there with a very great want.

Making every allowance for the exaggerations of a man who had a very keen sense of humour, things remained very slack, even after the beginning of Joint ownership, until the serious head-on collision near Radstock in August 1876 alerted the joint owners to the general state of affairs, and reform began.

In the previous chapter the introduction of the Johnson 0—4—4 tank engines was described. Contrary to what one might have expected these engines were put on the main-line trains between Bath and Wimborne and the connecting works from Wimborne to Bournemouth. Those of the 2—4—0 tender engines that were not sold out of stock were put on the branch between Evercreech and Highbridge.

The Johnson 0—4—4 tanks had to do some quite fast running with the express trains put on from the summer of 1880. The fastest service was the northbound 11.50 a.m. from Wimborne, which covered the sixty-four miles to Bath in exactly two hours with two intermediate stops, at Blandford and Shepton Mallet. The down afternoon train leaving Bath at 2.30 p.m. was an even harder proposition from the locomotive point of view. It was allowed 2h. 3m. to Wimborne, but made three stops, including the awkward run into Templecombe, and the subsequent reversal.

These trains were the outcome of Midland enterprise, and included through carriages from as far afield as Bradford and Newcastle. Ahrons wrote of personal experience in the trains not long after the line from Evercreech to Bath was opened. At that time the 0—4—4 tank engines had not been built, and the old 2—4—0s used to make very heavy weather of the long 1 in 50 banks. He wrote:

> As they could do little more than crawl up one side of the bank, the drivers made amends by letting the engine out for all they were worth down the other side. Further, since the trains consisted of four-wheeled coaches, the age of which was extremely uncertain, the side-to-side motion was somewhat appalling, especially between Binegar and Evercreech Junction, where I more than once thought that my days were about to end.

Fast downhill running did not end with the relegation of the old 2—4—0s to the Highbridge line. At a later date one driver was 'on the carpet' before the great Alfred Whitaker for speeding. When asked why he had run so recklessly, this old worthy replied, in a free translation of the vernacular: 'Well, the faster you run, the less time there is to come off the road!'

THE 4—4—0s

Joking apart, the times scheduled from 1880 onwards were not bettered, in general, throughout the life of the railway; but before the turn of the century there was one train booked to cover the twenty-one and three-quarter miles from Shepton Mallet to Bath in thirty-five minutes. This was quite a hard run, with an average speed of 37 m.p.h. By the time this train was put on, the new Johnson 4—4—0 engines were available, and these were far more suitable for brisk running on the more favourable stretches of line.

Over the heavy gradients crossing the Mendips there was naturally a good deal of piloting with through trains including Midland bogie corridor stock, and in LMS days, when the new 6 ft 9 in 4—4—0s Nos. 44, 45 and 46 were sharing the work with the 7 ft engines of 1914, Nos. 67 to 71, the maximum load permitted to an unassisted engine between Bath and Evercreech Junction, in each direction, was 200 tons. This permitted the normal mid-week and winter load of 'The Pines Express' to be worked unpiloted, though it involved some very hard pulling on the 1 in 50 banks.

This tonnage of 200 compares well with the loadings permitted with 4—6—0 locomotives over heavily-graded routes in Scotland. For example, 200 tons was the limit for the 'Castle' class 4—6—0s on the worst stretches of the Highland line, where the limit for a Stanier 'Black Five' was no more than 255 tons. Engines were expected to work very hard on the Somerset & Dorset, and yet the later engines were not loaded so proportionately heavily as the class 2 4—4—0s. The 6 ft 9 in variety of this latter class had a nominal tractive effort of 17,730 lb and when the 'Black Fives' arrived on the scene, with a nominal tractive effort of 25,455 lb, one could have expected that their limit over the Mendips would have been about 300 tons. Instead, their load was fixed at 270 tons.

The Somerset & Dorset was a line where nominal tractive effort, as a measure of the sheer strength of an engine in climbing the banks, could be most misleading. This became very evident when the Bulleid 'West Country' Pacifics were put on the job. With their nominal tractive effort of 31,000 lb it was hoped that they would be able to take at least ten coaches unassisted, about 320 tons tare. But their liability to fits of slipping banished any such hopes, and despite their increased tractive effort their load limit had to be fixed at the same figure as that of the Stanier 4—6—0s.

When the class 2 4—4—0s were at their zenith, the southbound 'Pines Express' was allowed thirty-nine minutes to pass Masbury, 18.7 miles. The actual summit point, on the crest of the Mendips, is about a quarter of a mile short of the station, and stands 811 ft above ordnance datum. The booked average speed for the ascent was thus 28.8 m.p.h., and required some very hard work. Sustained speeds on the long stretches of 1 in 50 gradient were rarely as much as 20 m.p.h. with maximum load trains, but this involved a drawbar pull equivalent to some 80 to 82 per cent of the nominal tractive effort of the engines.

Figures apart, one could not be other than tremendously impressed by the skilled enginemanship—on both sides of the footplate—shown in taking a maximum load train away from Bath, starting cold, and pounding successfully up that first back-breaking length of 1 in 50 from Bath Junction to Combe Down tunnel, negotiating that infernal Devonshire tunnel in the process. A narrow single track bore is not the pleasantest of incidentals on the footplate when an engine is being worked virtually 'all-out' at slow speed! Yet these relatively small engines used to climb the first stretch of 1 in 50 almost as fast as they climbed from Radstock to Chilcompton when they were nicely warmed up.

The northbound 'Pines Express' used to call at Shepton Mallet, with thirteen minutes allowed for the 4.5 miles from Evercreech Junction. Most of this distance is inclined at 1 in 50, with a good deal of curvature. Here the speeds were generally not so high as in the climbing from Radstock southwards, no doubt because of the curves; and the 4—4—0 engines did not always keep time on this section. The brief downhill run from Shepton Mallet to the viaduct gave the chance to attain about 30 m.p.h. before tackling the main part of the 1 in 50 ascent to Masbury summit, and the minimum speeds were sometimes above 20 m.p.h. The booked time was 12 min from the restart to passing Binegar, 4.8 miles, and just over a mile beyond the summit.

As on all sections of line where bank engine working is needed, the arrangements varied according to circumstances. In the southbound direction, if pilots were needed they usually worked through from Bath to Evercreech Junction, and a second 4—4—0 engine would be put on. Northbound, if there was likely to be a pilot wanted on a return trip, the engine would go through to Bath; but if no balanced working was needed, the pilot would assist only to Binegar, and then return light engine.

1938—1962

When the Stanier 4—6—0s were introduced, the heavier loads were conveyed on the same schedules without any noticeable difference in the speeds maintained on the heaviest gradients. Piloting at times of heavy traffic was reduced, but the only differences sometimes to be observed were on the faster-running stretches of the line south of Evercreech. Here the 4—6—0s seemed to hold an advantage. But these engines had not long been introduced when war broke out in September 1939, and all form of holiday traffic over this once-popular route ceased. Up to that time the only reinforcement to the 4—4—0s and 4—6—0s when extra trains had to be run had been through using the class 4F 0—6—0s. These engines naturally climbed the banks with ease, but were inclined to lose time south of Evercreech. The use of these engines, in case of need, was in keeping with practice elsewhere on the LMS.

The end of the war, and the relatively quick return to holiday conditions in the summer months, did not see a return to the traffic conditions of pre-war years. The general introduction of 'holidays with pay', together with continuing austerity in the form of petrol rationing and a shortage of motor cars, led for a time to some astonishing 'peaks' of holiday traffic from many parts of the Midlands to the south coast; and on summer Saturdays the number of extra trains required, and the heavy coach formations conveyed, strained the motive power resources of the Somerset & Dorset line almost to breaking point. With maximum tonnages of 200, with a 4—4—0 or 0—6—0, and 270 with a 4—6—0, practically every train required double-heading between Bath and Evercreech Junction. Engines from the North, awaiting return workings at Bath, were commandeered as pilots, and at times even the standard LMS 0—6—0 shunting tank engines were pressed into service as main-line pilots.

So far as numbers were concerned, the motive power situation was helped by the drafting of some new class 4 2—6—0 engines of the '3000' class to the Somerset & Dorset line; but these engines, as first delivered, were poor steamers, and in actual practice were little better than the 4—4—0s. One of the most useful innovations was the decision to use the special SDJ 2—8—0 freight engines on passenger service on summer Saturdays. Although these engines lacked the speed necessary to run the trains south of Evercreech with full mastery over the schedules, the main thing about them was that they could be relied on to haul ten coach trains without assistance between Evercreech and Bath. The maximum load for any train was limited to twelve corridor coaches. With the heavy modern stock used on the principal expresses to the north, sometimes including twelve-wheel dining cars, this meant about 390 tons tare. This was well below the combined maximum tonnage of a class 2 4—4—0 and a class 5 4—6—0, so that in general there was time in hand. Use of the 2—8—0s lessened the amount of piloting needed over Masbury summit.

It is a little ironical to reflect that it was only in the years of declining traffic on the line that the motive power position was finally resolved, and locomotives provided that were capable of handling maximum loads unassisted over any part of the line. The British Railways 9F 2—10—0s were first introduced on the Somerset & Dorset line in 1960, and from the outset they did remarkably good work. Here again was a case where nominal tractive effort meant little in assessing the capabilities of the engines for load haulage over the banks of the S & D. It is interesting to set down the actual limits for the classes of locomotives regularly used:

Engine class	Nominal T.E. at 85% B.P. lb	Max. tare load tons	Ratio load/T.E. in tons
Class 2 4—4—0	17,730	200	26
Class 5 4—6—0	25,455	270	24
Southern 4—6—2	31,000	270	19.5
BR9 2—10—0	39,667	420	23.5

PERFORMANCE OVER THE DORSET

The standard 2—10—0s, in relation to their nominal tractive power, took loads roughly the same as those of the Stanier class 5 4—6—0s; but much more than the Bulleid Pacifics. The following table gives details of actual running of three of the above classes, each loaded to near maximum. Unfortunately no particulars are available of any runs with the Bulleid Pacifics working without assistance.

On the run with the 2—10—0, a very experienced observer of locomotive performance, Baron G. Vuillet of Paris, was on the footplate, and he recorded the engine working in full detail in addition to the running times and the speeds. The engine was worked with the regulator full open for all the heavy climbing, and the cut-off was advanced from 35 to 42 per cent on the 1 in 50 ascent to Combe Down Tunnel, and a maximum of 48 per cent was used on the long climb above Radstock. On this section the equivalent drawbar horsepower was no less than 2,000, while on the entire climb from Radstock to Masbury the average output was 1,840 e.d.h.p.

Attention has so far been concentrated on the line over the Mendips, where the hardest-sustained locomotive effort was required. But the southern end of the line was far from a sinecure, with numerous sharp intermediate gradients. The line was single-tracked from Templecombe No. 2 box to Blandford, but the passing loops were laid out so as to permit full speed running by non-stopping trains in the northbound direction but with severe slacks going south.

The Whitaker mechanical tablet-exchanging apparatus could be satisfactorily worked at speeds up to 60 m.p.h., if necessary. The cut-off line from Corfe-Mullen Junction to Broadstone was also sharply graded, and drivers used to interpret the speed restriction at the former place somewhat liberally to get a 'run' at the 1 in 80 bank that followed. But by far the worst ascent on the southern part of the line was the 1 in 60 up from Poole harbour towards Branksome. Here, with journey's end in sight, drivers used to throw in all they had. Engines of all kinds were flogged to the limit, though one would imagine the climax was reached on the occasion when Baron Vuillet rode on the footplate of the 9F 2—10—0 No. 92000.

SOMERSET & DORSET LINE

Bath—Evercreech Junction

Run No.		1	2	3
Engine No.		697	5440	92000
„ type		4—4—0	4—6—0	2—10—0
„ class		2P	5	BR9
Load tons E/F		179/190	255/270	416/450
Dist.		Actual	Actual	Actual
Miles		min sec	min sec	min sec
0.0	BATH	0 00	0 00	0 00
2.5	Milepost 2	7 57	7 05	—
4.3	Midford	10 55	9 50	10 10
10.7	Radstock	19 13	17 27	19 40
12.5	Midsomer Norton	23 52	22 19	22 50
14.5	Chilcompton	29 50	29 30	27 52
17.5	Binegar	35 29	35 27	32 25
—		—	—	—
21.9	Shepton Mallet	41 55	42 10	—
26.4	EVERCREECH JUNCTION	7 05	7 00	46 00
Speeds:		m.p.h.	m.p.h.	m.p.h.
	At Milepost 2	20	17½	24
	Chilcompton	20	15	22
	Binegar	37	37	36
	Masbury	30	28	30

From the stop at Poole there is just a mile of level to get a run at this bank, and the engine was worked with regulator full open and 49 per cent cut-off from the start. There was no linking up as the engine roared into speed, and at the foot of the bank where speed had risen to 47 m.p.h. the cut-off was *increased* to 52 per cent. The 1 in 60 gradient was taken in terrific style, with no lower speed than 41 m.p.h., and Branksome, 3.1 miles, was passed in the extraordinary time of 5m. 10s. This tremendous effort, with a trailing load of 450 tons, was perhaps exceptional; but it was typical of the 'all-out' manner in which this bank used to be tackled. On passing Branksome only one and a quarter miles remained before the terminus was reached at Bournemouth West.

Two Notes on Signalling

SIGNALS

The original signalling on the line reflected upon the respective origins of the northern and southern sections. The Somerset Central, as a broad-gauge line, and one which was confidently expected in early days to fall into the Great Western empire, was signalled on standard Brunellian lines with disc and crossbar signals exactly like those on the Bristol & Exeter Railway and on the Great Western itself. Display of the red disc facing the train was the proceed signal; the outfit turned through a right angle, to place the disc edge-on and display the crossbar at right angles to the track, was the stop indication. These disc and crossbar signals were used throughout the Somerset Central portion, from Burnham to Cole.

On the Dorset Central section of the line, London & South Western influence was apparent. A different type of disc signal was used which, in the absence of any positive indication in the clear position, was typical of the majority of signals in the earliest days of railways. In the danger position a red half-disc was shown to the driver—only the upper half of the complete signal. The outer periphery of the circle was continued round the bottom half, but the interior portion below the horizontal centre line was open. In the proceed position the disc was turned edge-on, and virtually no positive indication was shown to the driver. The distant signals on the Dorset Central part of the line, when they were introduced, were of similar construction to the stop signals except that the division between the red half-disc and the open portion was made on the vertical centre line, instead of the horizontal, and the left-hand portion was red, with the right-hand portion open.

On the single-line sections there were certain stations having no crossing loops. These came in the middle of single-line block sections, and accordingly were not equipped with signals of any kind. At the same time the scheduled stops at some of these stations were conditional only, and after their removal from the original block posts on the Somerset Central part of the line, some of the old disc and crossbar signals were installed at these intermediate stations to indicate when a station stop was required. It is certainly a tribute to the long visibility of these creations of Brunel that they could give sufficiently good warning to a driver. At the same time speeds on the Somerset & Dorset, even after Joint ownership, were not very high.

After the setting-up of Joint ownership, the London & South Western took over responsibility for civil engineering and signalling, and standard LSW semaphore signalling practice became established. While many wooden posts remained until the grouping era, the

Junction Signals.

At the Junctions of a Branch with the Main Lines, in addition to the ordinary Signals

Double Discs, and Crossbars by Day, and Double Lamps by Night, are fixed for signalling the Branch Trains—Thus

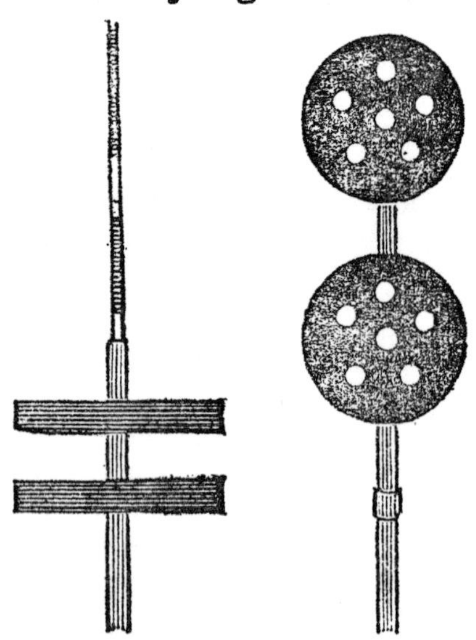

Disc and crossbar signals—from the S & D Rule Book, 1864

majority of the actual masts were of the standard South Western lattice pattern. In Southern Railway days when there was an acute shortage of steel, many of the older posts, when due for renewal, were replaced by a new standard type developed on the Southern, using two old rails braced together. Gradually too the old LSW semaphores were replaced by modern upper-quadrant arms. In the last few years of the line's operation a few Great Western type semaphores were erected as replacements—the down starting signal at Midford, for example, and the down distant at Masbury—representing an entirely different tradition and managing to look extraordinarily incongruous in their new setting.

THE WHITAKER TABLET-EXCHANGING APPARATUS

The tablet-exchanging apparatus used on the Somerset & Dorset was designed by Alfred Whitaker during his term as locomotive superintendent of the Joint line. A very similar apparatus was designed by James Manson of the Great North of Scotland Railway, but Whitaker's invention was patented at about the time when it was first brought into use (British Patent Specification No. 861 of 1905).

On the engine was a combined deliverer and receiver. When out of use this was close to the side of the engine and was pushed out when required. The tablet to be given up was placed in a leather pouch with a steel ring, carried at the rear end of the apparatus, and kept in position by a spring clip. The receiver consisted of a gunmetal jaw with two triggers in the front and with a rubber pad at the back. At the lineside at the tablet station were mounted the familiar standards. The jaws of the apparatus on the engine engaged with the loop of the tablet pouch carried on the lower arm of the standard, and a similar receiver on the upper arm of the standard seized the loop of the tablet pouch from the engine.

The arms of the standard were normally parallel with the running line, and were turned to a right angle with the line by the signalman when putting out a tablet ready for exchange. The standard was provided with two bevel wheels, but these had teeth on only a quarter of their faces and were provided with a stop to prevent them moving further than the correct distance. When that point was reached, the weighted lever was slightly past the perpendicular. The shock given by the receipt of the tablet into the receiver was such as to throw the weight over the centre. It then fell, and the bevel wheels turned the standard so that the arms were cleared of the running line. This was a very good feature, and the apparatus in general gave excellent service with speeds of exchanging sometimes even in excess of 60 m.p.h.

The margin of error was limited with a pouch loop of such small diameter. When the apparatus was fitted on the tender, variations in height caused by weak springs or track undulations which caused the tender to roll at the critical moment would result in a 'miss'. Drivers were always prepared for this with a hand raised toward the brake handle. If the enginemen were smart, very little loss of time occurred by the fireman having to turn back for the tablet after stopping. In placing the tablet into, or removing it from, the engine catcher, the fireman had to expose himself to some danger, but in the history of the line there was no record of anything worse than a badly bruised arm sustained by a fireman who had left his action so late that he was struck by a lineside catcher.

To ascertain whether the catchers were correctly aligned, a locomotive inspector on the engine would insert a circle of cardboard into the pouch hoop prior to delivery from the engine. The cardboard was secured to the end of a length of string by which it was drawn back on to the footplate after delivery of the pouch; the cardboard would then bear an imprint showing where the lineside catcher had struck it, and if the imprint was not central, the catcher had to be checked with a special gauge.

Engines not fitted with catchers had to exchange tablet pouches by hand, in which case the code word 'POUCH' was relayed to all signalmen, who then made use of the pouches with large hoops. Bath locomotive department kept a stock of clamp-on catchers which could be fitted at short notice to any engine arriving from the North which had to be pressed into service over the S & D.

CARRIAGE DEVELOPMENT

(50) *Four-wheeled first class carriage No. 1*

(51) *Six-wheeled composite No. 19 with luggage compartment*

(52) *Non-corridor bogie composite with lavatory compartment*

SIGNAL CURIOSITIES

(53) *Disc and crossbar signal at Spetisbury in the 1890s, at 'clear'*

(54) *Guarding the Clandown colliery branch at Radstock*

(55) *Standard at Binegar for picking up the banking engine staff*

(56) *Reversing arm at Evercreech Junction; Betty Lambert was the only woman working as signal lampman on the* LMS

Appendices

1: AUTHORISATION AND OPENING DATES

Lines owned or worked as part of the Somerset & Dorset system

Line	Authorised	Company	Opened to public traffic
Highbridge-Glastonbury	17 June 1852	Somerset Central	28 Aug 1854 (a) (b)
Highbridge-Burnham	30 July 1855	Somerset Central	3 May 1858 (b)
Glastonbury-Wells	30 July 1855	Somerset Central	15 Mar 1859 (b) (c)
Wimborne Junction-Blandford	29 July 1856	Dorset Central	1 Nov 1860 (d) (e) (f)
Glastonbury-Cole	21 July 1856	Somerset Central	3 Feb 1862 (g)
Cole-Templecombe	10 Aug 1857	Dorset Central	3 Feb 1862 (g) (h)
Templecombe-Blandford	10 Aug 1857	Dorset Central	31 Aug 1863 (i)
Templecombe Upper-Templecombe No. 3	16 July 1866	Salisbury & Yeovil	Mar 1870
Evercreech Junction-Bath Junction	21 Aug 1871	Somerset & Dorset	20 July 1874
Corfe Mullen Junction-Broadstone	20 Aug 1883	LSWR and MR	14 Dec 1885 (j)
Edington Junction-Bridgwater	18 Aug 1882	Bridgwater (k)	21 July 1890

Lines over which running powers were exercised

Line	Company	Opened	Used by S & D
Wimborne-Poole (Hamworthy)	Southampton & Dorchester (l)	1 June 1847	31 Aug 1863
Broadstone-Poole (New)	LSWR	2 Dec 1872	2 Dec 1872
Poole-Bournemouth West	Poole & Bournemouth	15 June 1874	15 June 1874
Bath Junction-Bath (Queen Square)	MR	4 Aug 1869 (m)	20 July 1874

NOTES

(a) formal opening 17 August 1854
(b) worked by Bristol & Exeter until 3 February 1862
(c) formal opening 3 March 1859
(d) formal opening 31 October 1860
(e) temporary station at Blandford St Mary
(f) worked by LSW until 31 August 1863
(g) formal opening 18 January 1862
(h) worked by Somerset Central until 1 September 1862
(i) opened by Somerset & Dorset
(j) for goods only; opened for passenger traffic 1 November 1886
(k) acquired by LSW 1 January 1923
(l) absorbed by LSW 22 July 1848
(m) temporary station until opening of Queen Square 7 May 1870

2: DISTANCES (1930)

MAIN LINE

	miles	
Bath Queen Square (LMS)	0	LMS block
Bath Junction (LMS)	½	
Midford	4¼	Single-line, electric tablet
Wellow	6¾	
†Shoscombe & Single Hill Halt	8½	
Writhlington & Braysdown	9¾	
Radstock (East)	10½	
Radstock (West)	10¾	
Midsomer Norton & Welton	12½	
Chilcompton	14½	
Moorewood	15¾	
Binegar	17	
Masbury	18¾	
Winsor Hill	20	
Shepton Mallet	21¾	
Evercreech New	25	
Evercreech Junction (North)	26¼	
Evercreech Junction (South)	26½	
Cole	29¼	
Wincanton	33½	
Templecombe No. 3	36¼	
Templecombe No. 2	36¾	
Templecombe B	37	SR block
Templecombe (SR)	37	

Templecombe No. 2		
†Henstridge	38¾	Single-line, electric tablet
Stalbridge	40¼	
Sturminster Newton	44¼	"
Shillingstone	47¼	"
**Stourpaine*	49¾	
†Stourpaine Halt	50¼	"
Blandford	52¾	
†Charlton Marshall Halt	54½	

Signalbox	Miles	Working
*Spetisbury	56	
Bailey Gate	59	
Corfe Mullen Junction	60¾	Single-line, electric tablet
Wimborne Junction (SR)	63¾	
Wimborne (SR)	64	SR block

Signalbox	Miles	Working
Corfe Mullen Junction		Single-line, electric tablet
†Corfe Mullen Halt	62	
Broadstone Junction (SR)	63¾	
Holes Bay Junction	66½	SR block
Poole	67¼	
Parkstone	69	
Branksome	70¼	
Bournemouth West Junction	70¾	
Bournemouth West	71½	

NOTES. Distances are given to the nearest quarter of a mile. The names of intermediate signalboxes are shown in italics. The names of signalboxes at manned crossings which were not block posts have not been included.

† Not a block post * Not a regular block post

BRANCHES (all single-line)

BURNHAM - EVERCREECH

	miles	
Burnham-on-Sea	0	Train staff and ticket
Highbridge C	1¼	Single-line block, no staff
Highbridge B	1½	GWR single-line block, no staff
Highbridge (*West*) GWR	1¾	GWR double-line block
†Highbridge	1¾	
Highbridge Loco	1¾	Electric tablet
†Bason Bridge	3¼	
Edington Junction	6¾	,,
Shapwick	9	,,
†Ashcott	10¾	
Glastonbury & Street	13½	,,
West Pennard	18¾	,,
†Pylle	22¼	
Evercreech Junction (*North*)	24	Double-line block
Evercreech Junction (South)	24¼	

BRIDGWATER BRANCH

	miles	
Edington Junction	0	Electric tablet
†Cossington	3	
†Bawdrip Halt	4¼	
Bridgwater	7¼	

WELLS BRANCH

	miles	
Glastonbury & Street	0	Electric tablet
†Polsham	3	
*Wells	5½	

NOTES. Distances are given to the nearest quarter of a mile. The names of intermediate signalboxes are shown in italics. The names of signalboxes at manned crossings which were not block posts have not been included.

† Not a block post

* Wells station was controlled by the GWR single line block without a staff between Tucker Street and East Somerset signalboxes

3: CLOSURES

March 1870	Templecombe Lower-junction with Salisbury & Yeovil line (part retained as a siding)
16 January 1887	Templecombe Lower station and No. 1 Junction
11 July 1920	Corfe Mullen Junction-Wimborne Junction closed for passenger traffic; closed for goods traffic 17 June 1933, except for the section from Corfe Mullen to Carter's Siding which was closed 19 September 1959
5 May 1950	Templecombe Lower Yard
29 October 1951	Glastonbury-Wells closed for all traffic
29 October 1951	Highbridge-Burnham closed for passenger traffic; used for excursions until 8 September 1962. Closed for goods 20 May 1963, except for the section from Highbridge East to Highbridge Wharf which was closed 2 November 1964
1 December 1952	Edington Junction-Bridgwater closed for passenger traffic; used for goods until 1 October 1954
17 September 1956	Charlton Marshall, Corfe Mullen, Spetisbury and Stourpaine & Durweston Halts closed

At various dates between 1963 and 1965 freight facilities were withdrawn from the majority of stations on the main line and on the branch. The following sections of the line were then closed for goods traffic:

14 June 1965	Wincanton-Blandford
3 January 1966	Radstock-Wincanton (except for coal traffic from Midsomer Norton until 19 February)
	Highbridge-Evercreech Junction
7 March 1966	Bath Junction-Broadstone, and Evercreech Junction-Highbridge closed for passenger traffic
	Bath Co-op Siding-Writhlington, Radstock-Blandford, Evercreech Junction-Bason Bridge closed completely, leaving the following sections still open: Bath Junction-Co-op Siding (coal traffic) Writhlington-Radstock (coal traffic) Bason Bridge-Highbridge (milk traffic) Blandford-Broadstone (goods and milk traffic)

4: OFFICERS

SOMERSET CENTRAL RAILWAY
(amalgamated with Dorset Central 1 September 1862)

Chairmen	1852-55	Philip Pleydell Bouverie
	1855-62	George Warry
Secretaries	1852-53	J. F. Giles
	1853-62	R. A. Read
Engineers	1852-62	C. H. Gregory
	1861-62	F. G. Slessor (Resident Engineer)
Locomotive Superintendent	1862	R. Andrews
Traffic Superintendent	1862	A. Patey

DORSET CENTRAL RAILWAY
(amalgamated with Somerset Central 1 September 1862)

Chairman	1856-62	Henry Danby Seymour
Secretary	1856-62	R. A. Read
Engineers	1856-62	C. H. Gregory
	1861-62	F. G. Slessor (Resident Engineer)

Between 3 February 1862 and 1 September, pending amalgamation, the locomotive superintendent and the traffic superintendent of the Somerset Central were also in charge of the working of the Dorset Central between Cole and Templecombe.

SOMERSET & DORSET RAILWAY

Chairmen	1862-66	Lord Rivers
	1866-67	George Warry
	1867-71	Charles Waring
	1871-73	George Warry
	1873-75	Charles Waring
Secretaries	1862-72	R. A. Read
	1872-75	A. Difford
Engineers	1862-75	C. H. Gregory (Engineer-in-Chief & Consulting Engineer)
	1862-75	F. G. Slessor (Resident Engineer)
	1875-76	H. S. Chapman
Locomotive Superintendents	1862-68	R. Andrews
	1868-74	F. G. Slessor
	1874-75	B. S. Fisher
Traffic Superintendents	1862-63	A. Patey
	1863-75	A. Difford
General Manager	1862-75	R. A. Read (Managing Director 1872-74)

SOMERSET & DORSET JOINT RAILWAY

Chairmen
- 1875-88 Charles Waring
- 1888-91 William Waring
- New board nominated by MR and LSW 1 December 1891

Secretary & General Manager for the Joint Committee
- 1875-91 R. A. Read

Engineers
- 1875-76 H. S. Chapman
- 1876-1900 A. Colson
- 1900-04 O. A. G. Edwards
- 1904-08 J. Tyler
- 1908-16 E. R. Roche
- 1916 T. E. Maidment†
- 1917-30 W. E. Fox*

† Died before taking office
* Assistant Engineer under Western District Engineer LSW

Locomotive Superintendents
- 1875-83 B. S. Fisher
- 1883-89 W. H. French
- 1889-1911 A. H. Whitaker
- 1911-13 M. F. Ryan
- 1913-30 R. C. Archbutt

Traffic Managers (or Superintendents of the line)
- 1875-76 A. Difford
- 1876-1902 R. A. Dykes
- 1902-20 G. H. Eyre
- 1920-22 A. S. Redman
- 1922-30 G. H. Wheeler

5: SHIPPING

THE SOMERSET & DORSET FLEET

Date of p'chase	Vessel	Description	Built	Tonnage Gross /net	Owner	
1860	*Ruby*	Iron paddler	1854 Renfrew	155/98		Sold 1864
1863	*Defiance*	Iron paddler	1856 Glasgow	150/96	Burnham Tidal Harbour Co.	Sold for scrap 1871
1864	*Heather Bell*	Iron paddler	1858 Glasgow	152/95		Sold 1867
1866	*George Reed*	Iron screw	1866 Cubitt Town	170/115	George Reed	Sold 1867
1873	*Railway*	Wood ketch	1855 Strood	59	S & D	Wrecked at Cardiff 1886
1873	*Julia*	Wood ketch	1863 Milton, Kent	69	S & D	Sold 1904
1873	*Richard and Emily*	Wood ketch	1862 Lewes	82	S & D	Sank off Nash Light 1886
1874	*Leopard*	Iron screw	1861 Bristol	67/42	S & D	'Unfit for further use 1890' Sold 1896
1879	*Alpha*	Iron screw	1877 Maryhill	82/48*	SDJ	Scrapped 1925
1884	*Sherbro*	Wood paddler	1870 Cowes	239/119	SDJ	Sold 1888
1904	*Julia*	Steel screw	1904 Woolston	197/78	SDJ	Scrapped 1934
1925	*Radstock*	Steel screw	1925 Saltney	195/78	SDJ	Sold 1934

* *Alpha* was twice lengthened, in 1884, making her tonnage 94/55, and again in 1905, making her tonnage 111/76

SOMERSET & DORSET FERRY SERVICES

(a) Burnham—Cardiff

	Vessel	Description	Owner
1858-60	*Taliesin*	Wood paddler built Mostyn 1842 158 tons gross, 85 net	Cardiff Steam Navigation Co.
1860-63	*Ruby*		Burnham Tidal Harbour Co.
1863-71	*Defiance*		Burnham Tidal Harbour Co.
1864-67	*Heather Bell*		Burnham Tidal Harbour Co.
1866-67	*George Reed*		George Reed (for Burnham Tidal Harbour Co.)
1871-79	*Flora*	Iron paddler built Govan 1851 119 tons gross, 42 net	F. C. Winby, Cardiff H. Cousins, Cardiff
1879-84	*The Lady Mary*	Iron paddler built Glasgow 1868 179 tons gross, 90 net	John Boyle, Cardiff (for Bute Trustees)
1884-88	*Sherbro*		SDJ

NOTE. Other steam packets were chartered from time to time for relief work while the regular packets were being overhauled: for example, in July 1882, *Wye* (an iron paddler built at Bristol in 1861, tonnage 108 gross, 54 net) was deputising for *The Lady Mary*.

(b) Poole—Cherbourg

	Vessel	Description	Owner
1865-66	*Albion*	Iron paddler built Glasgow 1860 307 tons gross, 152 net	P. L. Henderson (Liverpool)

Cargo vessels chartered by the Somerset & Dorset

	Vessel	Description	
1875-76	*Lincolnshire*	Built Newcastle 1867 88 tons gross, 54 net	
1876-77	*Terrier*	Built Whiteinch 1865 91 tons gross, 79 net	Lost with all hands on Swansea-Highbridge run 14 October 1877

6: FINANCES

(a) Capital

At the time of the lease to the MR and the LSW the statement of capital authorised and created or sanctioned by the S & D read as follows (as at 31 December 1875):

Act of Parliament	Capital created or sanctioned		
	Stock and shares	Loans and deb. stock	Total
	£	£	£
Somerset Central 1855	140,000	43,000	183,000
Somerset Central 1856	100,000	33,000	133,000
Somerset Central 1859	75,000	24,000	99,000
Somerset Central 1861	45,000	73,000	118,000
Dorset Central 1856 & 1857	400,000	133,000	533,000
Somerset & Dorset 1864	100,000	33,000	133,000
Somerset & Dorset 1866	300,000	100,000	400,000
Burnham Tidal Harbour 1860	17,000		17,000
Additional capital authorised by scheme of arrangement enrolled 21 September 1870		414,920	414,920
Somerset & Dorset 1871 (Bath Extension)	360,000	120,000	480,000
Somerset & Dorset 1874	330,000	110,000	440,000
	1,867,000	1,083,920	2,950,920

The 1873 Act had authorised a further £60,000 in shares and £20,000 in loans. The stock and share capital created was organised as follows:

	£
Ordinary Stock	1,045,680
First 5% Preference	100,000
First 4½% Preference	99,960
Second 5% Preference	261,360
5% Extension Shares	360,000
	1,867,000

Of this total £1,207,784 had actually been received, while £1,006,768 had been raised by debenture stock.

(b) Revenue

The following figures give a fair picture of the financial position of the line at regular intervals in its history:

	Traffic receipts £	Working expenses £	Profit or loss £
1864 (half-year)	23,938	16,476	+ 7,462
1874 (half-year to June 30)	29,021	24,698	+ 4,323
(half-year to Dec 31*)	40,995	35,154	+ 5,840
1884	144,411	106,254	+38,157
1894	175,740	134,913	+40,827
1904	209,404	169,724	+39,680
1913†	255,763	194,792	+60,971
1924	439,672	462,693	−23,020
1934	265,410	301,607	−36,196

During the years 1939-46 when the railways were under Government control, the annual net revenue for the whole undertaking was fixed as showing a deficit of £79,414, payable in moieties by the SR and the LMS.

NOTES. * Bath Extension opened 20 July 1874
† On the authority of the Board of Trade no figures were published in the 1914 report

SOURCES OF THE ILLUSTRATIONS

PLATES

I am grateful to the following for courteously allowing me to reproduce photographs in their possession and of which in some cases they hold the copyright: Mr R. Andrews, 34; Bath Railway Society, 37; *Bath & Wilts Chronicle & Herald*, 30; Mr G. Braithwaite, 1; British Rail, London Midland Region, 6, 7, 10, 25, 27, 29, 35, 36, 38-52, 56; Col Rixon Bucknall, frontispiece; C. & J. Clark Ltd, 13, 31; Capt J. Dew, 4; Miss D. Eyre, 15; Locomotive & General Railway Photographs, 16, 32, 33, 34, 53; Mr G. Luxon, 5; Mr G. W. Purvis, 11; Mr P. Riley, 24; Mr R. E. Toop, 18; Mr S. C. Townroe, 17, 26, 28; University of Reading Museum of Rural Life, 8; Mrs M. S. Warry and the Somerset Constabulary, 12; Mr P. J. Williams, 54.

The following supplied me with photographs taken specially for this book: Mr K. F. Marchant, 21, 22, 23; Mr D. Milton, 2, 3, 19, 20, 55; Moorhouse-Presley, 4, 11, 14, 15.

The frontispiece is reproduced from an oil painting by Mr V. Welsh from a photograph by Dr T. F. Budden.

LINE DRAWINGS

British Rail, London Midalnd Region, 40, 75; British Transport Historical Records, 65, 68, 140, 142, 151; *The Illustrated London News*, 22; Mr F. Kemp, 14, 33, 109, 115, 146, 174; *The Railway Magazine*, 89; Mr F. Redman, 103.

Bibliography and Acknowledgements

Although the fame of the Somerset & Dorset was far greater than its size or importance would have appeared to justify, surprisingly little has been written about its history. *The Somerset & Dorset Railway* by D. S. Barrie and C. R. Clinker, Oakwood Press, 1948, is the only self-contained history and description of the line; where I differ from Messrs Barrie and Clinker on matters of fact, it is only after prolonged research in primary sources or in the face of incontrovertible evidence.

Among the printed sources I have consulted, the most important are: E. T. MacDermot's *History of the Great Western Railway*, revised by C. R. Clinker, Ian Allan, 1964; C. F. Dendy Marshall's *A History of the Southern Railway*, Ian Allan, 1962; David St John Thomas's *A Regional History of the Railways of Great Britain, Vol 1—The West Country*, David & Charles, third edition 1966; L. T. C. Rolt's *Red for Danger*, David & Charles, 1966; Grahame Farr's *Somerset Harbours*, Christopher Johnson, 1954, and his *West Country Passenger Steamers*, Tilling, 1956. *A Family and a Railway*, C. & J. Clark, 1955, describes the 1954 Centenary celebrations.

A great deal of material is buried in the files of local newspapers, which are sometimes inaccessible, and of railway periodicals. A number of specific references are included in the text; the most important articles are to be found in *The Railway Magazine*—March 1899, interview with R. A. Dykes; January-February 1905, H. Rake; May 1917, H. L. Hopwood; February-March 1924, E. L. Ahrons (reprinted in *Locomotive & Train Working in the Latter Part of the 19th Century, Vol V*, Heffer, 1953); October 1931, E. C. B. Ashford; December 1932, R. B. Fellows; and February 1966, D. W. Winkworth. The Editor of *The Railway Magazine* has kindly allowed me to quote from the interview with R. A. Dykes, and also to make use of material which appeared in my own article on the Radstock accident in December 1962. A series of exceptionally interesting articles by J. Thornton Burge, then stationmaster at Templecombe, appeared in *Railway & Travel Monthly* for November 1911, July-October 1913, and March-April 1914.

I have made considerable use of S & D and SDJ Rule Books, Appendices to Working Timetables, and Notices such as Signal

Instructions. Apart from *Bradshaw's Guide*, a number of SDJ public and working timetables are available at the British Transport Historical Records, 66 Porchester Road, London, W.2, where the Minute Books and the large collection of original records referring to the Somerset & Dorset line are deposited. Other manuscript sources consulted include the diaries of George Warry (by kind permission of Mrs M. S. Warry of Shapwick), and those of Thomas Foster and George Tucker (by kind permission of Mr G. A. V. Foster of Radstock).

It is impossible for me to thank adequately all those who have helped me either in the collection of material or in the actual writing of this book. The Public Relations and Publicity Officers of the Southern and Western Regions of British Railways made it possible for me to visit all installations on the line where I invariably met with the greatest friendliness and co-operation from railwaymen of all ranks: while it would be invidious to mention any individuals by name, I can only say that collectively and individually I remain deep in their debt. My typescript has been read by Mr P. B. Pearman and by Mr S. C. Townroe (sometime District Manager, Southampton) who saved me from a number of gratuitous errors of fact, and for whose wise advice on many points I am sincerely grateful; for any remaining errors of fact, or for any opinions expressed, I of course remain entirely responsible. The same applies to Mr David Milton who has ungrudgingly helped me at every stage with his intensive knowledge of the line, especially the branches. I must also thank many other members of the Somerset & Dorset Circle, whose monthly bulletins are becoming an increasingly valuable repository of historical material and personal reminiscences.

I also wish to thank the Archivist (Mr E. Atkinson) and his indefatigable staff for their ready assistance on my many visits to the British Transport Historical Records; the Somerset County Archivist (Mr I. P. Collis); the Dorset County Archivist (Miss M. Holmes); the Bristol City Librarian (Mr W. S. Haugh); the Director of the City of Bath Municipal Libraries (Mr Peter Pagan) and all their staffs; Mr George Ottley of the British Museum; and Mr Grahame Farr, without whose generous help it would have been quite impossible for me to compile the Appendix on Somerset & Dorset shipping.

Last but not least I take great pleasure in acknowledging my debt to Mr O. S. Nock for so readily agreeing to contribute two chapters of technical matter on the locomotive history, practice and performance on the S & D with which I was not myself competent to deal; also to my son, Mr Charles Atthill, who undertook the compilation of the Index; and to my daughter-in-law, Mrs Charles Atthill, who has typed and retyped my manuscript for me at every stage.

Chilcompton,
March 1967.

NOTE TO SECOND IMPRESSION

Shortly before this new impression was due to go to the printers, a lot of important material relating to the early history of S & DR locomotives from 1861 to 1871 was published as a result of the researches of Mr D. L. Bradley in the S & DR locomotive register at Derby works. In the light of this information, some corrections have been made on pages 155 and 156, but confusion is often made worse confounded by the S & D malpractice of continually renumbering their engines. Readers who wish to pursue these minutiae of locomotive history are referred to Mr Bradley's article in the *Journal* of the Stephenson Locomotive Society for March 1968 (Vol 44 No 512), though even here no cognisance is taken of the later numbers under which almost every engine masqueraded.

Chilcompton,
April 1968.

Index

Illustrations are indicated by heavy type